ENCOUNTERS
Chinese Language and Culture

Use the Access Code below to register for the
Encounters: Chinese Language and Culture Website.

1. Go to: www.EncountersChinese.com

2. Click "Register" and follow the instructions

3. Use this code

D1716641

318nyf3u35

Yale UNIVERSITY PRESS
New Haven and London

yalebooks.com/languages

ENCOUNTERS
Chinese Language and Culture

Student Book 3

ENCOUNTERS

Chinese Language and Culture

Student Book 3

汉语和中国文化

▶ **Cynthia Y. Ning**
University of Hawai'i at Mānoa

▶ **Stephen L. Tschudi**
University of Hawai'i at Mānoa

▶ **John S. Montanaro**
Yale University

Instructor's Annotations by **Amy Shen**
Berkshire School

Audio Program by **Cynthia Y. Ning** and the **Confucius Institute**
University of Hawai'i at Mānoa

Yale UNIVERSITY PRESS
New Haven and London

华语教学出版社
SINOLINGUA

Published with assistance from the Office of the President, Yale University.

Project Developers: Mary Jane Peluso and Timothy J. Shea
Project Director: Sarah Miller
Editorial Assistant: Ashley E. Lago
Developmental Editor: Martin Yu
Project Manager: Karen Hohner
Copy Editor: Jamie Greene
Managing Editor: Jenya Weinreb
Designer and Compositor: Wanda España/Wee Design Group
Illustrator: Nora Guo
Cover Designers: Sonia Shannon and Wanda España/Wee Design Group
Art Managers: Melissa Flamson and Poyee Oster
Production Controller: Maureen Noonan
Digital Product Manager: Sara Sapire
Digital Product Assistant: Thomas Breen
Marketing Managers: Karen Stickler and Dawn Angileri

Printed in the United States of America.

ISBN: 978-0-300-16164-9 (student edition)
ISBN: 978-0-300-16168-7 (annotated instructor's edition)
Library of Congress Control Number: 2015932953

A catalogue record for this book is available from the British Library.

This paper meets the requirements of ANSI/NISO Z39.48-1992 (Permanence of Paper).

10 9 8 7 6 5 4 3 2 1

We dedicate *Encounters* to the memory of John DeFrancis, who began his seven-decade career as the first Ph.D. student in Chinese Studies at Yale University and who then published numerous books and articles on the subject of China and the Chinese language. He was a gentle man who lived a full, good life and gave so much to so many.

Contents

Unit 21: "It seems an old friend has come to visit"
似是故人來　*Sì shì gùrén lái*
Getting reacquainted with old friends

Unit 22: "Seeking a physician and inquiring about medicine"
尋醫問藥　*Xúnyīwènyào*
Handling illnesses—a visit to the doctor

Unit 28: "The Eight Immortals display their personal magic"

八仙過海，各顯神通　*Bāxiānguòhǎi, gèxiǎnshéntōng*
Personalities and appearances

Unit 29: "Filial piety is the foundation of all virtues"

孝，德之本也　*Xiào, dé zhī běn yě*
Family relationships

Preface

Congratulations, you've reached Level 2 of *Encounters: Chinese Language and Culture!* We hope that by now, you have a grounding in useful language skills that allow you to communicate well enough to meet many basic needs: ask for the price of an item, find out simple directions, meet and greet someone new. Level 2 will build on that foundation and take you further. We hope that your sentences will become slightly more complex, you'll be able to meet daily survival needs with more facility, and you will get to know more about people and allow them to get to know you better. Book 3 takes you further afield in daily life than you had ventured in Level 1. We visit a health clinic, find out about using banking services, sample the offerings at a hair and beauty salon, shop for a cell phone, visit shopping malls, and get deeper into dealing with personal relationships.

As in Level 1, Book 3 takes a four-skill approach to learning Chinese. You will work on listening, speaking, reading, and writing—all in a cultural context—but as in Books 1 and 2, the curriculum emphasizes listening and speaking. We believe that these skills will help you build the strongest foundation to develop competency in Chinese.

Book 3 integrates content from the dramatic series, filmed in present-day Beijing. The episodes, available at *www.EncountersChinese.com*, provide the basic content of each unit. You will find that you are able to understand much more of the language used in these episodes than you did in Books 1 and 2. The language in the episodes is useful both for training in comprehension and as the basis for picking up new vocabulary and grammar and developing functional competence. As in the past, though, don't try to learn *everything* in each unit; there is simply too much.

We have introduced an innovation in Book 3. In addition to reading realia (real-life examples of written Chinese), each lesson includes a generally humorous, illustrated, self-contained story linked to the theme of the unit. It is our hope that the story will inspire you to write your own stories and that these texts can become additional reading material for your class. Selected student texts may, with permission, be uploaded to the *Encounters* website in the future, so that students can choose freely and extensively among texts of high interest, to further develop reading ability.

At this level, we are not providing a workbook to teach stroke order, since the basic principles relating to stroke order will have been internalized by now. If you need stroke order support, please use the *Encounters* Character Trainer App that is accessible via *www.EncountersChinese.com*.

We wish you continuing success on your journey of learning Chinese!

—Cynthia Y. Ning
—Stephen L. Tschudi
   University of Hawai'i at Mānoa

Academic Committee

Acknowledgments

Cynthia Y. Ning dedicates her work to the memory of her parents, Grace and Chung Fong Ning, who made her conversant in Chinese in a decidedly non-Chinese environment; to the memory of her husband, Allan Ngai Lim Yee, who died too young; to her talented and loving daughter, Robyn Yee; to her brother and frequent dining companion, Sam Ning; to her yoga, dining, movie, and adventure buddies, Myrtle Wong, Janeen Kuhn, Robert Kohn, and Robert Brumblay; and to her mentor in filmmaking, Eric Gustafson.

Stephen L. Tschudi dedicates his work to his amazing parents, Martha and Morton Wood, who by their example taught him to love life, music, dance, and nature; to his husband, Daniel Tschudi, who delicately imposes a modicum of order on Stephen's chaos; and to the friends in China who were his earliest and best teachers.

The authors and publishers thank their professional friends and colleagues, including the staff of the Center for Chinese Studies at the University of Hawai'i and in particular its Confucius Institute; the University's Department of East Asian Languages and Literatures, Center for Language and Technology, and National Foreign Language Resource Center; and the following individuals: Li Qikeng, Zha Yunyun, Dong Xu, Qu Yaojia, Liu Meiyi, Zhai Mengying, Yang Jia, Zhang Zihe, Frederick Lau, Sun Jialin, Samuel Ning, Amy Shen, Chunman Gissing, Kristine Wogstad, Joanne Shang, Terry Waltz, Reed Riggs, and Martin Yu.

Introduction

Overview

The comprehensive *Encounters* program:

- Includes two complete levels of two books each (Level 1: Books 1 and 2; Level 2: Books 3 and 4).
- Employs a functional, task-based approach.
- Presents authentic language and culture through engaging dramatic video episodes.
- Focuses on communication in the spoken language.
- Includes reading material in both traditional and simplified characters.
- Links cultural video interviews to language functions.
- Presents clearly focused grammar instruction and practice.
- Adheres to ACTFL Proficiency Guidelines.
- Assists teachers with a fully annotated instructor's edition, materials to excite students' interest, and a wide selection of useful tools in various media.

Program Components

The *Encounters* program comprises:

- A beautifully produced *video series*, filmed entirely on location in China and featuring a dramatic story line and segments devoted to Chinese culture and history.
- A full-color *student textbook*, completely integrated with the video series and other *Encounters* components.
- An *annotated instructor's edition* of the textbook, packed with teaching tips, extra classroom activities, and suggestions for using the program in the classroom.
- *Screenplays* containing the transcripts of the dramatic episodes.
- An *audio program* to assist students with listening comprehension, pronunciation, vocabulary, and model conversations.
- A *website, www.EncountersChinese.com,* that offers students and teachers streaming video and audio content, and other resources for speaking, reading, and writing Chinese.

Level 1 Recap

The 20 units in Level 1 (Books 1 and 2) touched on making introductions and sharing personal information; dealing with time and money; talking about travel, foreign languages, and currency; discussing school, study, and daily routines; arranging for food and eating; discussing leisure activities; comparing living arrangements; moving around town and going on excursions; and chatting about the experience of learning Chinese.

Level 1 followed the experiences of expatriates living and learning in China, a pair of visitors to China, and the Chinese professionals and students they came to know. Some of these people you will meet again, several years later, in Level 2. There were also 20 mini-documentaries in Level 1, which presented the points of view of a diverse range of people on the topics covered in each unit. The mini-documentaries are expanded in Level 2.

▶ The Cast of Characters

MAO ZHIPENG (Máo Zhìpéng, 毛志鵬／毛志鹏) In Level 2, Mao Zhipeng returns as a core character. He is no longer working with Chen Feng but has instead become a professor at the Communications University of China (the true profession of the actor who plays him).

LUO XUETING (Luó Xuětíng, 羅雪婷／罗雪婷) Professor Mao is now engaged to a Chinese American physician, Luo Xueting, played by a woman previously interviewed in the mini-documentary section of Level 1. Dr. Luo is interning at the clinic of the Communications University of China.

MICK (Mǐkè, 米克) Also returning is Mick, the Australian tea connoisseur. The actor who plays him is really a tea connoisseur and the owner of a real-life establishment called *The Hutong*, which also figures in Level 2. Mick is now dating Lynn, who does not appear in Level 2.

FANG LAN (Fāng Lán, 方蘭／方兰) New to Level 2 are two dynamic characters. The first is the puckish Fang Lan, a student of Professor Mao. She is outspoken and strong-minded, and she has an opinion about everything. She lives at home with her parents, who also appear in the series.

EMMA (Àimǎ, 艾瑪／艾玛) Emma, the second new character, is an American exchange student at the Communications University of China and is living at the home of Fang Lan and her parents. Emma has a positive outlook and is not afraid of making mistakes, but she does succumb to bouts of homesickness and occasional physical illnesses.

TANG YUAN (Táng Yuǎn, 唐遠／唐远) Tang Yuan comes to the capital as well, with A-Juan, now his wife. He is a successful artist seeking to establish himself in the art community in Beijing.

 **A-JUAN** (Ā-Juān, 阿娟)   A-Juan is now married to Tang Yuan and expecting their first child. The character is played by a different actress than in Level 1 (the original actress left the cast to start a family).

 **CHEN FENG** (Chén Fēng, 陳峰／陈峰)   Chen Feng is still in advertising, and although he and Xiao Mao are no longer partners, he still calls on his old friend for help with an occasional project.

 **XIAO FEI** (Xiǎo Fēi, 小飛／小飞)   Chen Feng's cousin, Xiao Fei, still works for Chen Feng's company but is now almost presentable as a member of the team.

A number of other memorable characters round out the cast: Fang Lan's real-estate agent mother and opera-singing father, a comic chef, a cool spa manager, Fang Lan and Emma's school friends, Professor Mao's colleagues, a famous actress, and an agile martial arts instructor and his students. All work together to portray life in the rich and diverse communities of metropolitan Beijing.

▶ The Dramatic Story Line

The lives of all the major characters intersect in the course of an academic year. Xiao Mao and Luo Xueting reconnect with Mick, Fang Lan helps Emma settle in, Emma joins Xiao Mao's media class, Xiao Mao introduces Fang Lan to Chen Feng as a potential intern, Xiao Fei develops a crush on Fang Lan, and Xiao Mao suffers through a massage. The characters experience many of the normal ups and downs of life at home, in school, and at work.

▶ The Mini-documentaries

The content of the documentary series could constitute a parallel and completely independent textbook. Here, the documentaries serve to enrich the video offerings of Level 2 significantly. Via a plethora of interviews intercut with footage of sites, products, and activities, the depth of Chinese culture pertaining to each topic in the textbook is explored. We hope you will take the time to savor the wealth of knowledge on offer in this documentary series and come away with a much fuller sense of the breadth and depth of contemporary Chinese culture.

❭ A Unit Tour

The ***Encounters*** textbook presents a carefully structured and cumulative approach to learning Mandarin Chinese. Students progress from listening and speaking activities to the more challenging skills of reading and writing Chinese characters. The emphasis is on communicative skills, as the primary goal of the ***Encounters*** program is to foster proficiency in everyday Chinese.

Each unit offers an inviting combination of in-class, individual, pair, and group activities. Humor, music, and a lighthearted attitude encourage learners to approach the study of Chinese with enthusiasm and confidence. "FYI" boxes provide in-depth glimpses into Chinese language and culture, and appealing illustrations keep interest levels high. By weaving cultural information throughout the text—rather than relegating it only to end-of-unit notes—***Encounters*** reinforces the notion that language is inseparable from culture.

Unit titles are presented in English, in Chinese characters, and in pinyin. Traditional characters are used here to evoke decorative calligraphy, which is often presented only in the traditional form, even in China.

The introductory page for each textbook unit features a photograph from the corresponding video episode. Skills taught and practiced in the unit are related to the events that students observe in the episode.

A list of skills to be covered in the unit clarifies learning goals and helps students stay organized.

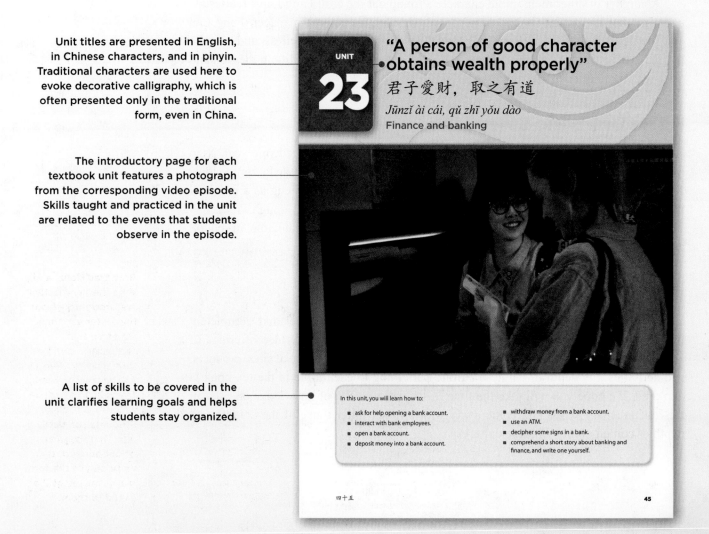

UNIT

23

"A person of good character obtains wealth properly"

君子愛財，取之有道

Jūnzǐ ài cái, qǔ zhī yǒu dào
Finance and banking

In this unit, you will learn how to:

- ask for help opening a bank account.
- interact with bank employees.
- open a bank account.
- deposit money into a bank account.

- withdraw money from a bank account.
- use an ATM.
- decipher some signs in a bank.
- comprehend a short story about banking and finance, and write one yourself.

四十五

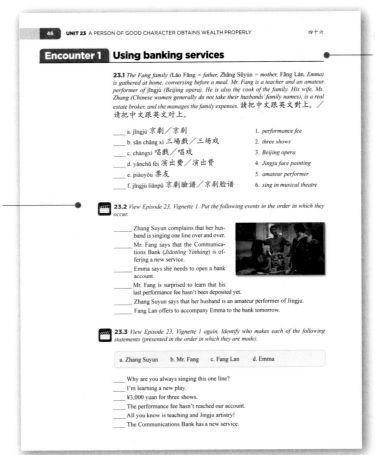

Each unit contains several interesting and enlightening "Encounters," presenting material that covers common real-life situations.

Various listening and learning activities are enriched by their connections to the ongoing video and by their insights into Chinese culture.

46 UNIT 23 A PERSON OF GOOD CHARACTER OBTAINS WEALTH PROPERLY 四十六

Encounter 1 Using banking services

23.1 *The Fang family (Lǎo Fāng = father, Zhāng Sùyún = mother, Fāng Lán, Emma) is gathered at home, conversing before a meal. Mr. Fang is a teacher and an amateur performer of jīngjù (Beijing opera). He is also the cook of the family. His wife, Ms. Zhang (Chinese women generally do not take their husbands' family names), is a real estate broker, and she manages the family expenses.* 请把中文跟英文对上。／請把中文跟英文對上。

____ a. jīngjù 京劇／京剧   1. performance fee
____ b. sān chǎng xì 三場戲／三场戏   2. three shows
____ c. chàngxì 唱戲／唱戏   3. Beijing opera
____ d. yǎnchū fèi 演出費／演出费   4. Jingju face painting
____ e. piàoyǒu 票友   5. amateur performer
____ f. jīngjù liǎnpǔ 京劇臉譜／京剧脸谱   6. sing in musical theatre

23.2 *View Episode 23, Vignette 1. Put the following events in the order in which they occur.*

____ Zhang Suyun complains that her husband is singing one line over and over.
____ Mr. Fang says that the Communications Bank (Jiāotōng Yínháng) is offering a new service.
____ Emma says she needs to open a bank account.
____ Mr. Fang is surprised to learn that his last performance fee hasn't been deposited yet.
____ Zhang Suyun says that her husband is an amateur performer of Jingju.
____ Fang Lan offers to accompany Emma to the bank tomorrow.

23.3 *View Episode 23, Vignette 1 again. Identify who makes each of the following statements (presented in the order in which they are made).*

a. Zhang Suyun   b. Mr. Fang   c. Fang Lan   d. Emma

____ Why are you always singing this one line?
____ I'm learning a new play.
____ ¥3,000 yuan for three shows.
____ The performance fee hasn't reached our account.
____ All you know is teaching and Jingju artistry!
____ The Communications Bank has a new service.

四十七   ENCOUNTER 1 **47**

____ They inform you by text message.
____ That sounds convenient.
____ Is this a Halloween mask?
____ Our teacher mentioned it today.
____ We paint this mask on our faces.
____ We don't need to open a new account.
____ I need an account at a Chinese bank.
____ You're a good father and a good husband.
____ Go cook!

FYI boxes provide relevant cultural information that will both fascinate students and deepen their understanding of the Chinese language and the culture and people of China.

FYI 供你参考

Beijing opera

Fang Lan's father is an amateur singer of *jīngjù* 京劇／京剧, which is also called Beijing opera. He sings a male role—in this case, specifically the part of Zhūgě Liàng 諸葛亮／诸葛亮, a legendary military strategist in Chinese history and a frequent subject of Jingju. Jingju actors represent role types more than individualized characters; for example, "dignified older male," "virtuous upper-class woman," "handsome young man," "vivacious young female," "martial larger-than-life male," and "clown." The martial larger-than-life males sport colorful painted faces, with each of the colors indicating a distinct personality trait—red for loyalty, white for trickery, black for integrity, green for chivalry, yellow for cruelty, purple for wisdom, and so on. All the actors speak, sing, and move in time to music played by a live orchestra.

Both traditional and simplified characters are used throughout the materials. Only 20 percent of characters have two forms, and students will encounter both forms in areas where Chinese is spoken. Students can easily learn to recognize both but need to write only in the form that is meaningful or useful to them.

23.4 *View Episode 23, Vignette 1 again.* 請把中文跟英文對上。／請把中文跟英文对上。

____ a. dàozhàng 到賬／到账   1. been deposited
____ b. Jiāotōng Yínháng 交通銀行／交通银行   2. funds
____ c. guǎnggào 廣告／广告   3. convenient
____ d. yínháng zhànghù 銀行帳戶／银行帐户   4. Communications Bank
____ e. zījīn 資金／资金   5. direct deposit into the account
____ f. tōngzhī 通知   6. advertisement, commercial
____ g. fāngbiàn 方便   7. inform
____ h. kāi yí ge xīn zhànghù (hùtóu) 開一個新帳戶（戶頭）／开一个新户户（户头）   8. bank account
____ i. zhíjiē dǎ dào yínháng hùtóuli qù 直接打到銀行戶頭裡去／直接打到银行户头里去   9. open a new account

Suggestions for practice conversations appear throughout each unit. Students build confidence and practical conversational skills through these entertaining oral exercises.

By incorporating materials found in real life—signs in a bank, for example—lessons provide practical information enabling students to perform everyday tasks in Chinese.

五十一   ENCOUNTER 1   51

23.12 *Pair work: Work with a partner to practice the following guided dialogue between a customer and a bank teller. Switch roles and repeat when you are done.*

Bank teller	Customer
Greet the customer.	Greet the teller. Say you'd like to open an account.
Confirm that he/she is opening an account.	Confirm. Ask if there's a charge.
Say there is a ¥15 charge.	Say that's not a problem.
Ask for his/her ID.	Hand over your ID and say what it is. (*jiàshǐzhèng* 駕駛證／驾驶证 driver's license)
Say you'll make a photocopy. Ask him/her to wait.	Say that's not a problem.
Hand over a form and ask him/her to fill it out.	Say OK. Ask where you should sign.
Tell him/her to sign in the lower right corner.	Say OK. Say you're done. (*Tián hǎo le* 填好了)
Ask how much he/she wants to deposit.	Say you want to deposit ¥1,000.
Confirm the amount.	Confirm.
Ask if he/she wants a bank card.	Say that you want a bank card.
Hand over the bank card. Say it has ¥1,000 on it.	Say thank you. Ask if you should pay the ¥15 now.
Say yes.	Hand over ¥15.
Say thanks. Hand over a receipt and say what it is. (*shōujù* 收據／收据 receipt). Ask if he/she needs anything else.	Say thanks, no, you're all done.
Thank him/her for choosing your bank. Ask him/her to come again.	Say thanks. Say good-bye.

五十三   ENCOUNTER 2   53

▶ **Reading real-life texts**

23.14 *These are some signs Fang Lan and Emma saw at the bank.*

ⓐ *The name of the bank is written in traditional characters, for elegance. Write the pinyin.*

_____ _____ _____ _____

交通银行
BANK OF COMMUNICATIONS

ⓑ *The Chinese for this sign is rhymed, and it says more than the English. Fill in the blanks in the translation.* 用英文填空。

Jìnmén qǐng shuākǎ, wúxū shū mìmǎ.
To enter the door, please _____;
there's no need to enter a _____.

进门请刷卡
无需输密码
Swipe the Card to ...

ⓒ *Again, the English is terse, and the Chinese says more.* 用拼音填空。

Nín yǐ _____
24 _____ jiānkòng qūyù.
You have entered an area under 24-hour surveillance.

您已进入
24小时监控区域
VIDEO

ⓓ *This counter offers a list of charges for various services.* 用英文填空。

Fúwù jiàgé zīxúnchù
Jiāotōng Yínháng
Nín de cáifù guǎnlǐ yínháng
Jiāotōng Yínháng fúwù shōufèi mínglù
2012 nián 3 yuè
_____ *prices inquiry (counter)*
Bank of Communications
Your _____ *for wealth management*
Bank of Communications _____ _____ *roster*
March 2012

服务价格咨询处
交通银行服务收费名录
2012年3月
交通银行
BANK OF COMMUNICATIONS

Beautifully illustrated stories written in characters facilitate intensive reading and develop reading comprehension skills. The engrossing storyline also deepens students' understanding of the unit topic.

▶ Reading a story

23.16 故事：田裡的黃金。 *Work with a partner or in a small group to read the story below.*

 很久很久以前，在中國的一個小鄉村裡，有一對老夫婦，都是農民。他們家很窮 (qióng *poor*)，只能靠種自己的一塊地過日子。

這對老夫婦有一個兒子。這個孩子已經長大了，身體很好，身材也不錯，又高又壯 (zhuàng *strong*)。只可惜他生來就很懶 (lǎn *lazy*)。他看別居都比自己家有錢，覺得很不公平 (gōngping *fair*)。為什麼別人有錢，自己就沒有？

 有一天，媽媽看見兒子特別不高興，也不到地裡來幹活 (gànhuó *work*) 了，就跟他說：兒呀。其實我們家也有自己的財產 (cáichǎn *property, possessions*)。我們也有金子，是我們祖先留給我們的。

兒子聽到這話就高興地跳了起來，說：真的嗎？金子都在哪兒呢？為什麼不趕快拿出來用？

媽媽說：金子不能隨便放。我們把它藏 (cáng *hide*) 起來了，埋 (mái *bury*) 在田地裡，需要的時候才能去取。

 兒子很生氣地說：為什麼我們不能現在就去把金子找出來，開始花呢？那樣我們就可以跟別人一樣過上舒通 (shūshì *comfortable*) 的日子。媽，趕快告訴我，我們的金子在哪裡？我現在就去取。

媽媽回答：我不是說了嗎？金子都埋在田地裡，具體 (jùtǐ *specifically*) 哪兒我也說不清。你自己去找吧，去挖 (wā *dig*) 吧。

Encounter 3 Extension: Cultural mini-documentary

 View the cultural mini-documentary for this unit and complete the exercises below.

23.18 *The speakers in the video (0:00–1:52) first talk about generational differences among Chinese people's conception of money.* 請用拼音填空。／请用拼音填空。

a. Duì qián de kànfǎ, lǎo yídài hé wǒmen kěndìng _____, yīnwèi jīnglì de niándài bù yíyàng. Hái yǒu, jiùshì shuō, yìxiē guānniàn yě bù yíyàng. Tāmen rènwéi qián _____ zǎn chūlai de, wǒmen rènwéi qián shì zhèng chūlai de. Hái yǒu yí ge, xiànzài de huánjìng kěnéng shuō xiǎng _____ hěn nán, dànshì nǐ yào shuō xiǎng nǔlì qù _____, hái yǒu jīhuì.

对钱的看法，老一代和我们肯定不一样，因为经历的年代不一样。还有，就是说，一些观念也不一样。他们认为钱应该是攒出来的，我们认为钱是挣出来的。还有一个，现在的环境可能说想攒钱很难，但是你要说想努力去挣钱，还有机会。

*When it comes to attitudes toward money, the older generation is certainly **not the same** as we are, because they lived through a different time. And, I mean, some concepts are not the same. They think that money **should be** made by saving it; we believe that money is made by earning it. Also, you might say that in the current environment, **saving money** is difficult, but if you put a real effort toward **making money**, then there are opportunities.*

b. Shì fēicháng bù yíyàng de, wǒ juéde. Jiùshì, lǎonián rén, tāmen de sīxiǎng, yīnwèi shì cóng shèhuìzhǔyì guójiā guòlái de ma, jiùshì háishi dàizhe yìxiē _____, shì yǐ bǎoshǒu, jiùshì, wéi jīchǔ. Jiùshì, shéi jiāli dōu huì yǒu yìxiē _____ a, bāokuò shì zhànghù lǐ de, yínháng lǐ cún de qián a, _____ shì huì yǒu de, dànshì xiànzài de niánqīng rén jiùshì yǐ xiǎngshòu shēnghuó wéi, zuòwéi zìjǐ de yí ge, jiùshì shēnghuó fāngshì, tāmen jiùshì _____ míngtiān zěnmeyàng, jiùshì jīntiān kāixīn le jiù hǎo. Dànshì lǎoniánrén huì xuǎnzé bǐjiào _____ de nà zhǒng lǐcái fāngshì, zhè shì tāmen chuántǒng de nàge guānniàn zàochéng de.

是非常不一样的，我觉得。就是，老年人，他们的思想，因为是从社会主义国家过来的嘛，就是还是带着一些老思想，是以保守，就是，为基础。就是，谁家里都会有一些现金啊，包括是帐户里的，银行里存的钱，肯定是会有的，但是现在的年轻人就是以享受生活，作为自己的一个，就是生活方式，他们就是不在乎明天怎么样，就是今天开心了就好。但是老年人会选择比较保守的那种理财方式，这是他们传统的那个观念造成的。

*I think they are extremely different. I mean, older people, their way of thinking, because of their coming from a socialist country, they still carry some old **ways of thinking**; they are grounded in conservatism. I mean, everyone's family has some **cash** on hand, including what's in their accounts, the money they have put in the bank, they'll **definitely** have that. But young people nowadays take the enjoyment of life as their own sort of lifestyle. They just **don't care** how tomorrow will be, just as long as they are happy today, then fine. But older people will choose a relatively **conservative** style of money management; this is a product of their traditionalist worldview.*

Mini-documentaries extend students' control of the language and enrich their understanding of the unit topics. Authentic interviews offer a closer look into Chinese society and its people, encouraging students to investigate how Chinese culture is different from or similar to their own.

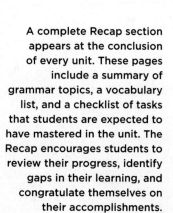

A complete Recap section appears at the conclusion of every unit. These pages include a summary of grammar topics, a vocabulary list, and a checklist of tasks that students are expected to have mastered in the unit. The Recap encourages students to review their progress, identify gaps in their learning, and congratulate themselves on their accomplishments.

UNIT 21

"It seems an old friend has come to visit"

似是故人來

Sì shì gùrén lái

Getting reacquainted with old friends

In this unit, you will learn how to:

- ask about and provide details about personal background.
- recap past connections with people you know.
- comment on details in the present situation of others.
- make arrangements to get together with new and old acquaintances.
- read brief statements about people's backgrounds.

- write a brief note about your experience learning Chinese.
- decipher some traffic, directional, and decorative signs posted in public places.
- read a simple story about friends.
- decipher people's personal backgrounds.
- decipher professional titles.

Encounter 1 Asking and providing details about personal backgrounds

21.1 *Xiao Mao and his fiancée Luo Xueting intend to sign up for a cooking class offered by a private school called* The Hutong. *To Xiao Mao's surprise, he finds that he knows the proprietor—an Australian named Mick. To prepare for watching the video, match the terms below.* 請把中文跟英文對上。／请把中文跟英文对上。

_____ a. hútòng
  胡同

1. *long time no see*

_____ b. chúyìkè(bān)
  廚藝課(班)／厨艺课(班)

2. *Australia*

_____ c. hǎoxiàng jiànguo
  好像見過／好像见过

3. *open a business*

_____ d. hǎojiǔ bújiàn
  好久不見／好久不见

4. *Sichuanese teacher*

_____ e. Měiguó Huárén
  美國華人／美国华人

5. *a traditional Beijing alleyway*

_____ f. kāi gōngsī
  開公司／开公司

6. *drink tea*

_____ g. Àodàlìyà
  澳大利亞／澳大利亚

7. *Chinese-American*

_____ h. yóuxiāng dìzhǐ
  郵箱地址／邮箱地址

8. *e-mail address*

_____ i. Sìchuān de lǎoshī
  四川的老師／四川的老师

9. *We seem to have met before.*

_____ j. hēchá
  喝茶

10. *business card*

_____ k. míngpiàn
  名片

11. *cooking class*

21.2 *View Episode 21, Vignette 1. Write (in English) two facts you learn about each of the characters below.*

Xiǎo Máo (Máo Zhìpéng) 小毛 (毛志鵬／毛志鹏)		
Luó Xuětíng 羅雪婷／罗雪婷		
Mǐkè (*Mick*) 米克		
Lín (*Lynn*) 琳		*She's away on business.*

 21.3 *Watch Episode 21, Vignette 1 again. Identify who makes each of the following utterances (presented in the order in which they are made).*

a. Xiao Mao	b. Luo Xueting	c. Mick

_____ Let's go. Let's step inside and take a look.

_____ See, it's here. The cooking class!

_____ You are Lynn's friend, right?

_____ Let me introduce you . . . this is my fiancée.

_____ I grew up in the United States and came here last year.

_____ She's been on a business trip.

_____ You ran a company with Chen Feng.

_____ I'm now teaching at the Communications University of China.

_____ My cooking isn't very good.

_____ A Chinese-American studies Chinese cooking in a class run by an Australian.

_____ Last year I studied Chinese for a semester at the Communications University of China.

_____ You'll come here to have some tea?

_____ I'll be able to confirm with you tomorrow.

_____ This is my business card.

21.4 *Watch Episode 21, Vignette 1 again.* 然後選一個答案來填空。／
然后选一个答案来填空。

a. Xiao Mao and Mick met before at the _____.
   (home of friends / Communications University of China)

b. Luo Xueting's parents emigrated from _____.   (Hong Kong / China)

c. Lynn is Mick's _____.   (girlfriend / wife)

d. Chen Feng is Xiao Mao's _____.   (ex-business partner / colleague at
   work)

e. Xiao Mao's cooking is _____.   (not too good / pretty good)

f. When Xiao Mao mentions *guójì dà dūshì,* he is referring to _____.
   (Shanghai / Beijing)

g. Xiao Mao and Luo Xueting met _____.   (at a friend's house / at a school
   event)

h. Luo Xueting is currently _____.   (interning in a hospital / studying
   Chinese)

i. The teacher from Sichuan will be teaching Chinese _____.   (language /
   cooking)

j. Xiao Mao says he has no afternoon classes _____.   (the day after
   tomorrow / tomorrow)

k. Xiao Mao comments that Mick's business is _____.   (not too good / pretty
   good)

FYI 供你参考

Lucky numbers in Chinese culture

After Mick gives his phone number (ten digits long, five of which are the number
8), Xiao Mao repeats the number 8 three times and concludes that it's no wonder
Mick's business is so good. The number 8 *(bā)* in Chinese is an auspicious number
because it sounds like *fā* 發／发, which means "flourishing, prosperous." Can you
believe the following about the number 8?

■ In 2003, a telephone number made up entirely with the number 8 was sold
   for ¥2.33 million (approximately $280,000) to Sichuan Airlines in Chengdu.

■ The opening ceremony of the 2008 Summer Olympic Games in Beijing began
   on 8/8/08 at 8 seconds and 8 minutes past 8 p.m. local time.

■ A man in Hangzhou offered to sell his license plate reading A88888 for ¥1.12
   million (roughly $164,000).

By contrast, the number 4 *(sì)* is unlucky because it is a homophone for an
inauspicious word (*sǐ* 死, "to die"). In the West, people tend to love 7 and fear 13 in
a similarly folkloric fashion.

21.5 *Guess the meaning of each of the terms below (presented in the order in which they appear).* 圈選正確的英文。／圈选正确的英文。 Quānxuǎn zhèngquè de Yīngwén. *(Circle the correct English term.)*

Part 1

a. jiùshì zhèr 就是這兒／就是这儿 *(It's right here. / It's only this.)*

b. wǒ hǎoxiàng rènshi nǐ 我好像認識你／我好像认识你 *(I'd like to get to know you. / I think I know you.)*

c. jiànguo miàn 見過面／见过面 *(met before / saw your face in passing)*

d. wǒ lái jièshào yíxià 我來介紹一下／我来介绍一下 *(Let me introduce you. / I'll come and explain it.)*

e. wèihūnqī 未婚妻 *(wife / fiancée)*

f. yímín dào Měiguó 移民到美國／移民到美国 *(visited the United States / emigrated to the United States)*

g. zài Měiguó zhǎngdà 在美國長大／在美国长大 *(grew up in the United States / grew old in the United States)*

h. huānyíng 歡迎／欢迎 *(welcome / please come again)*

i. chūchāi 出差 *(away on business / on vacation)*

j. wǒ jìde 我記得／我记得 *(I'm anxious. / I remember.)*

k. wǒ yǐjing gǎiháng le 我已經改行了／我已经改行了 *(I've changed my bank. / I've changed my profession.)*

l. jīngcháng zài yìqǐ 經常在一起／经常在一起 *(often get together / always get together)*

m. hézuò 合作 *(do again / collaborate)*

n. shēngyi búcuò 生意不錯／生意不错 *(idea is not bad / business is not bad)*

Part 2

a. guǎnggào 廣告／广告 *(advertisement / registration)*

b. hěn búcuò de chúshī 很不錯的廚師／很不错的厨师 *(a very bad cook / quite a good cook)*

c. jiāchángcài 家常菜 *(homestyle dishes / special dishes)*

d. tèbié náshǒu 特別拿手／特别拿手 *(particularly clingy / exceptionally adept)*

e. tài bàng le 太棒了 *(That's great! / That's OK.)*

f. Běijīng tèsè 北京特色 *(Beijing's colors / Beijing's distinguishing features)*

g. jiù zhèyàng 就這樣／就这样 *(That's the way it is. / It has to be that way.)*

h. zhè cái jiào 這才叫／这才叫 *(called him just now / this is what is called)*

i. guójì dà dūshì 國際大都市／国际大都市 *(a capital city / an international metropolis)*

j. nǐmen zěnme rènshi de 你們怎麼認識的／你们怎么认识的 *(How do you know that? / How do you know each other?)*

k. fàng hánjià qián 放寒假前 *(before the winter vacation / before the summer vacation)*

l. wǎnhuì 晚會／晚会 *(evening event / late meeting)*

m.nǐ hěn xìngyùn 你很幸運／你很幸运 *(You're very lucky. / You're very quick.)*

n. shíxí 實習／实习 *(studying / interning)*

Part 3

a. gǎnjǐn bàomíng 趕緊報名／赶紧报名 *(hurry up and register / quickly tell your name)*

b. liú xià nǐ de yóuxiāng dìzhǐ 留下你的郵箱地址／留下你的邮箱地址 *(forgot your e-mail address / leave [me] your e-mail address)*

c. jiāokè, jiǎngkè 教課,講課／教课,讲课 *(classroom, lecture hall / teach, lecture)*

d. hǎohāo liáoliao 好好聊聊 *(have a good look / have a good chat)*

e. gāi hǎohāo jùju 該好好聚聚／该好好聚聚 *(ought to spend some time together / ought to have a good meal)*

f. zhènghǎo méi kè 正好沒課／正好没课 *(just happen to have no classes / happy to have no classes)*

g. gěi nǐ fā yí ge duǎnxìn 給你發一個短信／给你发一个短信 *(I'll mail you a letter. / I'll send you a text message.)*

h. guàibude 怪不得 *(No wonder. / Don't blame me.)*

i. nǐ zhèr shēngyi zhème hǎo 你這兒生意這麼好／你这儿生意这么好 *(You've done so much here. / Your business is so good here.)*

j. wǒ gěi nǐ dǎguòqu 我給你打過去／我给你打过去 *(I'll give you a call. / I'll beat you up.)*

k. shōu dàole 收到了 *(received [it] / sent [it])*

l. jiù zhè yàng ba 就這樣吧／就这样吧 *(Let's leave it at that. / That's the way it is.)*

m.jīntiān jiù dào zhèr 今天就到這兒／今天就到这儿 *(Come over today. / That's it for today.)*

n. wǒmen xiān zǒu le 我們先走了／我们先走了 *(We'll be on our way. / We'll go by foot first.)*

FYI 供你参考

Idiomatic expressions (*shúyǔ* 熟語／熟语)

Idioms are popular in most languages, likely because they convey common ideas with power and elegance. English contains thousands of idioms, many of which you use often. For example, it's not raining hard—it's "raining cats and dogs." You know what you've done when you've "spilled the beans." Chinese speakers use idioms just as frequently, yet understanding idioms is often a challenge for language learners. This is mostly because the language is compressed (usually to just four characters) and sometimes uses allusions drawn from classical literature. In this unit, Xiao Mao uses two idioms, which are highlighted in red in the sentences that follow.

Exercise: Write the characters in the appropriate blanks to construct the two expressions below.

生 *be born*	徑／径 *path*	起 *arise*	幽 *quiet seclusion*
風／风 *wind*	曲 *winding*	水 *water*	通 *lead to*

1. Nǐ kàn zhèr huánjìng hái búcuò a, yǒudiǎnr qūjìngtōngyōu de gǎnjué.
   Look, this setting is pretty nice; it seems like the winding path is leading to a secluded spot. =
   _____ _____ _____ _____

2. Chén Fēng tǐng hǎo de, gōngsī zuò de fēngshēngshuǐqǐ de.
   Chen Feng is doing pretty well. His company is burgeoning. =
   _____ _____ _____ _____

qūjìngtōngyōu 曲徑通幽／曲径通幽 (*The winding path leads to a secluded place.*)

fēngshēngshuǐqǐ 風生水起／风生水起 (*The wind stirs and the water rises.* = *Things are really humming [in Chen Feng's business].*)

Here's another idiom you might remember from ***Encounters*** Student Book 2:

jiāchángbiànfàn 家常便飯／家常便饭 (*a simple, home-cooked meal*)

In addition to its literal meaning, this idiom is often used figuratively to mean "a commonplace or an ordinary thing." Can you guess why?

Exercise: By the way, 熟語／熟语 *shúyǔ* is also called 成語／成语 *chéngyǔ*. Both translate loosely into English as "idiomatic expressions." Following are some more 熟語／熟语 or 成語／成语 from ***Encounters*** Student Books 1 and 2. 把中文熟語跟英文對上。／把中文熟语跟英文对上。

a. sìhǎiyìjiā 四海一家 4

b. ānjūlèyè 安居樂業／安居乐业 1

c. jiàliánwùměi 價廉物美／价廉物美 5

d. chēshuǐmǎlóng 車水馬龍／车水马龙 2

e. xiāngjiànhènwǎn 相見恨晚／相见恨晚 5

1. *happy at home and work*

2. *heavy traffic*

3. *If only we had met sooner.*

4. *We're all one family.*

5. *good quality at a low price*

Grammar Bits 语法点滴

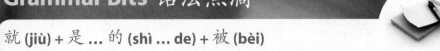

就 (jiù) + 是 ... 的 (shì ... de) + 被 (bèi)

In the video, Xiao Mao says: 我們就是被你的廚藝課廣告吸引過來的。/ 我们就是被你的厨艺课广告吸引过来的。 *Wǒmen jiù shì bèi nǐ de chúyìkè guǎnggào xīyǐn guòlái de.* (We are exactly [the people who have been] attracted here by your cooking class advertisement.) This is a complex sentence. It includes 就 *jiù* to express ease or "this is it," 是 ... 的 *shì + de* to express "we are the people who," and 被 *bèi* to mark the passive voice.

Exercise: To practice this structure, unscramble the pinyin sentences below to create an equivalent of the English translation. Then restate the sentence by replacing the underlined word with the prompt in brackets. The first one is done as an example.

1. Wǒ / nà yīnyuè / jiùshì bèi / de / xīyǐn guòlái
   (It's the <u>music</u> that attracted me.) [color]
   a. <u>Wǒ jiùshì bèi nà yīnyuè xīyǐn guòlái de.</u>
   b. <u>Wǒ jiùshì bèi nà yánsè xīyǐn guòlái de.</u>

2. Wǒ de shǒujī / tā tōu zǒu / jiùshì bèi / de
   (He's the one who stole my <u>cell phone</u>.) [money]
   a. _____
   b. _____

3. Wǒ de dàngāo / de / tā chī diào/ jiùshì bèi
   (He's the one who ate my <u>cake</u>.) [lunch]
   a. _____
   b. _____

4. Wǒ de guǒzhī / de / jiùshì bèi / tā hē diào
   (He's the one who drank my <u>juice</u>.) [milk]
   a. _____
   b. _____

5. jiùshì bèi / Zhè ge fángjiān / de / tā nòng luàn
   (He's the one who messed up this <u>room</u>.) [classroom]
   a. _____
   b. _____

Note: The agent of the action—the words right after *bèi* (by)—is the part that receives the most emphasis. This is reinforced by *jiùshì*, which draws attention to the agent.

Now try filling in the blanks below.

6. *He's the one who drank my coffee.*
   Wǒ de kāfēi _____ tā hēdiào _____.

7. *My younger sister is the one who spoils our dog.*
   Wǒmen de _____ _____ wǒ mèimei chǒnghuài _____.
   (chǒnghuài = *spoil*)

Now try producing a sentence with the same pattern. Write it below, check it with your teacher, and then share it with other students.

_____

21.6 *Mingling:* *Pretend that you and your classmate, like Mick and Xiao Mao, are meeting again after having known each other in the past. Try to figure out how you knew each other previously (pretend, if necessary), and share some details about your lives now. Repeat with more than one classmate, if time permits. Begin by trying out the sentences below and brainstorming more as appropriate.*

Wǒ hǎoxiàng rènshi nǐ. 我好像認識你。／我好像认识你。 *(I think I know you.)*

Wǒmen shì zěnme rènshi de? 我們是怎麼認識的？／我们是怎么认识的？ *(How do we know each other?)*

Nǐ bú shì shàngguo yī niánjí de Zhōngwén kè ma? 你不是上過一年級的中文課嗎？／你不是上过一年级的中文课吗？ *(Didn't you take first-level Chinese?)*

Nǐ de míngzi jiào X, duìbuduì? 你的名字叫X, 對不對？／你的名字叫X, 对不对？ *(Your name is X, right?)*

_____

_____

_____

21.7 *Prepare a brief presentation of how you came to be in this intermediate Chinese class. Take notes so you can deliver at least three sentences about your background in Chinese.*

Encounter 2   Reading and writing

21.8 *The following notes were written by Chinese language students about their own language-learning backgrounds. Highlight the parts you can understand.*

重慶／重庆
Chóngqìng *(Chongqing)*

費城／费城
Fèichéng *(Philadelphia)*

三藩市
Sānfānshì *(San Francisco)*
also translated as 舊金山／
旧金山 Jiùjīnshān

a 我父母是中国人。我生在重庆，我们一家人在我六岁的时候来到了美国。我爸爸妈妈常常跟我说中文，可是我回答的时候通常说英文。我中文说得还可以，可是阅读能力不太好。我的汉字写的更差。

b 我家在費城。我爸爸媽媽是做進出口的。我們的鄰居是從台灣來的。我從小就跟鄰居的小孩一起上中文學校，每個星期六早上學中文。那時候我很不高興，不想週末還上學。現在我特別喜歡寫漢字，因為會寫漢字的美國人不多！

c 我們家人住在三藩市。我爺爺奶奶在家裡說廣東話。我聽得懂廣東話，也會說一點，可是說得不太好。我爸媽很希望我能學好中文。我覺得廣東話很不像普通話／國語，所以中文課對我來說很不容易，特別是我的發音。老師常說我的發音不對。

d 我只会说英文，不会说其他语言。我觉得中文很难，要花很多时间学。

e 我是日本人。我看得懂中文，也会写汉字。可是我的听力不好，中国人说话我很难听懂。我自己说的话别人也听不懂。我常常要用写的，别人才知道我想说什么。

f 我去过很多国家，会很多语言。我在学校学了一年的中文了。我希望还可以再学一年，然后去中国留学。我觉得中文有些方面比其它语言容易，有些方面比其它语言难。所有的语言都很有意思，可是都不容易学。但是学好外语很有用。

Label each of the following sentences a–f, depending on the note to which it corresponds.

____ My father and mother own an import-export business. Our neighbors are from Taiwan. Since I was little, I learned Chinese with the neighbors' kids.

____ I think that in some respects, Chinese is easier than other languages; in some respects, it is harder than other languages. All languages are interesting, but they are not all easy to learn. However, learning a foreign language is very useful.

____ My grandpa and grandma speak Cantonese at home. I can understand Cantonese, and I can speak a little, but I can't speak it very well. My mom and dad would really like me to learn Chinese.

____ Other people can't understand what I say, either. Often, I have to use writing to make them understand what I want to say.

____ My family came to the United States when I was six years old. My mother and father often speak Chinese to me, but I generally answer them in English.

____ I think Chinese is very hard. I have to spend a lot of time studying it.

____ Now I really like writing Chinese characters, because there aren't many Americans who know how!

____ I can read and write Chinese characters, but my listening comprehension isn't good. When Chinese people speak, I have a hard time following.

____ I can speak Chinese OK, but my reading comprehension isn't too good. I'm even worse at writing Chinese characters.

____ I've been to a lot of countries, and I know a lot of languages. I've studied Chinese in school for a year so far. I'd like to study it for another year, and then I'll go study in China.

____ I can only speak English. I can't speak any other languages.

____ I think that Cantonese is really not like Putonghua/Mandarin, so it's not easy for me in Chinese class, especially my pronunciation. My teacher often says my pronunciation isn't right.

21.9 *Using characters, write a note—such as the ones in 21.8—that briefly describes your previous experiences learning Chinese.*

▶ **Reading real-life texts**

21.10 *Here are some signs Xiao Mao and Luo Xueting saw as they made their way to Mick's school.*

a 請用拼音填空。／请用拼音填空。

Zhù _____

_____tōng _____

Pay attention to traffic safety.

b 請把中文跟英文對上。／请把中文跟英文对上。

North Dongsi Avenue

1. 大街 dàjiē   A. *north*

2. 东四 Dōngsì   B. *Eastern Quad (a district in Beijing)*

3. 北 běi   C. *avenue*

c 請寫英文。／请写英文。

Běi Xīn Qiáo

_____ _____ Bridge

d *Check the appropriate boxes for these two signs.*

màn

☐ *Go Slowly*

☐ *Stop*

ràng

☐ *Right Turn Only*

☐ *Yield*

JIUDAOWAN BEIXIANG

Nine-bend North Alley

e *This is the alley in which* The Hutong *is located. Insert the missing tone marks.*

Jiudaowan Bei Xiang

f *When Xiao Mao and Luo Xueting enter* The Hutong, *they are attracted by this sign.* 請把中文跟英文對上。／请把中文跟英文对上。

1. 厨艺班 chúyìbān   A. *has begun*

2. 报名 bàomíng   B. *registration*

3. 开始了 kāishǐ le   C. *cooking class*

g *This decorative lantern in* The Hutong *is imprinted with a stylized wish for good fortune that combines the following four characters:*

招 财 进 寶

zhāo cái jìn bǎo

beckon wealth (and) bring in treasure

Circle and label each of these four characters on the replica below. Watch out for the overlap.

21.11 *Mick's school is simply called* The Hutong *(*胡同 *hútòng) at* #1 Jiǔdàowān hútòng zhōngxiàng. *On a separate sheet of paper, design a poster for the school. Make sure you include as many Chinese characters as you can.*

▶ **Reading a story**

21.12 故事： 老朋友跟新朋友。 *Work with a partner or in a small group to read the story that follows.*

小紅跟小蘭從小就認識。她們在一起讀小學、中學、大學；現在她們開始工作了，也還是朋友。她們結婚以後是鄰居，經常見面,真是老朋友。

小蘭的先生對她說："為什麼你老跟小紅在一起？你不能交一些新朋友嗎？" 小蘭說："你不就是我的新朋友嗎？"她先生說："我是你丈夫，不能算是朋友。"小蘭說："妻子和丈夫不就是最要好的朋友嗎？"她先生說："不，丈夫是丈夫，朋友是朋友。不一樣。"小蘭說："好。我去認識一些新朋友。""

小紅和小蘭在一起的時候，小蘭說："小紅，我們得去認識一些新朋友。"小紅說："為什麼？老朋友才是真的朋友。新朋友有什麼好？"

小蘭說："沒關係。時間久了，新朋友也就變成老朋友了。"

通過別人介紹，小紅和小蘭認識了小玉和小立。她們四個人非常談得來，不久，就變成非常要好的朋友了。四個人老在一起。

有一天，小蘭的先生又不高興了。他說："你為什麼老跟小紅他們在一起？都沒有時間在家裡。"

小蘭説："哦，我明白了。問題不在老朋友和新朋友，問題是朋友和先生。下次我跟朋友們在一起的時候，你也來，好不好？"她先生説："我跟你的朋友没有話説。"　小蘭説："那我們去看電影，你就不用説話了。"她先生説："你們喜歡看的電影我不會喜歡的。"　　小蘭説："我們星期六去看一部美國老電影，叫《教父》，是馬龍・白蘭度演的。我想你會喜歡的。"

她先生説："哦，《教父》，我知道那部電影。很有名，我一直想看。馬龍・白蘭度是個非常好的演員。好吧！我跟你們一起去看。"

小蘭説，"好極了！那麼我的老朋友就可以變成你的新朋友了！"

21.13 *Write a short story about old and/or new friends. Have it edited by your teacher or someone else who is fluent in Chinese. Illustrate your story as best as you can before sharing it with your classmates.*

21.14 *Extra Listening Practice: View Episode 21, Vignette 2, and mark the statements below* True *or* False.

	True	False
a. *Gōngfuchá* has nothing to do with martial arts.	☐	☐
b. Luo Xueting's father is a physician.	☐	☐
c. Mick had a bike accident recently.	☐	☐
d. Luo Xueting says that acupuncture (針灸／针灸 *zhēnjiǔ*) needles are very thin.	☐	☐
e. Xiao Mao never lets his fiancée practice acupuncture on him.	☐	☐
f. Mick doesn't mind needles.	☐	☐

Encounter 3   Extension: Cultural mini-documentary

 In this video, you will hear various bits of personal information, such as names, ages, places of origin, personal titles, and so on. View the cultural mini-documentary for this unit and complete the exercises below.

21.15 *Listen to the first part of the video (0:00–0:24), and add tone marks to the following names.*

a. Liu Jiefeng

b. Lin

c. Zhao Xiangpeng

d. Xiao Shenshen

e. Wang Wei

f. Cai Huali

g. Jin Xin

h. Huang Jingjing

i. Luotuo

21.16 *Watch the next part of the video (0:24–0:38), and fill in the blanks.*

在這六個人當中，有___ 個二十七歲， ___ 個三十歲， ___ 個七十二歲，還有___ 個要保密 (bǎomì, *keep it a secret*)。／

在这六个人当中，有___个二十七岁， ___个三十岁， ___个七十二岁，还有___个要保密 (bǎomì, *keep it a secret*)。

21.17 *The next topic (0:39–1:40) is about places of origin. Consult the map. Fill in the number from the map that corresponds to each person's province of origin. Remember, people usually say the province first when saying where they are from.*

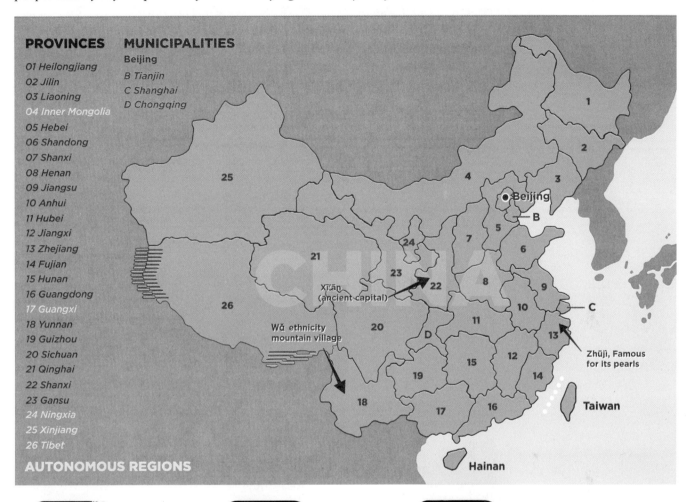

PROVINCES

01 Heilongjiang
02 Jilin
03 Liaoning
04 Inner Mongolia
05 Hebei
06 Shandong
07 Shanxi
08 Henan
09 Jiangsu
10 Anhui
11 Hubei
12 Jiangxi
13 Zhejiang
14 Fujian
15 Hunan
16 Guangdong
17 Guangxi
18 Yunnan
19 Guizhou
20 Sichuan
21 Qinghai
22 Shanxi
23 Gansu
24 Ningxia
25 Xinjiang
26 Tibet

MUNICIPALITIES

Beijing
B Tianjin
C Shanghai
D Chongqing

AUTONOMOUS REGIONS

Xī'ān (ancient capital)

Wǎ ethnicity mountain village

Zhūjì, Famous for its pearls

Taiwan

Hainan

a. _____

b. _____

c. _____

d. _____

e. _____

f. _____

21.18 *Next in the video (1:40–2:22), people mention their personal titles. Note that in Chinese, the organization or company comes first, whereas in English, the person's title often comes first. For each of the following personal titles that appear in the video, match the pinyin, English, and Chinese. (You will not use two each of the pinyin and English choices.)*

Pinyin	English	
		北京磊石跨文化發展有限公司總經理／北京磊石跨文化发展有限公司总经理
		北京中醫藥大學基礎醫學院副院長／北京中医药大学基础医学院副院长
		中國青年報社常務副社長／中国青年报社常务副社长
		CET學術項目學術主任／CET学术项目学术主任
		北京中原地產房地產經紀有限公司望京西園三區店店長／北京中原地产房地产经纪有限公司望京西园三区店店长

a. Zhōngguó Qīngnián Bàoshè Chángwù Fùshèzhǎng

b. CET Xuéshù Xiàngmù Xuéshù Zhǔrèn

c. Běijīng Zhōngyuán Dìchǎn Fángdìchǎn Jīngjì Yǒuxiàn Gōngsī Wàngjīng Xīyuán Sān Qū Diàn Diànzhǎng

d. CET Xuéshù Xiàngmù Chángwù Fùyuànzhǎng

e. Běijīng Lěishí Kuàwénhuàfāzhǎn Yǒuxiàn Gōngsī Zǒngjīnglǐ

f. Běijīng Zhōngyīyào Dàxué Jīchǔ Yīxuéyuàn Fùyuànzhǎng

g. Běijīng Lěishí Zhōngyīyào Yǒuxiàn Gōngsī Zǒngjīnglǐ

1. *Branch Manager, Wangjing West Garden Zone 3 Branch, Beijing Centaline Property Agency Ltd.*

2. *Vice Director, College of Preclinical Medicine, Beijing Central University of Chinese Medicine*

3. *Executive Vice Editor-in-Chief,* China Youth Daily

4. *Executive Vice Director, CET Academic Program*

5. *Academic Director, CET Academic Program*

6. *CEO, Beijing Boulder Chinese Medicine Co. Ltd.*

7. *CEO, Beijing Boulder Cross-Cultural Development Co. Ltd.*

21.19 *Beginning at about 2:22 in the video, listen and see how much you can understand. Take some notes on a separate sheet of paper.*

Recap

▶ Grammar

Activating your Chinese: Reviewing some familiar and unfamiliar structures

Chinese, as a verb-oriented language, presents ideas mostly in terms of verbs. Verbs equal action, so as a student of Chinese, you need to be clear about how actions are expressed in the language. Here are some sentences inspired by our lesson text that may help clarify various actions.

■ *Today I plan to paint a painting.*

Jīntiān wǒ xiǎng huà yì fú huàr.

今天我想畫一幅畫兒。／今天我想画一幅画儿。

ACTION: The subject does something; it's clear who's doing the action.

STRUCTURE: subject + simple verb + object

■ *After I finish it, I will show it to Mr. Zhang; perhaps he might want to buy it.*

Huà wán le yǐhòu, wǒ jiù bǎ huàr gěi Zhāng xiānsheng kànyikàn, yěxǔ tā huì mǎi.

畫完了以後，我就把畫兒給張先生看一看，也許他會買。／画完了以后，我就把画儿给张先生看一看，也许他会买。

ACTION: The subject acts upon something. (He shows the painting to Mr. Zhang.)

STRUCTURE: The uniquely Chinese *bǎ* pattern shifts the object (the painting) to a preverbal position. The verb always needs some sort of complement when *bǎ* is used. Here, the verb is reduplicated (*kànyikàn*), but many other types of complements are possible.

■ *As soon as Mr. Zhang saw it, he became entranced by it and really wanted to buy it.*

Zhāng xiānsheng yí kàn, jiù bèi zhè fú huàr xīyǐn le, yídìng yào mǎi.

張先生一看，就被這幅畫兒吸引了，一定要買。／张先生一看，就被这幅画儿吸引了，一定要买。

ACTION: The subject (Zhang) is acted upon by something, in this case the painting. (Zhang is entranced by the painting.)

STRUCTURE: The agent of the action is specified by *bèi*. This *bèi* structure is called the passive voice, which is very common in English but less so in Chinese. In addition, Chinese has other markers to indicate the passive that you might encounter elsewhere (e.g., *gěi* 給／给, *jiào* 叫, and *ràng* 讓／让).

■ *Usually, Mr. Zhang's friends do not come to his house (to visit), but that day many came to his house. Why? Because on that (particular) day, they were all attracted by the painting.*

Píngcháng Zhāng xiānsheng de péngyou hěn shǎo dào tā jiā qù, kěshì nèi tiān hěn duō péngyou dōu lái le. Wèishénme? Yīnwèi tāmen dōu shì bèi nà fú huà xīyǐn guòlai de.

平常張先生的朋友很少到他家去，可是那天很多朋友都來了。為甚麼？因為他們都是被那幅畫吸引過來的。／平常张先生的朋友很少到他家去，可是那天很多朋友都来了。为什么？因为他们都是被那幅画吸引过来的。

ACTION: The subject (Zhang's friends) is acted upon by something, in this case the painting. (It is the painting that attracts Zhang's friends.)

STRUCTURE: Again, *bèi* (by) appears, but this time it is accompanied by the *shì . . . de* pattern. Remember, *shì . . . de* highlights a specific aspect of action: it was the painting that brought the friends to visit Zhang.

Exercise: For practice, try translating the English below.

1. Please take my luggage outside. (Use 把.)
   _____

2. My luggage has been stolen! (Use 被.) _____
   _____

3. My stolen luggage was a gift from my father. (Construct a 是…的 sentence with a complex subject.) _____

How did you do? Match the Chinese below with the English above.

a. 我的行李被偷了。

b. 請把我的行李拿出去。／请把我的行李拿出去。

c. 我被偷的行李是我爸爸送的。

▶ Vocabulary

Starred items have appeared previously in *Encounters* Books 1 and 2. Please refer to page R-2 for a list of grammatical abbreviations used throughout this book.

. . . a 啊 P; **Chén Fēng a, tā búcuò.** 陳峰啊，他不错。／陈峰啊，他不错。 Oh, Chen Feng, he's fine.

Āi 哎 Um I

*Aòdàlìyà 澳大利亞／澳大利亚 Australia PW

bàng 棒 good; fine; excellent SV; **Tài bàng le! Zhēn bàng a!** 太棒了！真棒啊！ That's great!

bào yí ge bān 報一個班／报一个班 register for a class VP

bàomíng 報名／报名 sign up VO

*bèi 被 by (someone or some agent) [marker of passive voice; see grammar notes] P

cái 才 just (indicates emphatic tone) A

cháshì 茶室 tearoom N

chuánméi 傳媒／传媒 communications, media N

chūchāi 出差 be away on a business trip VO

chúyì 廚藝／厨艺 art of cooking N

chúyìbān/kè 廚藝班｜課／厨艺班｜课 cooking class N

dà dūshì 大都市 metropolis N

dādàng 搭檔／搭档 partner up (with); team up (with) VP; partner N

fā duǎnxìn 發短信／发短信 send a text message VP

fēngshēngshuǐqǐ 風生水起／风生水起 burgeoning; successful (said of an enterprise) IE

gǎiháng 改行 change to a new profession VO

*gǎnjǐn 趕緊／赶紧 hurriedly; losing no time A

gōngsī 公司 company; corporation N

gōngzuò rìlì 工作日曆／工作日历 work schedule N

guàibude 怪不得 no wonder; so that's why RV

guǎnggào 廣告／广告 advertisement N

guójì 國際／国际 international ATTR

hánjià 寒假 winter vacation N

hǎohāo liáoliao 好好聊聊 have a good chat/talk VP

hǎojiǔbújiàn 好久不見／好久不见 Long time no see! IE

hǎoxiàng 好像 seems; seems as if A

hézuò 合作 cooperate; work together; collaborate V

huánjìng 環境／环境 environment; surroundings N

hútòng 胡同 lane; alley N

*jiāchángcài 家常菜 homestyle cooking/food N

jiǎngkè 講課／讲课 teach; lecture VO

jiànmiàn 見面／见面 meet each other VO

*jīngcháng 經常／经常 frequently; constantly; regularly; often A

jù(ju) 聚(聚) get together (for a chat, meeting, etc.) V

kāi 開／开 open (a course) V

liúxià 留下 leave *(something for someone)* RV

...ma! 嘛 *(indicates that something speaks for itself)* P; **Nǐ de shēngyi búcuò ma!** 你的生意不錯嘛！／你的生意不错嘛！ Wow! Your business is certainly doing well!

máfan nǐ 麻煩你／麻烦你 May I trouble you to . . . ? Will you please . . . ? IE

Měiguó Huárén 美國華人／美国华人 American-born Chinese person N

míngpiàn 名片 business card N

náshǒu 拿手 be good at doing something SV

ng 嗯 *(indicates hesitation)* I

Ò, duì le 哦，對了／哦，对了 Oh, that reminds me *(expresses realization)* I

***qíshí** 其實／其实 in fact; as a matter of fact; actually A

quèrèn 確認／确认 confirm; identify with certainty V

qūjìngtōngyōu 曲徑通幽／曲径通幽 a winding path leading to a secluded spot IE

shāo děng yíxià 稍等一下 just a moment; a moment, please VP

shēngyi 生意 business; trade N

***shíjiānbiǎo** 時間表／时间表 schedule; timetable N

shíxí 實習／实习 work as an intern V

shōu 收 receive; accept V

Sìchuān 四川 *(province in southwestern China known for its very spicy cuisine)* PW

tèsè 特色 characteristic; special feature; hallmark N

wǎnhuì 晚會／晚会 evening event; soiree N

wèihūnqī 未婚妻 fiancée N

xiào yīyuàn 校醫院／校医院 school hospital; student health center N

xìngyùn 幸運／幸运 good fortune; good luck N; fortunate; lucky SV

xīyǐn 吸引 attract; draw one's attention to V

***xuéqī** 學期／学期 semester N

yālì 壓力／压力 pressure; burden; strain N

yàobu(shi) 要不(是) otherwise; or else C

yāoqǐng 邀請／邀请 request; ask of *(someone)*; invite V

yímín 移民 migrate, immigrate VO

(yīng) gāi (應)該／(应)该 ought to; should A

yìzhí 一直 *(indicates a constant state)* A; **Tā yìzhí chūchāi.** 她一直出差。 She's always away on business. *(indicates a constant direction)* A; **Yìzhí zǒu.** 一直走。 Go straight ahead.

yóuxiāng dìzhǐ 郵箱地址／邮箱地址 e-mail address N

zhāo(r) 招(兒)／招(儿) trick; device; move N

zhènghǎo 正好 happen to; as it happens VP

***zhuānmén** 專門／专门 special SV

zhǔchí 主持 take charge of; host; direct; manage V

zhǔchírén 主持人 host; hostess; anchorperson N

▶ Checklist of "can do" statements

After completing this unit, you should be able to perform each of the following tasks:

Listening and speaking

☐ Ask someone about his or her personal background.
☐ Tell several details about your own background.
☐ Ask and answer questions about past connections with people you know.
☐ Make polite comments about information that others share with you.
☐ Make arrangements to get together with old and new acquaintances.

Reading and writing

☐ Read brief statements about other people's backgrounds.
☐ Write a brief note about your own experience learning Chinese.

☐ Decipher some traffic, directional, and decorative signs.
☐ Read a simple story.
☐ Draft a simple story.

Understanding culture

☐ Talk about "lucky" and "unlucky" numbers in Chinese.
☐ Talk about the use of idiomatic expressions and give an example.
☐ Share some information about what people tend to tell you when they introduce themselves.

"Seeking a physician and inquiring about medicine"

尋醫問藥

Xúnyīwènyào

Handling illnesses—a visit to the doctor

In this unit, you will learn how to:

- state physical discomforts and illnesses.
- ask and answer questions about physical conditions.
- ask for and understand directions to move around a clinic.
- follow a health care provider's instructions.
- ask and answer follow-up questions about your health care.

- decipher some signs in a physician's office or clinic.
- comprehend a short story about health care and write one of your own.
- gain an understanding of some aspects of Chinese medicine.

Encounter 1 Visiting a doctor

22.1 *Write the pinyin for the expressions below. Add any other minor ailments you can think of.*

tired: _____

have a headache: _____

have a fever: _____

_____ : _____

_____ : _____

22.2 *View Episode 22, Vignette 1. Put the following events in the order in which they occur.*

_____ Emma says she's not feeling well, and she describes some symptoms.

_____ The teacher announces that there will be a quiz in the next class.

_____ The teacher texts his fiancée, who is an intern at the clinic.

_____ The teacher tells Fang Lan to take Emma to the university clinic.

_____ Emma says she's been waiting for Fang Lan at the library.

22.3 *View Episode 22, Vignette 1 again. Identify who makes each of the following statements (presented in the order in which they are made).*

> a. Fang Lan   b. Emma   c. Teacher Mao   d. The other student

_____ There's a lot I still don't understand.

_____ We got out of class late.

_____ You didn't eat breakfast, did you?

_____ What does "have the runs" mean?

_____ Should we take her to the hospital?

_____ You're married?

_____ I'll send her a text message.

_____ When you're sick, you need to drink a lot of water.

22.4 *View Episode 22, Vignette 1 again.* 請把中文跟英文對上。／请把中文跟英文对上。

____ a. dǎ pēntì 打噴嚏／打喷嚏

____ b. tóuténg 頭疼／头疼

____ c. duì huāfěn guòmǐn 對花粉過敏／对花粉过敏

____ d. tóuyūn 頭暈／头晕

____ e. méiyǒu wèikǒu 没有胃口

____ f. juéde ěxīn 覺得噁心／觉得恶心

____ g. tù 吐

____ h. dùzi bù shūfu 肚子不舒服

____ i. lā dùzi 拉肚子

____ j. fùxiè 腹瀉／腹泻

____ k. yízhèn yízhèn de téng 一陣一陣地疼／一阵一阵地疼

____ l. fāshāo 發燒／发烧

____ m. késòu 咳嗽

1. *feel dizzy*
2. *feel nauseous*
3. *have a headache*
4. *"have the runs"*
5. *throw up*
6. *sneeze*
7. *have diarrhea*
8. *feel waves of pain*
9. *have hay fever (be allergic to pollen)*
10. *have a fever*
11. *have an upset stomach*
12. *cough*
13. *have no appetite*

22.5 *Pair work: Pretend you are not feeling well. Pick three symptoms and write them here in pinyin:* _____, _____, *and* _____. *Now work with a partner. Begin by asking* Nǐ zěnme le? 你怎麼了？／你怎么了？ *(What's wrong with you?) Then guess his or her symptoms by asking* Nǐ X ma? *Answer your partner's questions by saying* Duì, wǒ X *or* Bù, wǒ bú (shì) X. *Continue until you've guessed all three symptoms. Then make one of the following suggestions to your partner:*

Wǒ juéde wèntí bú dà. Guò yìhuǐr jiù hǎo le. 我覺得問題不大。過一會兒就好了。／我觉得问题不大。过一会儿就好了。

Nǐ zuìhǎo huíjiā xiūxi. 你最好回家休息。

Nǐ zuìhǎo qù kàn yīshēng. 你最好去看醫生。／你最好去看医生。

What other advice might you give? 請寫拼音。／请写拼音。

_____

In response to the advice your partner gives you, say one of the following:

Hǎo de. Wǒ huì de. 好的。我會的。／好的。我会的。

Búyòng, méi nàme yánzhòng. 不用，没那麼嚴重。／不用，没那么严重。 *(No need; it's not that serious.)*

If there is time, repeat this exercise with more classmates.

22.6 *When Emma sneezed, one of the students in the class said* chángmìngbǎisuì—*literally, "(May you live) a long life of 100 years"—the equivalent of "Bless you!" in English. Number the characters below to form this phrase.*

___ 百   ___ 命   ___ 長／长   ___ 歲／岁

Walk around the classroom, pretending to sneeze and saying chángmìngbǎisuì *to the sneezers.*

22.7 *In Episode 22, Vignette 2, Emma and Fang Lan go to the university clinic. Write (in English) three things you predict will happen there.*

_____

_____

_____

Try to write the Chinese for these predictions, with help from an online dictionary or your teacher.

_____

_____

_____

22.8 *View Episode 22, Vignette 2. Put the following events in the order in which they occur.*

_____ Emma's classmates call to ask about her.

_____ Luo Xueting checks on Emma.

_____ The doctor writes out a prescription.

_____ The doctor takes Emma's temperature.

_____ The doctor checks Emma's blood pressure.

_____ Emma pays ¥1 for a treatment record booklet.

22.9 *View Episode 22, Vignette 2 again. Answer the following questions.*

Part 1

a. *The clerk who registers Emma notes the following:*

Liúxuéshēng yīnggāi shì zìfèi de. 留學生應該是自費的。／留学生应该是自費的。

So, who is paying for Emma's treatment? Circle one item. 圈選一項。／圈选一项。 Quānxuǎn yí xiàng.

    insurance   Emma herself   the Foreign Student Office

b. *Does Emma eventually register for Chinese or Western treatment?* 圈選一項。／圈选一项。

    Zhōngyī 中醫／中医   Xīyī 西醫／西医

c. *What is the expression for "internal medicine"?* 用拼音填空。

    nèi_____ 内科

d. *Fang Lan and Emma say the following:* Tā yìzhí ěxīn, dàn tā hǎoxiàng yìzhí tù bù chūlái. 她一直噁心，但她好像一直吐不出來。／她一直恶心，但她好像一直吐不出来。 *What does this mean?* 用英文填空。

    She is constantly _____, but all along she doesn't seem to be able to _____.

Part 2

What are Emma's and Fang Lan's answers to each of the following questions posed by the doctor? Circle the correct items. 圈選正確的項目。／圈选正确的项目。 Quānxuǎn zhèngquè de xiàngmù.

1. What seems to be the problem?   (dizziness / stomachache / sneezing / nausea / runny nose / headache)
2. Do you have a fever?   (a little bit / very high fever / no)
3. Did you eat something that didn't agree with you yesterday?   (No. / We ate out. / We ate cold items. / We ate spicy food.)
4. Did you catch a chill?   (yes / no / I don't remember.)
5. How many times did you have the runs?   (none at all / once / many times)
6. Does your stomach hurt?   (sometimes / not at all / constantly)
7. Are you nauseous?   (sometimes / not at all / constantly)
8. Did any of your friends have the same problem?   (yes / no)

Part 3

Now match the Chinese below to their English equivalents in Part 2 on page 27. 請把中文跟英文對上。／请把中文跟英文对上。

_____ Nǐ lā le jǐ cì dùzi? 你拉了幾次肚子？／你拉了几次肚子？

_____ Nǐ zuótiān chī le shénme bù héshì de ma? 你昨天吃了甚麼不合適的嗎？／你昨天吃了什么不合适的吗？

_____ Nǐ shòuliáng le ma? 你受涼了嗎？／你受凉了吗？

_____ Nǐ dùzi téng ma? 你肚子疼嗎？／你肚子疼吗？

_____ Nǐ juéde ěxīn ma? 你覺得噁心嗎？／你觉得恶心吗？

_____ Nǐ péngyou yǒu méiyǒu tóngyàng wèntí de? 你朋友有沒有同樣問題的？／你朋友有没有同样问题的？

_____ Nǐ nǎr bù shūfu? 你哪兒不舒服？／你哪儿不舒服？

_____ Nǐ fāshāo ma? 你發燒嗎？／你发烧吗？

FYI 供你参考

Chinese medicine

Chinese medical practices have been developed over the course of millennia and are documented in classical texts such as the *Huángdì Nèi Jīng* 黃帝內經／黃帝内经 (*Inner Canon of the Yellow Emperor*) and the *Běncǎogāngmù* 本草綱目／本草纲目 (*Compendium of Materia Medica*). Chinese medicine focuses on maintaining one's health through dietary practices, gentle exercise, "right" living, and treatment when necessary through blends of herbs and other natural products, massage, acupuncture, moxibustion (the use of burning mugwort—a small, spongy herb—to facilitate healing), and so on.

Chinese medical practitioners say that they target the root cause of illnesses, which arise from imbalance and disharmony both within the human body and between people and the environment. Although Chinese treatments may not yield immediate results, followers believe that they are better in the long term.

Chinese medical schools offer training in both Western and Chinese medicine, and many hospitals allow patients to choose how they prefer to be treated. In fact, many prescribed courses of treatment will include both approaches: Western for immediate relief and Chinese for long-term benefit.

22.10 請把中文跟英文對上。／请把中文跟英文对上。

___ a. tǐwēnbiǎo 體溫表／体温表

___ b. liáng tǐwēn 量體溫／量体温

___ c. liáng xuèyā 量血壓／量血压

___ d. xuèyā zhèngcháng 血壓正常／血压正常

___ e. huàyàn dàbiàn 化驗大便／化验大便

___ f. kāiyào 開藥／开药

___ g. ná yào 拿藥／拿药

___ h. bìngrén 病人

___ i. zhèngzhuàng 症狀／症状

___ j. guàhào 掛號／挂号

1. *check blood pressure*

2. *thermometer*

3. *normal blood pressure*

4. *take a temperature*

5. *write out a prescription*

6. *analyze a stool specimen*

7. *patient*

8. *fill a prescription*

9. *check in; register (to see a doctor)*

10. *symptom*

22.11 *Pair work: Work with a partner to recite the following guided dialogue between a doctor and a patient. Switch roles and repeat when you are done.*

Doctor	Patient
Ask what the problem is.	Say you have a headache, stomachache, and diarrhea.
Ask if he/she feel nauseous.	Say you're nauseous but can't throw up.
Ask if he/she has a fever.	Say you're a little warm.
Say you'll take his/her temperature.	Say OK. Ask if your temperature is normal.
Say he/she has a slight fever. Say you'll check his/her blood pressure.	Ask if your blood pressure is OK.
Say that his/her blood pressure is normal.	Say your stomach really hurts.
Ask where it hurts.	Point to a spot and say that's where it hurts.
Say you'll write a prescription for some medicine.	Ask what your illness (*bìng* 病) is.
Say there's no real problem (*méi shénme wèntí* 没甚麼問題／没什么问题). Say he/she will be better with some medicine.	Say you don't quite understand. Ask if you'll need to take medicine.
Explain again that you'll write a prescription for some medicine.	Ask another follow-up question, such as: • How long will I need to take the medicine? • Is it Chinese or Western medicine? • Is it expensive?
Make up reasonable answers to all of his/her questions. Ask if there are any more questions.	Say that you understand and there are no more questions. Thank the doctor.
Say, "You're welcome."	Say good-bye.

Grammar Bits 语法点滴

Conjunction junction

You are now at the intermediate level of language learning where advancing to higher levels depends on understanding and creating more complex sentences. Critical to this skill is sentence and clausal linking. Chinese, like most languages, is well stocked with such linkages, most of which involve mastering conjunctions—words that connect or join. Here, we'll review a few old links and learn some new ones. (See Grammar Recap for more conjunctions.)

- **Inferring something with** *jìrán* 既然 **(since)**

Lǎoshī shuō: **Jìrán** Àimǎ bù shūfu, jiù jiào tā bié shàngkè le.

老師說：既然艾瑪不舒服，就叫她別上課了。／老師说：既然艾瑪不舒服，就叫她别上课了。

*(The teacher said: **Since** Emma isn't feeling well, tell her not to come to class.)*

- **Expressing a condition with** *zhǐyào* 只要 **(as long as) and** *zhǐyǒu* 只有 **(only if)**

Nǐ de bìng bù yánzhòng, **zhǐyào** nǐ xiǎoxīn, jiù bú huì chū shénme wèntí.

你的病不嚴重，只要你小心，就不會出甚麼問題。／你的病不严重，只要你小心，就不会出什么问题。

*(Your illness is not serious; **as long as** you're careful, you won't have any problems.)*

Zhǐyǒu nǐ hǎohāor xiūxi, chī zhè ge yào, cái néng bǎ bìng zhìhǎo.

只有你好好兒休息，吃這個藥，才能把病治好。／只有你好好儿休息，吃这个药，才能把病治好。

*(**Only if** you rest well and take this medication will you be able to treat your illness.)*

Zhǐyǒu nǐ xuéhǎo Zhōngwén, cái néng dào Zhōngguó qù gōngzuò.

只有你學好中文，才能到中國去工作。／只有你学好中文，才能到中国去工作。

*(**Only if** you learn Chinese well can you go work in China.)*

- **Expressing a noncondition with** *bùguǎn* 不管 **and** *wúlùn* 無論／无论 **(no matter if/whether)**

Àimǎ shuō: **Bùguǎn** bìng le háishi méi bìng, yīnwèi jīntiān kǎoshì, suǒyǐ tā hái děi qù shàngkè.

艾瑪說：不管病了還是沒病，因為今天考試，所以她還得去上課。／艾瑪说，不管病了还是没病，因为今天考试，所以她还得去上课。

*(Emma said: **No matter whether** she is sick or not, since there's a test today, she has to go to class.)*

Wúlùn nǐ yǒukòng méikòng, nǐ háishi děi qù kàn tā.

無論你有空沒空，你還是得去看他。／无论你有空没空，你还是得去看他。

*(**Whether** you have the time or not, you have to go see him.)*

■ **Expressing concession with** *jiùsuàn* 就算 **(even if)**

Wǒ zhīdao wǒ bìng le, **jiùsuàn** qù shàngkè yǒu yìdiǎn wēixiǎn, wǒ háishi děi qù.

我知道我病了，就算去上課有一點危險，我還是得去。／我知道我病了，就算去上课有一点危险，我还是得去。

*(I know I'm sick; **even if** going to class is a little dangerous, I still have to go.)*

....

Exercise: Chinese is a language flexible enough both to express composite sentences with conjunctions and to do without them. Here are some examples of expressing thoughts similar to those in the previous sentences but without explicit conjunctions. Just for fun, change these sentences by adding the appropriate conjunctions.

1. Tiānqì zài bù hǎo, wǒmen yě yào qù.

   天氣再不好，我們也要去。／天气再不好，我们也要去。

   _____

2. Tāmen lái le, wǒmen dāngrán yào qǐng tāmen chīfàn.

   他們來了，我們當然要請他們吃飯。／他们来了，我们当然要请他们吃饭。

   _____

3. Bǎ zuòyè xiěwán yǐhòu wǒ cái huì qù shuìjiào.

   把作業寫完以後我才會去睡覺。／把作业写完以后我才会去睡觉。

   _____

4. Guāfēng háishi xiàyǔ, wǒ dōu yào qù kàn qiúsài.

   刮風還是下雨，我都要去看球賽。／刮风还是下雨，我都要去看球赛。

   _____

Encounter 2   Reading and writing

22.12 *Here are some notes written by people who aren't feeling well. Read them and then fill out the chart that follows by checking who has what symptoms.*

ⓐ 我早上一起來就覺得有一點不對勁 (bú duìjìn *not quite right*)。全身發冷，喉嚨 (hóulóng *throat*) 癢癢的 (yǎngyǎng de *itchy, scratchy*)。一天下來 (yì tiān xiàlai *through the course of the day*) 開始咳嗽、打噴嚏、流鼻涕 (liú bítì *have a runny nose*)。到了晚上開始發燒了。真難受！我晚飯也沒吃就上床睡覺了。我吃了三天的感冒藥 (gǎnmàoyào *cold medicine*) 才好。

b 每年一到春天我就开始打喷嚏、咳嗽、流鼻涕、眼睛肿 (yǎnjing zhǒng *swollen eyes*)。真不幸 (búxìng *unlucky*)，我对花粉 (huāfěn *pollen*) 过敏。没办法。我要是吃抗过敏药 (kàng guòmǐn yào *anti-allergy medicine*) 的话，会觉得很困很困，所以不喜欢吃。只能继续 (jìxù *continue*) 打喷嚏、咳嗽、流鼻涕、眼睛肿！

c 我因为年龄大了（我今年六十多岁了），所以血压也高。医生让我吃降低 (jiàngdī *lower*) 血压的药，可是吃这种药会让我咳嗽。吃药都有副作用 (fùzuòyòng *side effect*) 的。但是降血压很要紧 (yàojǐn *important*)，所以我只好继续吃药了！

d 我真倒霉 (dǎoméi *be unlucky*)，會暈車 (yūnchē *get carsick*)！一坐上別人開的車，我就開始頭暈，噁心，可是一直吐不出來。要是真的吐出來還會好一點，問題就在吐不出來。所以我只好自己開車。我要是自己開車的話，就不暈車了。真奇怪 (qíguài *strange*)，我不暈飛機，也不暈船，只暈車！

	a	b	c	d
1. *get the chills*				
2. *have a scratchy (itchy) throat*				
3. *have a cough*				
4. *sneeze*				
5. *have a runny nose*				
6. *have a fever*				
7. *have a cold*				
8. *have swollen eyes*				
9. *have hay fever*				
10. *have high blood pressure*				
11. *be carsick*				
12. *be dizzy*				
13. *be nauseous*				

22.13 *Write a note such as the ones in 22.12, briefly describing an occasion when you did not feel well.*

_____

▶ Reading real-life texts

22.14 *Here are some signs Fang Lan and Emma saw at the university clinic.*

a *What do these signs say?* 請把中文跟英文對上。／请把中文跟英文对上。

1. 校医院 xiàoyīyuàn   A. *urgent medical treatment*

2. 急诊 jízhěn   B. *university clinic*

b 1. *The blue headline of this sign states "Today's emergency on-duty (personnel)."* 請用拼音填空。／请用拼音填空。

_____ _____ zhíbān

2. *The line in red indicates three types of professionals on duty: doctors, nurses, and pharmacists.* 請用拼音填空。／请用拼音填空。

_____ _____ yàofáng

3. *Which individuals are on duty? Match the columns.*

a. 医生   1. 杜晋雅 Dù Jìnyǎ

b. 护士   2. 孙同军 Sūn Tóngjūn

c. 药房   3. 张兰琴 Zhāng Lánqín

c *Emma and Fang Lan begin their visit in front of this window.*

1. *What two things do they have to do here?*

☐ *make inquiries*

☐ *register*

☐ *pay*

2. 請把中文跟英文對上。／请把中文跟英文对上。

a. 挂号 guàhào	1. *place*
b. 处 chù	2. *cashier*
c. 收费 shōufèi	3. *registration*

3. *The message in small blue print states the following:* 为您服务 (wèinínfúwù). *Check what this means, approximately:*

☐ *Here to serve you.*

☐ *Ask for a receipt.*

d *What do Emma and Fang Lan do at this window?*

1. ☐ *get a treatment*

☐ *fill out medical records*

☐ *fill a prescription*

2. 請用拼音填空。／请用拼音填空。

Qǔ _____ _____

e *If Emma has to return to the clinic to hand in a stool specimen, she would come first to the window at the top and then to the room at the bottom.*
請把中文跟英文對上。／请把中文跟英文对上。

1. 便 biàn (*short for* 大便 dàbiàn)	A. *analyze*
2. 杯 bēi	B. *room*
3. 化验 huàyàn	C. *cup*
4. 室 shì	D. *stool*

CARE FOR YOURSELF

f *This slogan on the wall is only half translated. What does the other half mean? Try to figure it out using the terms below, and then write in the missing English expressions.*

珍惜　zhēnxī　*cherish*

青春　qīngchūn　*youth*

关爱　guān'ài　_____

自己　zìjǐ　_____

"_____ your _____ and care for yourself."

22.15 *Work alone or with your classmates to make a poster in Chinese advertising the health care services offered at your school. Have your teacher or a Chinese speaker check your draft before finalizing it, and then share it with your classmates.*

▶ Reading a story

22.16 故事：我們的貓生病了。 *Work with a partner or in a small group to read the story below.*

我們家的小貓叫咪咪 (Mīmī)。它非常喜歡吃東西。要是我們給它很多貓食(*cat food*) 的話，它會變得 (biànde *become*) 很胖很胖。所以我們要小心 (xiǎoxīn *be careful*) 不給它太多貓食，不希望它變得太胖。目前 (mùqián *currently*) 咪咪不胖也不瘦，剛剛好 (gānggāng hǎo *just right*)。

白天 (báitiān *during the day*) 沒人在家的時候，咪咪吃完自己的貓食以後，會到處 (dàochù *everywhere*) 去找其他東西吃。我們不讓它出門到外面去抓 (zhuā *to catch*) 鳥 (niǎo *bird*) 啊、老鼠 (lǎoshǔ *mouse*) 啊、或者其他的小動物 (xiǎo dòngwù *small animals*)，只能在屋子 (wūzi *house*) 裡面找吃的。

有一天晚上，我們一家人吃晚飯的時候吃了很多蝦還有魚。吃完了以後，我們把蝦殼 (xiāké *shrimp shells*) 和魚骨頭 (gǔtou *bones*) 倒到一個垃圾袋 (lājīdài *garbage bag*) 裡頭，可是忘了把垃圾袋扔出去 (rēngchūqu *throw out*)。那天晚上，在大家都睡了以後，咪咪吃完了自己的貓食，又到處去找東西吃了。它聞到 (wéndào *smell*) 了垃圾袋裡頭的蝦殼和魚骨頭，就把垃圾袋抓破 (pò *broken, torn*) 了，咬 (yǎo *bite*) 破了，然後把裡面的蝦殼和魚骨頭都吃了。

第二天早上，我們起來一看，覺得小貓好像病了。它在夜裡拉了很多次肚子，也吐了很多次。我們看見了破垃圾袋，就知道它把蝦殼和魚骨頭吃了。我們知道咪咪對蝦有一點過敏，所以它現在一定很不舒服，肚子疼。

我們把它帶去看獸醫 (shòuyī *veterinarian*)。咪咪很不喜歡坐車，可能是因為它在車上會頭暈，一直 "喵喵喵" (miāo miāo miāo) 地大叫，叫了一路。可是沒辦法，獸醫的診所 (zhěnsuǒ *clinic*) 離我們家很遠，只能開車帶小貓去。

到了獸醫的診所，咪咪很不聽話 (tīnghuà *obedient*)，到處抓，到處咬。可是獸醫很能幹 (nénggàn *competent*)，沒被抓到、咬到。她檢查 (jiǎnchá *check*) 了咪咪，量了它的體溫，化驗了它的大便，問了我們很多問題。然後她給咪咪開了藥方。

咪咪回家以後吃了兩天的藥就好了，可是比以前瘦了一點。不過沒關係！過幾天它一定又會胖回來，因為咪咪太愛吃東西了！

22.17 *Write a short story about a visit to the doctor. Have it edited by your teacher or someone else who is fluent in Chinese. Illustrate your story as best as you can before sharing it with your classmates.*

Encounter 3　Extension: Cultural mini-documentary

 View the cultural mini-documentary for this unit and complete the exercises below.

22.18 *The first nine people in the video talk about their strategies for dealing with minor illnesses (0:00–0:50). Check the strategy each speaker mentions.*

Speaker	Do nothing / Natural cure	Self-treat / Buy OTC medicine	Go to a clinic or hospital	Notes
				pharmacy
				home
				káng ("I just stand it.")
				rěn zhe ("toughing it out")
				pharmacy
				school clinic
				depends on your body's ability to adjust
				cheap and reimbursable
				buy medicine

22.19 請把中文跟英文對上。／请把中文跟英文对上。

___ a. zìjǐ zhì 自己治

___ b. mǎi diǎnr yào 買點兒藥／买点儿药

___ c. zìjǐ tiáohé 自己調和／自己调和

___ d. qù xiào yīyuàn 去校醫院／去校医院

___ e. dào yàodiàn qù 到藥店去／到药店去

1. *go to the school clinic*

2. *treat it myself*

3. *go to the pharmacy*

4. *self-adjust*

5. *buy some medicine*

22.20 *In the second part of the video (0:50–1:41), the speakers talk about dealing with major illnesses. Check the statement made by each speaker.*

☐ I'll go to a hospital if the illness is complicated or serious.	☐ I'll go to a hospital if my wife says so.	☐ I'll go to a hospital if I have a fever.	☐ I'll go to a hospital if I need an IV drip.
☐ I'll go to a hospital if I'm near school.	☐ I'll go to a hospital if I feel really bad.	☐ I'll go to a hospital if I can't treat it myself.	☐ I'll go to a hospital if I can get an appointment.
☐ I'll go to a hospital if I'm throwing up.	☐ I'll go to a hospital if I can't treat it myself.	☐ I'll go to a hospital if my friend can take me.	☐ I'll go to a hospital if my fever lasts many days.
☐ If the illness is serious, I'll go to a hospital near school.	☐ If the illness is serious, I'll go to a local clinic.	☐ If the illness is serious, I'll go to a pharmacy.	☐ If the illness is serious, I'll go to my parents' home.
☐ I'll go see a doctor if my family thinks it's OK.	☐ I'll go see a doctor if a clinic is nearby.	☐ I'll go see a doctor if I really can't stand it.	☐ I'll go see a doctor if I have insurance.
☐ If the illness is serious, I'll go to a hospital.	☐ If the illness is serious, I'll ask a friend.	☐ If the illness is serious, I'll call a nurse for advice.	☐ If the illness is serious, I'll call the clinic.
☐ I'll go to a hospital if there's an accident.	☐ I'll go to a hospital if I have a fever.	☐ I'll go to a hospital if I have difficulty breathing.	☐ I'll go to a hospital if it's a major illness.
☐ If it's a major illness, I'll go to a famous hospital.	☐ If it's a major illness, I'll go to one of the larger hospitals.	☐ If it's a major illness, I'll go to a government hospital.	☐ If it's a major illness, I'll go to a private hospital.

| | ☐ If it's a major illness, I'll go to a famous hospital. | ☐ If it's a major illness, I'll go to one of the larger hospitals. | ☐ If it's a major illness, I'll go to a government hospital. | ☐ If it's a major illness, I'll go to a private hospital. |
| ☐ If it's a major illness, I'll go to a famous medical facility. | ☐ If it's a major illness, I'll go to one of the larger medical facilities. | ☐ If it's a major illness, I'll go to a government medical facility. | ☐ If it's a major illness, I'll go to a private medical facility. |

22.21 請把中文跟英文對上。／请把中文跟英文对上。

_____	a. fùzá yìdiǎnr de 複雜一點兒的／复杂一点儿的	1. *a hospital near school*
_____	b. lí xuéxiào jìn de yīyuàn 離學校近的醫院／离学校近的医院	2. *one of the larger hospitals*
_____	c. shízài kángbuzhù 實在扛不住／实在扛不住	3. *if it's a major illness*
_____	d. rúguǒ shì dà bìng de huà 如果是大病的話／如果是大病的话	4. *more complicated*
_____	e. dà yìdiǎnr de yīyuàn 大一點兒的醫院／大一点儿的医院	5. *really can't stand it*

22.22 *In the third part of the video (1:41–3:14), the speakers talk about procedures at the hospital. Mark the statements below* True *or* False, *according to what the speakers say.*

	True	False
a. You may be able to make an appointment in advance.	☐	☐
b. You only have to wait in line one time.	☐	☐
c. At the hospital, you proceed directly to the department/clinic that you need for your illness.	☐	☐
d. One registration desk handles registration (掛號／挂号 guàhào) for multiple departments/clinics.	☐	☐
e. If you need lab tests, you will have to return to the doctor's office after getting the results.	☐	☐
f. Lab test fees are included in the cost of your registration.	☐	☐

22.23 *Here are some of the phrases used by the speakers.* 請用英文填空。／ 请用英文填空。

draw blood	*make a payment*	*wait at the office door*
give you a number	*pick up medicine*	*wait in line*
go really early	*check in; register*	*write a prescription*
have a lab test done	*see the doctor*	
make an appointment in advance	*take your temperature*	

Appointments and registration

guàhào 掛號／挂号 _____

yùyuē 預約／预约 _____

gěi nǐ yí ge hàomǎ 給你一個號碼／给你一个号码 _____

jiāo qián 交錢／交钱 _____

At the hospital

hěn zǎo hěn zǎo qù 很早很早去 _____

liángyiliáng tǐwēn 量一量體溫／量一量体温 _____

páiduì 排隊／排队 _____

zài yīshēng de ménkǒu děng 在醫生的門口等／在医生的门口等

_____

kàn yīshēng 看醫生／看医生 _____

Lab work and prescriptions

chōu xiě 抽血 _____

huàyàn 化驗／化验 _____

kāi yàofāng 開藥方／开药方 _____

lǐng yào 領藥／领药 _____

Recap

▶ Grammar

Linking your thoughts

Here are some more linking words—some are single words, whereas others occur in related pairs. Let's see how both types work in the following categories.

■ Contrasting

Àimǎ hěn xiǎng shuì, **kěshì** shuìbuzháo.

艾瑪很想睡，可是睡不著。／艾玛很想睡，可是睡不着。

*(Emma really wanted to sleep, **but** she couldn't fall asleep.)*

Àimǎ **suīrán** hěn xiǎng shuì, **kěshì** shuìbuzháo.

艾瑪雖然很想睡，可是睡不著。／艾玛虽然很想睡，可是睡不着。

Although *Emma really wanted to sleep, she couldn't fall asleep.*

Fāng Lán shuō: Àimǎ, wǒmen kuài zǒu, **fǒuzé** kànbúdào Luó Yīshēng.

方蘭説：艾瑪,我們快走，否則看不到羅醫生。／方兰说：艾玛,我们快走，否则看不到罗医生。

*Fang Lan said, "Emma, let's go quickly **or else** we won't see Dr. Luo."*

Fāng Lán shuō: Àimǎ, **chúfēi** wǒmen xiànzài qù, **fǒuzé** kànbúdào Luó Yīshēng.

方蘭説：艾瑪，除非我們現在去，否則看不到羅醫生。／方兰说：艾玛，除非我们现在去，否则看不到罗医生。

*Fang Lan said, "Emma, **unless** we go now, we won't see Dr. Luo."*

■ Choice

Guàhào yuán shuō: Fù xiànjīn **huòzhě** kāi zhīpiào, dōu xíng.

掛號員説：付現金或者開支票，都行。／挂号员说：付现金或者开支票，都行。

*The registrar said, "Pay by cash **or** write a check; both are OK."*

Guàhào yuán shuō: Nǐ **huòzhě** fù xiànjīn **huòzhě** kāi zhīpiào **huòzhě** shuākǎ, dōu xíng.

掛號員説：你或者付現金或者開支票或者刷卡，都行。／挂号员说：你或者付现金或者开支票或者刷卡，都行。

*The registrar said, "Pay by cash **or** write a check **or** use a credit card; all are OK."*

■ Cause and effect

Àimǎ bìng le, **suǒyǐ** méi lái cānjiā wǎnhuì.

艾瑪病了，所以沒來參加晚會。／艾玛病了，所以没来参加晚会。

*Emma got sick, **so** she didn't attend the party.*

Yīnwèi Àimǎ zuìjìn shuìbuhǎo jiào, **suǒyǐ** bìng le.

因為艾瑪最近睡不好覺，所以病了。／因为艾玛最近睡不好觉，所以病了。

Because *Emma hasn't been sleeping well, she got sick.*

Àimǎ tūrán bìng le, **yīnwèi** chī le bù héshì de dōngxi. (tūrán 突然 *suddenly*)

艾瑪突然病了，因為吃了不合適的東西。／艾玛突然病了，因为吃了不合适的东西。

*Emma suddenly got sick, **because** she ate something that didn't agree with her.*

■ Expressing "apart from / in addition to"

Dàifu duì Àimǎ shuō: **Chúle** chī zhèi ge yào **yǐwài**, nǐ hái děi xiūxi yì liǎng tiān.

大夫對艾瑪説：除了吃這個藥以外，你還得休息一兩天。／大夫对艾玛说：除了吃这个药以外，你还得休息一两天。

*The doctor said to Emma, "**In addition** to taking this medication, you also have to rest for a day or two."*

Chúle yào jiāo gōngkè **yǐwài**, wǒmen hái yào zuò yí ge xiǎo cèyàn.

除了要交功課以外，我們還要做一個小測驗。／除了要交功课以外，我们还要做一个小测验。

Besides *turning in the assignment, we also have to take a quiz.*

■ **Expressing supposition**

Lǎoshī, **rúguǒ** méiyǒu cèyàn (de huà), nà jiù hěn wánměi le.

老師，如果沒有測驗（的話），那就很完美了。／老师，如果没有测验（的话），那就很完美了。

*Teacher, **if** there weren't a test, it would be perfect.*

Àimǎ, **yàoshi** nǐ yuànyi, wǒ kěyǐ dài nǐ qù kàn yīshēng.

艾瑪，要是你願意，我可以帶你去看醫生。／艾玛，要是你愿意，我可以带你去看医生。

*Emma, **if** you like, I can take you to see the doctor.*

▶ Vocabulary

Please refer to page R-2 for a list of grammatical abbreviations used throughout this book.

āsīpǐlín 阿司匹林 aspirin N

bìnglì(běn) 病曆(本)／病历(本) medical record; case history N

bìngrén 病人 patient N

bìyào 必要 need N; necessary; indispensable SV

cèyàn 測驗／测验 test; examination N; **xiǎo cèyàn** 小測驗／小测验 quiz

chángdào 腸道／肠道 intestines N

chángmìngbǎisuì 長命百歲／长命百岁 bless you *(said when someone sneezes)* IE

chūxiàn 出現／出现 appear; arise; emerge V

dǎ pēntì 打噴嚏／打喷嚏 sneeze VO

dàbiàn 大便 feces N

dàifu 大夫 doctor; physician N

dùzi 肚子 stomach; belly N

èn 摁 press with hand or fingertip V

ěxīn 噁心／恶心 feel nauseated; feel like vomiting; be sick VO

fàngxīn 放心 feel relieved; set one's mind to rest RV

fànwéi 範圍／范围 scope; extent; range; limits N

fāshāo 發燒／发烧 have a fever VO

fùxí 複習／复习 review *(what has been learned)* V

fùxiè 腹瀉／腹泻 diarrhea N

gǎnrǎn 感染 infect V; infection N

gēbo 胳膊 arm N

guàhào 掛號／挂号 check in; register (to see a doctor) VO

guānxīn 關心／关心 be concerned about; worry about V

guānzhào 關照／关照 look after V

gūjì 估計／估计 estimate; appraise; looks as though V

guòmǐn 過敏／过敏 have an allergy V; allergy N

héshì 合適／合适 suitable; appropriate SV

huāfěn 花粉 pollen N

huàyàn 化驗／化验 have a lab test V

jiā dào yèxià 夾到腋下／夹到腋下 place something in the armpit VP

jiǎnchá 檢查／检查 inspect; examine V

jìdé 記得／记得 remember V

jié 節／节 *(for classes)* M

jìnxíng 進行／进行 carry out; conduct V

kāiyào 開藥／开药 prescribe; write out a prescription VO

kànbìng 看病 see a doctor; see a patient VO

kàngshēngsù　抗生素　antibiotic　N

kǎochá　考察　check over; examine　V

késòu　咳嗽　cough　V

lā dùzi　拉肚子　suffer from diarrhea; have loose bowels　VO

liáng　量　measure　V

liú bítì　流鼻涕　have a runny nose　VO

liúxuéshēng　留學生／留学生　foreign student; student studying abroad　N

ná yào　拿藥／拿药　fill a prescription　VO

nào dùzi　鬧肚子／闹肚子　have diarrhea　VO

nèikē　內科　internal medicine　N; **wàikē**　外科　surgical department

nèiróng　內容　content; essence　N

nòng　弄　make; do; handle　V

páichú　排除　eliminate　RV

qíngkuàng　情況／情况　situation; condition; state of affairs　N

qīngwēi　輕微／轻微　trivial　SV

shòuliáng　受涼／受凉　catch a chill/cold　VO

tàng　燙／烫　burning hot　SV

téng　疼　ache; painful　SV

tǐwēnbiǎo　體溫表／体温表　thermometer　N

tóuténg　頭疼／头疼　have a headache　VO

tóuyūn　頭暈／头晕　dizzy　VP

tù　吐　vomit; throw up　V

wánměi　完美　perfect; flawless　SV

wèikǒu　胃口　appetite　N

wǒ méishì　我没事　I'm fine; nothing wrong; no problem　IE

xīyī　西醫／西医　Western medicine; a doctor trained in Western medicine　N

xuéshengzhèng　學生證／学生证　student ID　N

xuèyā　血壓／血压　blood pressure　N

yánzhòng　嚴重／严重　serious; grave; critical　SV

yàodiǎn　要點／要点　main points; essentials; gist　N

yīyuàn　醫院／医院　hospital　N

yízhèn yízhèn de　一陣一陣地／一阵一阵地　wave after wave (of pain)　A

zhèngcháng　正常　normal　SV

zhèngjiàn　證件／证件　credentials; ID　N

zhèngzhuàng　症狀／症状　symptoms　N

zhēnjiǔ　針灸／针灸　acupuncture and moxibustion (traditional Chinese medicine made from mugwort)　N

Zhōngcǎoyào　中草藥／中草药　Chinese herbal medicine　N

Zhōngyī　中醫／中医　traditional Chinese medicine; a doctor trained in traditional Chinese medicine　N

zhǔyào　主要　main; principal; major; chief　ATTR; primarily　A

zhùyì　注意　pay attention; take note of　V

zìfèi　自費／自费　pay one's own expenses　V

zǐxì　仔細／仔细　careful; attentive; meticulous　SV; carefully; with care　A

▶ Checklist of "can do" statements

After completing this unit, you should be able to perform each of the following tasks:

Listening and speaking

☐ Understand some details when someone says he or she is not feeling well.

☐ Make statements about your own condition, if you are not feeling well.

☐ Ask to go see a doctor.

☐ Describe key symptoms to a doctor.

☐ Follow instructions given in a clinic.

☐ Figure out a doctor's instructions by listening and asking follow-up questions, if necessary.

☐ Begin to use conjunctions to link sentences in your speech.

Reading and writing

☐ Understand a note written by someone who isn't feeling well, and write one yourself.

☐ Decipher some signs in a clinic.

☐ Read a short story about illness, and write one of your own.

Understanding culture

☐ Be able to make 2–3 accurate statements about Chinese medicine.

☐ Be able to make 2–3 accurate statements about what Chinese people tend to do when they don't feel well.

"A person of good character obtains wealth properly"

君子愛財，取之有道

Jūnzǐ ài cái, qǔ zhī yǒu dào

Finance and banking

In this unit, you will learn how to:

- ask for help opening a bank account.
- interact with bank employees.
- open a bank account.
- deposit money into a bank account.

- withdraw money from a bank account.
- use an ATM.
- decipher some signs in a bank.
- comprehend a short story about banking and finance, and write one yourself.

Encounter 1   Using banking services

23.1 *The Fang family (Lǎo Fāng = father, Zhāng Sūyún = mother, Fāng Lán, Emma) is gathered at home, conversing before a meal. Mr. Fang is a teacher and an amateur performer of* jīngjù *(Beijing opera). He is also the cook of the family. His wife, Ms. Zhang (Chinese women generally do not take their husbands' family names), is a real estate broker, and she manages the family expenses.* 請把中文跟英文對上。／ 请把中文跟英文对上。

_____ a. jīngjù 京劇／京剧   1. *performance fee*

_____ b. sān chǎng xì 三場戲／三场戏   2. *three shows*

_____ c. chàngxì 唱戲／唱戏   3. *Beijing opera*

_____ d. yǎnchū fèi 演出費／演出费   4. *Jingju face painting*

_____ e. piàoyǒu 票友   5. *amateur performer*

_____ f. jīngjù liǎnpǔ 京劇臉譜／京剧脸谱   6. *sing in musical theatre*

23.2 *View Episode 23, Vignette 1. Put the following events in the order in which they occur.*

_____ Zhang Suyun complains that her husband is singing one line over and over.

_____ Mr. Fang says that the Communications Bank (*Jiāotōng Yínháng*) is offering a new service.

_____ Emma says she needs to open a bank account.

_____ Mr. Fang is surprised to learn that his last performance fee hasn't been deposited yet.

_____ Zhang Suyun says that her husband is an amateur performer of Jingju.

_____ Fang Lan offers to accompany Emma to the bank tomorrow.

23.3 *View Episode 23, Vignette 1 again. Identify who makes each of the following statements (presented in the order in which they are made).*

a. Zhang Suyun	b. Mr. Fang	c. Fang Lan	d. Emma

_____ Why are you always singing this one line?

_____ I'm learning a new play.

_____ ¥3,000 yuan for three shows.

_____ The performance fee hasn't reached our account.

_____ All you know is teaching and Jingju artistry!

_____ The Communications Bank has a new service.

_____ They inform you by text message.

_____ That sounds convenient.

_____ Is this a Halloween mask?

_____ Our teacher mentioned it today.

_____ We paint this mask on our faces.

_____ We don't need to open a new account.

_____ I need an account at a Chinese bank.

_____ You're a good father and a good husband.

_____ Go cook!

FYI 供你参考

Bejing opera

Fang Lan's father is an amateur singer of *jīngjù* 京劇／京剧, which is also called Beijing opera. He sings a male role—in this case, specifically the part of *Zhūgě Liàng* 諸葛亮／诸葛亮, a legendary military strategist in Chinese history and a frequent subject of Jingju. Jingju actors represent role types more than individualized characters; for example, "dignified older male," "virtuous upper-class woman," "handsome young man," "vivacious young female," "martial larger-than-life male," and "clown." The martial larger-than-life males sport colorful painted faces, with each of the colors indicating a distinct personality trait—red for loyalty, white for trickery, black for integrity, green for chivalry, yellow for cruelty, purple for wisdom, and so on. All the actors speak, sing, and move in time to music played by a live orchestra.

23.4 *View Episode 23, Vignette 1 again.* 請把中文跟英文對上。／请把中文跟英文对上。

_____ a. dàozhàng 到賬／到账

_____ b. Jiāotōng Yínháng 交通銀行／交通银行

_____ c. guǎnggào 廣告／广告

_____ d. yínháng zhànghù 銀行帳戶／银行帐户

_____ e. zījīn 資金／资金

_____ f. tōngzhī 通知

_____ g. fāngbiàn 方便

_____ h. kāi yí ge xīn zhànghù (hùtóu) 開一個新帳戶（戶頭）／开一个新帐户（户头）

_____ i. zhíjiē dǎ dào yínháng hùtóuli qù 直接打到銀行戶頭裡去／直接打到银行户头里去

1. *been deposited*

2. *funds*

3. *convenient*

4. *Communications Bank*

5. *direct deposit into the account*

6. *advertisement, commercial*

7. *inform*

8. *bank account*

9. *open a new account*

23.5 *Do you have a bank account? If so, in what bank is it? Make a statement in Chinese about your account, and say something about your bank. If you don't have a bank account yet, where would you open one? Why?* 請寫漢字或者拼音。／请写汉字或者拼音。

_____

_____

Converse with a partner, and exchange information in Chinese. Which bank do you think is better? Why? Write your conclusion below. 請寫漢字或者拼音。／请写汉字或者拼音。

_____

_____

23.6 *Fang Lan speaks about "killing two birds with one stone"—making one trip to the bank to meet Emma's and her parents' needs.*

yījǔliǎngdé

一舉兩得／一举两得

"one lift two attainments"

yīshí'èrniǎo

一石二鳥／一石二鸟

"one stone two birds"

Walk around the classroom and practice these expressions with your classmates. If someone says yījǔliǎngdé, *then you should respond with* yīshí'èrniǎo, *and vice versa. Speak to everyone in the room.*

23.7 *Following are some terms relating to Halloween.*

guǐ 鬼 *ghost*	Wànshèngjié 萬聖節／万圣节 *Halloween*
jiāngshī 殭屍／僵尸 *zombie*	wūpó 巫婆 *witch*
kěpà 可怕 *scary*	xiàrén 嚇人／吓人 *frightening*
kǒngbù 恐怖 *terrifying*	xīxuèguǐ 吸血鬼 *vampire*
nánguā dēng 南瓜燈／南瓜灯 *jack-o'-lantern*	

Make up 2–3 sentences in Chinese about any one of these images and share them with your classmates. See if they can guess which picture you are describing. You do the same for their sentences.

_____

_____

_____

How would you say "Happy Halloween"? Write the pinyin for the characters below:

萬聖節快樂！／万圣节快乐！　_____

Pretend it's Halloween. Walk around and wish your teacher and each of your classmates a Happy Halloween.

23.8 *In Episode 23, Vignette 2, Emma and Fang Lan go to the bank. Check which of the following vocabulary terms you think you will encounter in this segment.*

☐ cúnkuǎn　存款　*deposits*
☐ qǔkuǎn　取款　*withdrawals*
☐ zìdòng qǔkuǎnjī　自動取款機／自动取款机　*ATM*
☐ huòbì duìhuàn　貨幣兌換／货币兑换　*foreign exchange*

23.9 *View Episode 23, Vignette 2. Put the following events in the order in which they occur.*

_____ The reception manager asks for Emma's ID.
_____ Emma creates a secret password.
_____ The teller takes ¥1,000 from Emma to deposit in her account.
_____ The reception manager says there are fees to open an account.
_____ Emma withdraws ¥200.

23.10 *View Episode 23, Vignette 2 again. Answer the following questions.* 圈選一項。／圈选一项。

a. *To open a bank account, there is an activation fee of ¥5 and another fee of ¥10. What is the ¥10 for?*

　　administrative fee　　　　checking fee　　　　annual fee

b. *What document does Emma offer to prove her identity?*
　　shēnfènzhèng 身份證／身份证 *(personal ID card)*
　　hùzhào 護照／护照 *(passport)*

c. *The reception manager says that Fang Lan can fill out the form for Emma, with one proviso. What is it?*
　　Emma needs to sign the application form herself.
　　Emma needs to sign an authorization for Fang Lan.

d. *What is it that Emma has to input twice?*
　　e-mail address　　　　user name　　　　password

e. *How will Emma pay the ¥15 fee?*
　　in cash　　　　automatic deduction

f. *What does Emma say she will do after she withdraws ¥200?*
　　She'll pay back Fang Lan.　　　　She'll treat Fang Lan to a meal.

FYI 供你参考

Personal ID card

It is common practice for people in Taiwan and China to carry around a personal ID card—the equivalent of a driver's license or a state ID card in the United States. Since a smaller percentage of the population drives, these personal ID cards prove one's identity in a variety of situations, such as in banks, hospitals, and government branches.

姓 名　张明
性 别　男　民 族 汉
出 生　1985 年 4 月 22日
住 址　吉林省长春市二道区
　　　　解放路302号

公民身份号码　220105195504221669

23.11 請把中文跟英文對上。／请把中文跟英文对上。

_____ a. bàn yínháng zhànghù 辦銀行帳戶／办银行帐户

_____ b. fèiyòng 費用／费用

_____ c. qǔ hào 取號／取号

_____ d. tián biǎo 填表

_____ e. dài xīnghàor de 帶星號兒的／带星号儿的

_____ f. hēitǐ zì 黑體字／黑体字

_____ g. shēnfènzhèng 身份證／身份证

_____ h. hùzhào 護照／护照

_____ i. zhèngjiàn 證件／证件

_____ j. fùyìn 複印／复印

_____ k. qiānzì 簽字／签字, qiānmíng 簽名／签名

_____ l. shēnqǐng biǎo 申請表／申请表

_____ m. cúnqián 存錢／存钱, cúnkuǎn 存款

_____ n. mìmǎ 密碼／密码

_____ o. àn "quèrèn" 按 "確認"／按 "确认"

_____ p. yòuxià jiǎo 右下角

_____ q. qǔqián 取錢／取钱, qǔkuǎn 取款

1. _fee, charge, expense_

2. _fill out a form_

3. _get a number_

4. _open a bank account_

5. _personal ID_

6. _photocopy_

7. _passport_

8. _boldfaced letter_

9. _sign a name, signature_

10. _asterisked_

11. _identification (document)_

12. _lower right corner_

13. _password_

14. _press "confirm"_

15. _make a withdrawal_

16. _application form_

17. _make a deposit_

23.12 *Pair work:* Work with a partner to practice the following guided dialogue between a customer and a bank teller. Switch roles and repeat when you are done.

Bank teller	Customer
Greet the customer.	Greet the teller. Say you'd like to open an account.
Confirm that he/she is opening an account.	Confirm. Ask if there's a charge.
Say there is a ¥15 charge.	Say that's not a problem.
Ask for his/her ID.	Hand over your ID and say what it is. (*jiàshǐzhèng* 駕駛證／驾驶证 driver's license)
Say you'll make a photocopy. Ask him/her to wait.	Say that's not a problem.
Hand over a form and ask him/her to fill it out.	Say OK. Ask where you should sign.
Tell him/her to sign in the lower right corner.	Say OK. Say you're done. (*Tián hǎo le* 填好了)
Ask how much he/she wants to deposit.	Say you want to deposit ¥1,000.
Confirm the amount.	Confirm.
Ask if he/she wants a bank card.	Say that you want a bank card.
Hand over the bank card. Say it has ¥1,000 on it.	Say thank you. Ask if you should pay the ¥15 now.
Say yes.	Hand over ¥15.
Say thanks. Hand over a receipt and say what it is. (*shōujù* 收據／收据 receipt). Ask if he/she needs anything else.	Say thanks, no, you're all done.
Thank him/her for choosing your bank. Ask him/her to come again.	Say thanks. Say good-bye.

Encounter 2   Reading and writing

23.13 *Following are five text messages. Match them up with the responses that follow.*

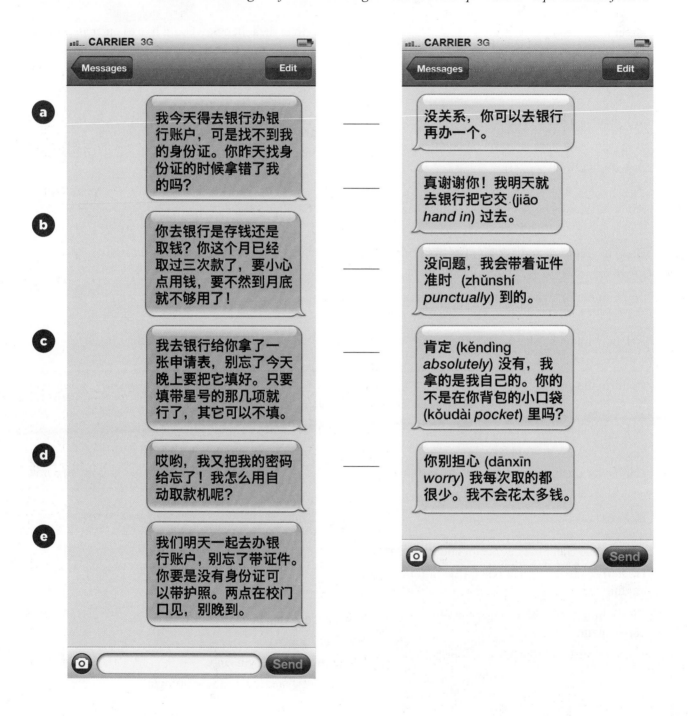

a 我今天得去银行办银行账户，可是找不到我的身份证。你昨天找身份证的时候拿错了我的吗？

b 你去银行是存钱还是取钱？你这个月已经取过三次款了，要小心点用钱，要不然到月底就不够用了！

c 我去银行给你拿了一张申请表，别忘了今天晚上要把它填好。只要填带星号的那几项就行了，其它可以不填。

d 哎哟，我又把我的密码给忘了！我怎么用自动取款机呢？

e 我们明天一起去办银行账户，别忘了带证件。你要是没有身份证可以带护照。两点在校门口见，别晚到。

没关系，你可以去银行再办一个。

真谢谢你！我明天就去银行把它交 (jiāo *hand in*) 过去。

没问题，我会带着证件准时 (zhǔnshí *punctually*) 到的。

肯定 (kěndìng *absolutely*) 没有，我拿的是我自己的。你的不是在你背包的小口袋 (kǒudài *pocket*) 里吗？

你别担心 (dānxīn *worry*) 我每次取的都很少。我不会花太多钱。

▶ Reading real-life texts

23.14 *These are some signs Fang Lan and Emma saw at the bank.*

a *The name of the bank is written in traditional characters, for elegance. Write the pinyin.*

_____ _____ _____ ____

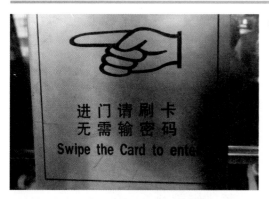

b *The Chinese for this sign is rhymed, and it says more than the English. Fill in the blanks in the translation.* 用英文填空。

Jìnmén qǐng shuākǎ, wúxū shū mìmǎ.

To enter the door, please _____;
there's no need to enter a _____.

c *Again, the English is terse, and the Chinese says more.* 用拼音填空。

Nín yǐ _____
24 _____ jiānkòng qūyù.
You have entered an area under 24-hour surveillance.

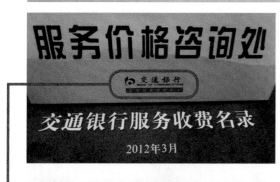

d *This counter offers a list of charges for various services.* 用英文填空。

Fúwù jiàgé zīxúnchù
Jiāotōng Yínháng
Nín de cáifù guǎnlǐ yínháng
Jiāotōng Yínháng fúwù shōufèi mínglù
2012 nián 3 yuè

_____ *prices inquiry (counter)*
Bank of Communications
Your _____ *for wealth management*
Bank of Communications _____ _____ *roster*
March 2012

e *What kind of exchange is available here?*
用英文填空。

Huòbì duìhuàn

_____ exchange

f *Write the pinyin for this sign over a service window.* 用拼音填空。

_____

Now serving #064

g *When Emma was done creating and entering her password, she selected "Enter"* (quèrèn 确认) *[rather than "Cancel"* (qǔxiāo 取消)]*. Fang Lan then told her to press the blue button on the bottom row. What are they selecting by pressing the blue button?* 圈選一項。／圈选一项。

extremely satisfied   not satisfied   basically satisfied
[with the service they have received; 满意 = *mǎnyì*]

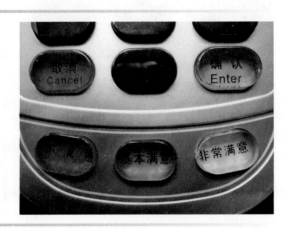

h *The Visa Pacific Card is the credit card offered by the Bank of Communications. Write the correct tones over the pinyin.*

Huanying shiyong Jiaotong Yinhang Taipingyang ka.

i *This poster in the bank is requesting that everyone join in the effort against counterfeit currency.* 用拼音填空。

(jiǎ 假 *fake;* zé 责 *responsibility*)

Fǎn jiǎ _____

_____ _____ yǒu zé

Àihù Rénmínbì, fǎn jiǎ Rénmínbì.

Guarding against counterfeit currency is everyone's responsibility. Protect the RMB; guard against counterfeit RMB.

j *Based on this sign, match the columns below.*
把中文跟英文對上。／把中文跟英文对上。

1. 客户 kèhù   A. *telephone*
2. 服务 fúwù   B. *opinion, suggestion*
3. 电话 diànhuà   C. *customer*
4. 意见 yìjiàn   D. *box*
5. 箱 xiāng   E. *service*

k *Can you decipher this sign with the help of the glossary below? Write the English below.* 請寫英文。／请写英文。

民警	mínjǐng	*People's Police*
提示	tíshì	*warning*
提取	tíqǔ	*withdraw*
防止	fángzhǐ	*guard against*
被尾随	bèi wěisuí	*be followed, be tailed*

_____

_____

l *Once again, the Chinese is wordier than the English translation. Write the correct tones over the pinyin, and fill in the blanks in the English translation.*

Jinzhi chongwu runei

Pets are _____ *to* _____.

23.15 *After they were finished inside the bank, Emma and Fang Lan went to the ATM to try out Emma's new bank card. Following are some of the screens they saw.*

a *The first screen states, "Please read your card in the card-reading area below."* 请在下方读卡区域读卡。

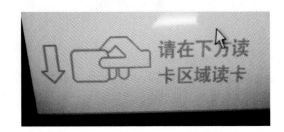

Please write the pinyin for the following:

below _____   read card _____

---

b *The next screen offers the following instructions.*

1. 用英文填空。

请选择服务项目 Qǐng xuǎnzé fúwù xiàngmù

_____ *items*

2. *Look at the glosses at the bottom of the page.* 然後把中文跟英文對上。／然后把中文跟英文对上。

跨行交易可能产生手续费，如需了解费率信息，请致电95559或联系发卡行

Kuàháng jiāoyì kěnéng chǎnshēng shǒuxùfèi, rú xū liǎojiě fèilǜ xìnxī, qǐng zhìdiàn 95559 huò liánxì fākǎ háng.

Transactions between banks can incur handling fees. If you wish to obtain information about fee schedules, please call 95559 or contact the bank that issued the card.

a. 交易 jiāoyì	1. *understand*
b. 手续费 shǒuxùfèi	2. *call by phone*
c. 了解 liǎojiě	3. *transaction*
d. 费率 fèilǜ	4. *information*
e. 信息 xìnxī	5. *fee schedule*
f. 致电 zhìdiàn	6. *bank that issued the card*
g. 联系 liánxì	7. *handling fee*
h. 发卡行 fākǎháng	8. *contact*

3. *The functions indicated by the buttons on the screen are glossed below.* 請把中文跟英文對上。／请把中文跟英文对上。

a. 代理缴费 dàilǐ jiǎofèi   1. *withdraw funds*

b. 取款 qǔkuǎn   2. *make a payment*

c. 余额查询 yú'é cháxún   3. *withdraw card*

d. 取卡 qǔkǎ   4. *check balance*

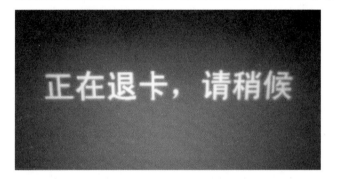

c *Can you decipher this message with the help of these hints?* 請寫英文。／请写英文。

zhèngzài   *in the midst of, in the process of*

tuìkǎ   *return the card*

shāohòu   *wait a while*

_____

d *This is a bad message to get. The first half states* Wúxiào zhōngduān *(Terminal not functioning). The rest of the message suggests* qǐng liánxì yínháng. *What is it telling you to do?* 請寫英文。／请写英文。

_____

e *If you see the following message on an ATM machine, you should move on.* 請把拼音跟英文對上。／请把拼音跟英文对上。

1. zàntíng fúwù   A. *This machine is undergoing maintenance.*

2. fēicháng bàoqiàn   B. *Please use other equipment of the Bank of Communications.*

3. běnjī zhèngzài wéihù   C. *Temporarily out of service.*

4. qǐng shǐyòng Jiāotōng Yínháng qítā shèbèi   D. *We are very sorry.*

▶ Reading a story

23.16 故事：田裡的黃金。 *Work with a partner or in a small group to read the story below.*

很久很久以前，在中國的一個小鄉村裡，有一對老夫婦，都是農民。他們家很窮 (qióng *poor*)，只能靠種自己的一塊地過日子。

這對老夫婦有一個兒子。這個孩子已經長大了，身體很好，身材也不錯，又高又壯 (zhuàng *strong*)。只可惜他生來就很懶 (lǎn *lazy*)。他看見鄰居都比自己家有錢，覺得很不公平 (gōngpíng *fair*)。為什麼別人有錢，自己就沒有？

有一天，媽媽看見兒子特別不高興，也不到地裡來幹活 (gànhuó *work*) 了，就跟他說：兒呀。其實我們家也有自己的財產 (cáichǎn *property, possessions*)。我們也有金子，是我們祖先留給我們的。

兒子聽到這話就高興地跳了起來，說：真的嗎？金子都在哪兒呢？為什麼不趕快拿出來用？

媽媽說：金子不能隨便放。我們把它藏 (cáng *hide*) 起來了，埋 (mái *bury*) 在田地裡，需要的時候才能去取。

兒子很生氣地說：為什麼我們不能現在就去把金子找出來，開始花呢？那樣我們就可以跟別人一樣過上舒適 (shūshì *comfortable*) 的日子了。媽，趕快告訴我，我們的金子在哪裡？我現在就去取。

媽媽回答：我不是說了嗎？金子都埋在田地裡，具體 (jùtǐ *specifically*) 哪兒我也說不清。你自己去找吧、去挖 (wā *dig*) 吧。

兒子聽到有金子埋在地裏就來勁 (láijìn *exciting, enthusiastic*) 了，提起工具就到田裡去挖了。從他們家那塊地的左上角開始挖，橫著過來，一行一行地挖到地的右下角，把所有的泥土 (nítǔ *earth*) 都翻過去了，可是什麼也沒找到。

可是他沒有放棄 (fàngqì *give up*)，又開始從地的左上角挖，這次挖得更深了，又一直挖到了右下角，可是還是沒有找到金子。

這時候，他爸爸默默 (mòmò *silently*) 地跟在他後面，把種子撒 (sǎ *sow*) 在他耕 (gēng *plow*) 好的田地裡，然後澆 (jiāo *irrigate, water*) 上水。

兒子勞動了很久也沒找到什麼金子，非常失望。他母親說：兒呀！你別失望。你先到鎮 (zhèn *town*) 上去，問問張叔叔這是怎麼回事，我們家的金子到哪兒去了？張叔叔是大夫，你去跟他學醫去。學完六個月以後，他肯定會告訴你，我們的金子到底在哪兒，然後你再回來告訴我們。

然後兒子就去鎮上，和張叔叔學了半年的醫術 (yīshù *medical skill*)。半年過去以後，張叔叔告訴他：你回家吧。你們家的金子就在那兒等著你呢。孩子聽了高興極了，趕快跑回家。

他到了家裡一看，地裡長滿了綠油油 (yóuyóu *luxuriant and dense*) 的一片菜田。他父母正在割 (gē *cut, harvest*) 菜，等到包好這些菜後就運到城裡去賣。他媽媽掏 (tāo *take out*) 出一大包錢來給兒子看，說：兒子！這不是金子嗎？你快把這錢拿到農業銀行去，存到我們的帳戶裡，然後回來開一個小診所，給我們村裡的鄰居們看病！

從此以後，兒子再也不懶了。每到春天，他就到田地裡去"找金子"，完了以後就回來開他的小診所，活得很高興！

23.17 *Write a short story about money. Have it edited by your teacher or someone else who is fluent in Chinese. Illustrate your story as best as you can before sharing it with your classmates.*

Encounter 3 Extension: Cultural mini-documentary

 View the cultural mini-documentary for this unit and complete the exercises below.

23.18 *The speakers in the video (0:00–1:52) first talk about generational differences among Chinese people's conception of money.* 請用拼音填空。／请用拼音填空。

a.
Duì qián de kànfǎ, lǎo yídài hé wǒmen kěndìng _____, yīnwèi jīnglì de niándài bù yíyàng. Hái yǒu, jiùshì shuō, yìxiē guānniàn yě bù yíyàng. Tāmen rènwéi qián _____ zǎn chūlai de, wǒmen rènwéi qián shì zhèng chūlai de. Hái yǒu yí ge, xiànzài de huánjìng kěnéng shuō xiǎng _____ hěn nán, dànshì nǐ yào shuō xiǎng nǔlì qù _____, hái yǒu jīhuì.

对钱的看法，老一代和我们肯定不一样，因为经历的年代不一样。还有，就是说，一些观念也不一样。他们认为钱应该是攒出来的，我们认为钱是挣出来的。还有一个，现在的环境可能说想攒钱很难，但是你要说想努力去挣钱，还有机会。

*When it comes to attitudes toward money, the older generation is certainly **not the same** as we are, because they lived through a different time. And, I mean, some concepts are not the same. They think that money **should be** made by saving it; we believe that money is made by earning it. Also, you might say that in the current environment, **saving money** is difficult, but if you put a real effort toward **making money**, then there are opportunities.*

b.
Shì fēicháng bù yíyàng de, wǒ juéde. Jiùshì, lǎonián rén, tāmen de sīxiǎng, yīnwèi shì cóng shèhuìzhǔyì guójiā guòlai de ma, jiùshì háishi dàizhe yìxiē lǎo _____, shì yǐ bǎoshǒu, jiùshì, wéi jīchǔ. Jiùshì, shéi jiālǐ dōu huì yǒu yìxiē _____ a, bāokuò shì zhànghù lǐ de, yínháng lǐ cún de qián a, _____ shì huì yǒu de, dànshì xiànzài de niánqīng rén jiùshì yǐ xiǎngshòu shēnghuó wéi, zuòwéi zìjǐ de yí ge, jiùshì shēnghuó fāngshì, tāmen jiùshì _____ míngtiān zěnmeyàng, jiùshì jīntiān kāixīn le jiù hǎo. Dànshì lǎoniánrén huì xuǎnzé bǐjiào _____ de nà zhǒng lǐcái fāngshì, zhè shì tāmen chuántǒng de nàge guānniàn zàochéng de.

是非常不一样的，我觉得。就是，老年人，他们的思想，因为是从社会主义国家过来的嘛，就是还是带着一些老思想，是以保守，就是，为基础。就是，谁家里都会有一些现金啊，包括是帐户里的，银行里存的钱啊，肯定是会有的，但是现在的年轻人就是以享受生活为，作为自己的一个，就是生活方式，他们就是不在乎明天怎么样，就是今天开心了就好。但是老年人会选择比较保守的那种理财方式，这是他们传统的那个观念造成的。

*I think they are extremely different. I mean, older people, their way of thinking, because of their coming from a socialist country, they still carry some old **ways of thinking**; they are grounded in conservatism. I mean, everyone's family has some **cash** on hand, including what's in their accounts, the money they have put in the bank, they'll **definitely** have that. But young people nowadays take the enjoyment of life as their own sort of lifestyle. They just **don't care** how tomorrow will be, just as long as they are happy today, then fine. But older people will choose a relatively **conservative** style of money management; this is a product of their traditionalist worldview.*

c.

Xiàng wǒ de bàba māma, tāmen shì méiyǒu xìnyòngkǎ, zhǐyǒu chǔxù kǎ, érqiě jiùshì jīběnshang jiùshì qù _____ hěn shǎo qǔqián, dōu shì _____, dànshì wǒmen zhè yídài ne, jiùshì yǐ _____ wéi zhǔ, jiùshì xiān qù xiāofèi, hòu qù cúnqián, jiùshì xiān bǎ hái méiyǒu zhèng dào de qián děngyú xiān huāle.

像我的爸爸妈妈，他们是没有信用卡，只有储蓄卡，而且就是基本上就是去银行很少取钱，都是存钱，但是我们这一代呢，就是以信用卡为主，就是先去消费，后去存钱，就是先把还没有挣到的钱等于先花了。

Take my parents, for example. They don't have credit cards, only debit cards, and you know, basically even if they go to the **bank***, they seldom withdraw money—it's all* **deposits***. But our generation, you know, mainly it's* **credit cards***, you know, consume first and save later, you know, it's like spending the money you haven't made yet.*

d.

Shàng yídài rén, tāmen huì bǎ qián _____, ránhòu huì huā de hěn shǎo, hěn jiéshěng, dànshì wǒmen _____ ne kěnéng huì pèngjiàn zìjǐ xǐhuan de dōngxi huì mǎi xiàlai, ránhòu, yǒu de shíhou yě huì bù jīngguò dànǎo, ránhòu zìjǐ hěn xǐhuan jiù zhíjiē _____ le, dànshì wǒ juéde shàng yídài de rén _____, huì hěn jīngdǎ-xìsuàn, ránhòu, hěn kòngzhì zìjǐ de nèixiē kāizhī a shénme de.

上一代人，他们会把钱存起来，然后会花得很少，很节省，但是我们这一代呢可能会碰见自己喜欢的东西会买下来，然后，有的时候也会不经过大脑，然后自己很喜欢就直接买下来了，但是我觉得上一代的人不会，会很精打细算，然后，很控制自己的那些开支啊什么的。

The prior generation, they would **save** *their money and then spend very little—very thrifty. But our* **generation***, if they come across something they like, they will probably buy it, and then, sometimes they'll just bypass the cerebral cortex, and since they really like it, they'll go ahead and* **buy** *it, but I think the prior generation* **wouldn't do that***; they would budget carefully and then really control their expenses and whatnot.*

23.19 *The second topic in the video (1:53–4:26) concerns differences between foreigners and Chinese in their relationships to money. Match each statement with its speaker.*

1. ____   2. ____   3. ____   4. ____   5. ____   6. ____   7. ____

a. Young people today have been influenced by several decades of the "reform and opening" [policy], whether it's been by a culture exchange or clash. I feel like whether they are Chinese or foreign, [members of] the younger generation seem to have pretty much the same attitude toward money. Basically, all of them are in the "moonlight" crowd. [*yuèguāngzú* 月光族; i.e., every month 月 they spend their paycheck until it is gone 光.]

b. Maybe it didn't use to be this way, because [back then] when it came to attitudes toward money, East and West were, it seems, different. The Chinese were relatively conservative about money and thought one definitely had to save money—and only then would they have a feeling of security. Maybe Westerners felt that money was meant for consumption—meant for fulfilling one's own needs or whatever. Their degrees of happiness were different. The Chinese assigned greater importance to money. But some young people now are no different from those in the West. You can spend in advance, and the attitude toward money is that it is earned [not saved]. There's no need to hold on to money.

c. But still, we have been influenced by our parents. So maybe in our minds we still have the concept of saving; that is, we will put a part of our income into the bank. Insurance, right?

d. There are a lot of things, such as "going Dutch" [splitting the bill], that—at least so I hear—spread here from abroad. But I am super into that and super willing to adopt things like this because I feel it's really good. It's a very careful way of doing things, and because . . . anyway, the way the people around me spent money when I was growing up, and looking back at it now, if you asked me to compare that way and going Dutch, I feel like I would now choose to go Dutch. Because it's comfortable that way. Very simple.

e. There's an old Chinese saying: "If people don't have distant concerns, then they'll definitely have nearby troubles." [i.e., People who do not take adequate precautions against distant eventualities will someday find themselves beset with difficulties.]

f. Chinese and foreigners' attitudes toward money are different. Foreigners are willing to spend money on things that make them happy, but Chinese pay more attention to the benefits that money can bring, and they will buy things that embody their personal worth and status, such as brand-name cars, brand-name watches, luxury goods, and so forth.

g. I think that now more and more [people] are like in the West, even to the extent of spending tomorrow's money today, going and getting loans and whatnot. And what's more, everyone is bolder about consuming—to spend a bit more on oneself and on one's happiness in the moment.

Recap

▶ Grammar

Not *le* again?! Yes, *le* again.

You've seen *le* many, many times before, but it's a good idea to review and refresh its usage. Here are the main features of this troublesome yet so powerful word.

1. It represents an accomplished fact—something that's over and done with. The object of the verb is usually generalized and nonspecific.

   PLACEMENT: end of a clause or sentence

2. It marks the completion of a specific action that took place in the past. It is verbal object specific and often numbered.

   PLACEMENT: suffixed to verb

3. It marks a newly arising situation and presents a change of what was in effect before. It's often marked with *xiànzài* 現在／现在.

   PLACEMENT: end of a clause or sentence

4. It indicates that an action in the first clause has been completed before something else is done.

   PLACEMENT: end of first clause

5. It indicates that something has gone to the extreme. It's often marked with *tài* 太.

6. It is habitually used with certain verbs that have a built-in ending point, such as "forget."

These are some of the most important uses, but there are others and we'll get to them later on. We will also review when *le* 了 is not used.

Exercise: In the following dialogue between Fang Lan and her father, *le* is used several times. Your task is to identify the reason for each usage by writing the appropriate number in parentheses. Compare your answers with your classmates'. Your teacher will resolve differences of opinion..

• Lǎo Fāng: Nǐ zuótiān dài Emma qù yínháng bàn kāi hùtóu de shìqing, dōu bàn hǎo le (___) ma?

  你昨天帶 Emma 去銀行辦開戶頭的事情，都辦好了嗎？／

  你昨天带 Emma 去银行办开户头的事情，都办好了吗？

• Lǎo Fāng: Nǐmen bàn wánshì yǐhòu, qù nǎr le (___)?

  你們辦完事以後，去哪兒了？／

  你们办完事以后，去哪儿了？

• Fāng Lán: Wǒmen qù le (___) sān ge dìfang, yòu bàn le (___) hǎo jǐ jiàn shì.

  我們去了三個地方，又辦了好幾件事。／

  我们去了三个地方，又办了好几件事。

• Lǎo Fāng: Nà tài hǎo le (___). Nàme nǐ jīntiān xiǎng zuò shénme?

  那太好了。那麼你今天想做甚麼？／

  那太好了。那么你今天想做什么？

• Fāng Lán: Wǒ jīntiān chī le (___) zǎofàn yǐhòu, děi qù yí tàng túshūguǎn.

  我今天吃了早飯以後，得去一趟圖書館。／

  我今天吃了早饭以后，得去一趟图书馆。

• Lǎo Fāng: Nǐ píngcháng bù chī zǎofàn, zěnme jīntiān tūrán yào chī le (___) ne?

  你平常不吃早飯，怎麼今天突然要吃了呢？／

  你平常不吃早饭，怎么今天突然要吃了呢？

• Fāng Lán: Wǒ píngcháng zǎoshang bú è, kěshì jīntiān è sǐ le (___), bù zhīdào wèishénme.

  我平常早上不餓，可是今天餓死了，不知道為甚麼。／

  我平常早上不饿，可是今天饿死了，不知道为什么。

- Lǎo Fāng: Hǎo, nǐ xiǎng chī jiù chī. Kěshì bié wàng le (___) chī wán yǐhòu yào shuāyá.

好，你想吃就吃。可是别忘了吃完以後
要刷牙。／

好，你想吃就吃。可是别忘了吃完以后
要刷牙。

Exercise: For the brave of heart, go through the transcripts of Unit 23, Vignettes 1 and 2 on the *Encounters* website, look for occurrences of *le*, and try to tell what they are doing there.

▶ Vocabulary

Please refer to page R-2 for a list of grammatical abbreviations used throughout this book.

āiyō 哎喲／哎哟 (*of surprise, pain*) I

àn 按 press down; push V

bànlǐ 辦理／办理 handle; set up V

běnrén 本人 oneself; in person N

biàndòng 變動／变动 change V/N

biǎo 表 chart; form; table; schedule N; **gōngkèbiǎo** 功課表／功课表 homework schedule

chā 插 insert; stick into V

chá 查 check; investigate; look up V; **chá zìdiǎn** 查字典 look it up in a dictionary

chǎng 場／场 (*for games, performances, etc.*) M

chūshì 出示 produce; show V

cún 存 save; deposit V

cúnkuǎn, cúnqián 存款, 存錢／存钱 deposit money VO

dài 帶／带 carry something V; **dài xīnghàor de zì** 帶星號兒的字／带星号儿的字 asterisked characters

dānzi 單子／单子 list; bill; form N

dàozhàng 到賬／到账 reach / been posted to [my/the] account VO

dé lìng 得令 receive / take an order VO

duìhuàn 兌換／兑换 exchange V

fèi 費／费 fee; charge N; **yǎnchūfèi** 演出費／演出费 performance fee

fèiyòng 費用／费用 fee; charge N

fúwù 服務／服务 service(s) N; **fúwùyuán** 服務員／服务员 attendant; **fúwùtái** 服務台／服务台 service counter

fùyìn 複印／复印 photocopy; copy; duplicate V

gōngběn(r)fèi 工本(兒)費／工本(儿)费 production / activation fee N

gōngnéng 功能 function N

guǐ 鬼 ghost N

guīnǚ 閨女／闺女 daughter (*unmarried*) N

héduì 核對／核对 check figures/sums; proof RV

hēitǐ zì 黑體字／黑体字 (*printing*) boldfaced letters N

huí 回 (*for times, occurrences*) M

huòbì 貨幣／货币 currency N

hùtóu 戶頭／户头 account N

hùzhào 護照／护照 passport N

jiā 加 plus V

jiàn 鍵／键 button; key (*of a piano, computer, etc.*) N

jiāngshī 殭屍／僵尸 zombie N

jiǎngxuéjīn 獎學金／奖学金 scholarship; stipend N

jiāoyì 交易 transaction; deal N

jīn'é 金額／金额 amount/sum of money N

jīngjìrén 經紀人／经纪人 broker; agent; middleman N

jù 句 (*sentence*) M; **yí jù huà** 一句話／一句话 a sentence; **zhèi jù huà** 這句話／这句话 this sentence; **jùzi** 句子 sentence

kǎ 卡　card　N

kāi kǎ 開卡／开卡　open a card *(account) (for ATM, etc.)*　VO

kěpà 可怕　scary　SV

kǒngbù 恐怖　fearful; horrible　SV

kòuchú 扣除　deduct　RV

liǎnpǔ 臉譜／脸谱　types of theatrical makeup; mask　N

mìmǎ(r) 密碼(兒)／密码(儿)　secret code; password　N

mǐngǎn 敏感　sensitive; susceptible; allergic　SV

nánguā dēng 南瓜燈／南瓜灯　jack-o'-lantern　N

nénggàn 能幹／能干　capable; competent　SV

niánfèi 年費／年费　annual fee/charge　N

piàoyǒu 票友　amateur performer　N

qiānzì, qiānmíng 簽字／签字, 簽名／签名　sign one's name, signature　VO/N

qǔ 取　get; take; obtain　V

quèdìng 確定／确定　be sure; confirm　V

qǔkuǎn, qǔqián 取款, 取錢／取钱　withdraw money　VO

ràng 讓／让　let; allow　CV

rēng 扔　throw away; discard; throw; toss　V

shēnfènzhèng 身份證／身份证　personal ID　N

shēnqǐng biǎo 申請表／申请表　application form　N

shèzhì 設置／设置　*(computers)* install　V

shūrù 輸入／输入　*(computers)* input　V

shùzì 數字／数字　numeral; number; figure; digit　N

suíshēn 隨身／随身　take or have with oneself　VO

suǒyǒu 所有　all; every　ATTR

tí 提　mention; refer to; bring up　V

tián 填　fill in/out *(a form, etc.)*　V

tígōng 提供　supply; furnish; offer　V

tōngzhī 通知　notify　V

tuì (chūlai) 退 (出來／出来)　quit; withdraw from; eject　V

tuīsòng 推送　promote　V

Wànshèngjié 萬聖節／万圣节　Halloween　N

wùpǐn 物品　articles; goods　N; **suíshēn wùpǐn** 隨身物品／随身物品　personal items

wūpó 巫婆　witch　N

xì 戲／戏　drama; play; show　N; **kàn xì** 看戲／看戏　watch a show

xiàngmù 項目／项目　project　N

xiàrén 嚇人／吓人　frightening　SV

xìnxī 信息　information; news; message　N

xìtǒng 系統／系统　system; process　N

xīxuèguǐ 吸血鬼　vampire　N

yǎn 演　perform; play　V

yǎnxì 演戲／演戏　put on or act in a play　VO

yào bùrán 要不然　otherwise; or else; or　C

yèwù 業務／业务　business　N

yèyú 業餘／业余　amateur; spare time　ATTR

yījǔliǎngdé 一舉兩得／一举两得　accomplish two results with one effort; kill two birds with one stone　IE

yīmóyīyàng 一模一樣／一模一样　be exactly alike　IE

yínháng 銀行／银行　bank　N

yīshí'èrniǎo 一石二鳥／一石二鸟　kill two birds with one stone　IE

yìshù 藝術／艺术　art; skill　N

yǒu qí mǔ bì yǒu qí nǚ 有其母必有其女　like mother, like daughter　IE; **yǒu qí fù bì yǒu qí zǐ** 有其父必有其子　like father, like son

yòu xiàjiǎo 右下角　lower-right corner　N

zhànghù 帳戶／帐户　*(business/bank)* account　N

zhènghǎo de 正好的　exactly　A

zìdòng 自動／自动　automatically　A

(zìdòng) qǔkuǎnjī （自動）取款機／（自动）取款机 ATM N

zījīn 資金／资金 fund; capital N

zǒuhuǒrùmó 走火入魔 be obsessed with something IE

zuòwèi 座位 seat; place N

▶ Checklist of "can do" statements

After completing this unit, you should be able to perform each of the following tasks:

Listening and speaking

☐ Ask for help opening a bank account.

☐ Ask and answer questions of bank employees.

☐ Open a bank account.

☐ Deposit money into a bank account.

☐ Withdraw money from a bank account.

☐ Make a comment about Halloween in the United States, and wish someone "Happy Halloween."

Reading and writing

☐ Decipher some signs in a bank.

☐ Use an ATM, following displayed instructions.

☐ Read some text messages related to banking.

☐ Read a short story about money, and write one yourself.

Understanding culture

☐ Make 2–3 accurate statements about Jingju and painted faces.

☐ Make 3–4 accurate statements about some Chinese people's perceptions about differences between their parents' generation and their own, regarding how they deal with money.

☐ Make 3–4 accurate statements about some Chinese people's perceptions about differences between how Chinese and Westerners deal with money.

"It's only natural to want to look beautiful"

愛美之心，人皆有之

Ài měi zhī xīn, rén jiē yǒu zhī

Personal care and appearance

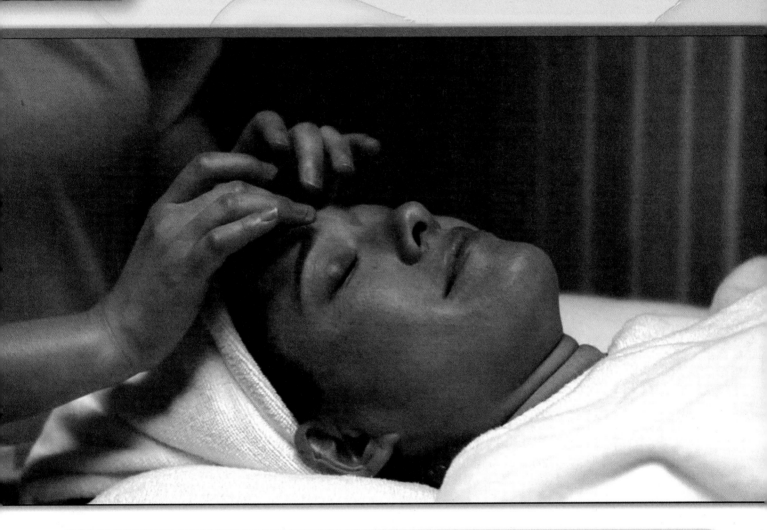

In this unit, you will learn how to:

- ask what personal-care services are available.
- specify what services you want.
- ask about prices of various services.
- give instructions for specific services.

- request adjustments as necessary.
- decipher some signs in a salon.
- comprehend a short story about salon services, and write one of your own.

Encounter 1   A visit to the salon

24.1 *Xiao Mao and Luo Xueting stop by a full-service salon that offers hair styling, facials, mani-pedis, and massages (i.e., spa services). To prepare for communication with the service personnel, match the terms below.* 請把中文跟英文對上。／ 请把中文跟英文对上。

_____ a. jiǎn tóufa 剪頭髮／剪头发   1. *relax*

_____ b. fàngsōng 放鬆／放松   2. *blow-dry*

_____ c. xǐtóu 洗頭／洗头   3. *manicure*

_____ d. chuīgān 吹乾／吹干   4. *haircut*

_____ e. miànbù hùlǐ 面部護理／面部护理   5. *massage*

_____ f. zhǐjia hùlǐ 指甲護理／指甲护理   6. *facial*

_____ g. ànmó 按摩   7. *wash (one's) hair*

24.2 *View Episode 24, Vignette 1. Put the following events in the order in which they occur.*

_____ A woman asks for a wash, cut, and blow-dry.

_____ Xiao Mao pretends to need a haircut.

_____ The salon attendant says he gets two facials a week.

_____ Luo Xueting says she'd like to have her hair cut shorter.

_____ Xiao Mao and Luo Xueting are offered a buy-one-get-one-free discount.

24.3 *View Episode 24, Vignette 1 again. Identify who makes each of the following statements (presented in the order in which they are made).*

> a. Attendant   b. Xiao Mao   c. Luo Xueting   d. Other woman

_____ Hey, the ambiance is pretty nice here.

_____ Do you have any packages here?

_____ I'd like to have my hair cut shorter.

_____ I like your hair long.

_____ Once you make a selection, let me know.

_____ So I could do all three together or each of them separately, right?

_____ So the cost of the perm depends on the texture of the hair?

_____ The price isn't bad either.

_____ We'll take the Beautiful Princess Spa package.

_____ This is for same-day service for your friend or family member.

_____ Beijing is so dry; you can give your skin a little drink.

_____ Can both of us go together?

_____ That's something you women need to do.

_____ Fine, fine. Where do we go then?

24.4 *View Episode 24, Vignette 1 again.* 請把中文跟英文對上。／请把中文跟英文对上。

_____ a. huānyíng guānglín 歡迎光臨／欢迎光临   1. *wash, cut, and blow-dry*

_____ b. lǐmiàn qǐng 裡面請／里面请   2. *discount*

_____ c. xūyào shénme fúwù 需要甚麼服務／需要什么服务   3. *what service do you need*

_____ d. shénme tàocān 甚麼套餐／什么套餐   4. *this way, please*

_____ e. xǐ jiǎn chuī 洗剪吹   5. *welcome*

_____ f. jiàgé 價格／价格   6. *have a facial*

_____ g. tàng tóufa 燙頭髮／烫头发   7. *dye (one's) hair*

_____ h. rǎnfà 染髮／染发   8. *price*

_____ i. yōuhuì 優惠／优惠   9. *please come in*

_____ j. xiǎngshòu ànmó 享受按摩   10. *enjoy a massage*

_____ k. zuòliǎn 做臉／做脸   11. *have a perm*

_____ l. zhè biān qǐng 這邊請／这边请   12. *what set menu (do you want)*

24.5 *Pretend you are going to a Chinese salon. What questions would you ask? List several.* 請寫拼音或者漢字。／请写拼音或者汉字。

_____

_____

_____

What instructions would you give to the stylist/attendant? List several. 請寫拼音或者漢字。／请写拼音或者汉字。

_____

_____

_____

Pretend you are an attendant in the salon. List several questions/statements you would expect to make while interacting with a customer who has just walked in. 請寫拼音或者漢字。／请写拼音或者汉字。

_____

_____

_____

Pair work: Have a brief exchange with a partner. One of you should pretend to be a salon attendant, and the other should be a customer. Ask and answer questions, and then decide on one or more services. Reverse roles and repeat when you are done.

24.6 *Luo Xueting is confused when Xiao Mao talks about getting a "spa package." She says, "Didn't you ask me to keep you company while you get a haircut?"* 請用拼音填空。／请用拼音填空。

Nǐ búshì yào wǒ _____ nǐ jiǎn tóufa ma?

你不是要我陪你剪頭髮嗎？／你不是要我陪你剪头发吗？

Following are some verbs you might know. Walk around the room, asking people to keep you company while you do something.

SUGGESTION: 你可以陪我 *[verb]* 嗎？／你可以陪我 *[verb]* 吗？

POSSIBLE RESPONSES: 可以，没問題/没问题，好 *or* 對不起／对不起，不行，我没時間／我没时间，我怕 [verb]。

qù kàn yīshēng 去看醫生／去看医生 *go to the doctor*

qù mǎicài 去買菜／去买菜 *go grocery shopping*

qù guàngjiē 去逛街 *go window shopping*

qù kàn diànyǐng 去看電影／去看电影 *go to the movies*

qù zhǎo Máo lǎoshī 去找毛老師／去找毛老师 *go see Professor Mao*

24.7 *Following are some terms relating to various salon services. Check those that you would be willing to try. Speak to some of your classmates and find out who would do what.*

Q: 你願意 (yuànyi) _____ 嗎？／你愿意 _____ 吗？

A: 我願意_____。／我愿意 _____。

我不願意_____。／我不愿意 _____。

	自己	同學 1／ 同学 1	同學 2／ 同学 2	同學 3／ 同学 3
a. xǐ jiǎn chuī 洗剪吹 *wash, cut, and blow-dry*	☐	☐	☐	☐
b. tàng tóufa 燙頭髮／烫头发 *perm the hair*	☐	☐	☐	☐
c. rǎnfà 染髮／染发 *color the hair*	☐	☐	☐	☐
d. tiǎorǎn 挑染 *highlight the hair*	☐	☐	☐	☐
e. rùnfū 潤膚／润肤 *skin hydration*	☐	☐	☐	☐

	自己	同學 1／ 同学 1	同學 2／ 同学 2	同學 3／ 同学 3
f. měibái 美白 *even out the skin tone*	☐	☐	☐	☐
g. shēncéng qīngjié 深層清潔／ 深层清洁 *deep clean the skin*	☐	☐	☐	☐
h. miànbù hùlǐ (zuòliǎn) 面部護理(做臉) ／面部护理 (做脸) *have a facial*	☐	☐	☐	☐
i. ànmó 按摩 *massage*	☐	☐	☐	☐
j. zhǐjia hùlǐ 指甲護理／ 指甲护理 *have a manicure/* *pedicure*	☐	☐	☐	☐

24.8 *View Episode 24, Vignette 2. Pay special attention to the instructions given to the masseuse.* 請把中文跟英文對上。／ 请把中文跟英文对上。

____ a. (qǐng àn) zhòng yìdiǎnr （請按）重一點兒／（请按）重一点儿   1. *(please press) harder*

____ b. (qǐng àn) qīng yìdiǎnr （請按）輕一點兒／（请按）轻一点儿   2. *(please press) lighter*

Work with a partner. Give each other shoulder massages. As the recipient of the massage, give instructions (lighter or harder) until the massage is just right. Switch roles.

Encounter 2   Reading and writing

24.9 *Following are some notes written by people about their hair. Read the notes, and then match each note with a picture.*

____ **a** 我每兩個月去剪一次頭髮。我的頭髮不長，短短的，有一點捲。每次剪的時候只剪半寸。有時間的話我就讓洗一下，很舒服。可是我不喜歡吹乾。吹了以後捲頭髮會變直了！

____ **b** 我头发不多，所以宁愿剃光头。这样也省钱，我不需要到理发店里去理，自己在家里就可以理了。我不用照镜子，只需要用电动刮胡刀全头摸着剃就行了。剃光头有个问题，那就是太阳晒了会烫，所以必需戴帽子。

____ **c** 我的头发很长，长到我腰部下面。长头发不好理，只有一位理发师能帮我剪好头发。这位理发师价格很高，可是没办法，我只好付了，因为对我来说，头发很要紧！

____ **d** 我一個月去一次美髮店裡染頭髮。我頭髮的自然顏色是棕色的，我不喜歡。我寧願染著比較奪目的顏色，像鮮紅色，或者大藍色，甚至紫色。我父母當然不贊成我這樣染頭髮，可是我的朋友們覺得很好玩。我朋友高興我也就高興了！

❱ **Reading real-life texts**

24.10 *These are some signs Luo Xueting and Xiao Mao saw at the salon.*

a *This sign says:*

永琪 SPA 生活馆欢迎您
(Yǒngqí SPA shēnghuóguǎn huānyíng nín)

永琪 *means approximately "forever like fine jade," which invokes lasting beauty.* 生活 *means "life," and* 馆 *is an establishment or institution, as in* 饭馆 *"restaurant." What would you say* 生活馆 *means?* 用英文填空。

_____

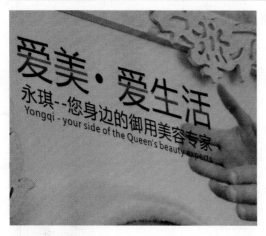

b *This commercial slogan on the wall is accompanied by a confusing English translation. See if you can provide a better one, using the following glosses as a guide.*

您身边	nín shēnbiān	*by your side*
御用	yùyòng	*used by the imperial court*
美容	měiróng	*beauty*
专家	zhuānjiā	*expert(s)*

爱美·爱生活
永琪--您身边的御用美容专家

Loving beauty, loving life
Yongqi— _____

c *The large characters on this storefront indicate that the salon offers two types of services.* 把中文跟英文對上。／把中文跟英文对上。

1. 美容 měiróng   A. *hair styling*
2. 美发 měifà   B. *health and beauty*

The smaller, scrolling characters on the bottom state the following:

以客户满意为标准，以……

If the section before the comma means "We take customer satisfaction to be our standard," then fill in the missing sections of these glosses. 用英文填空。

客户	kèhù	_____
满意	mǎnyì	_____
标准	biāozhǔn	_____
以……为	yǐ … wéi	*take . . . to be*

d *These are separate lists of services for* 美发 *and* 美容. *Work with a partner. Decipher at least three items on the "hair" menu and one item on the "health and beauty" menu.* 請寫英文。／请写英文。

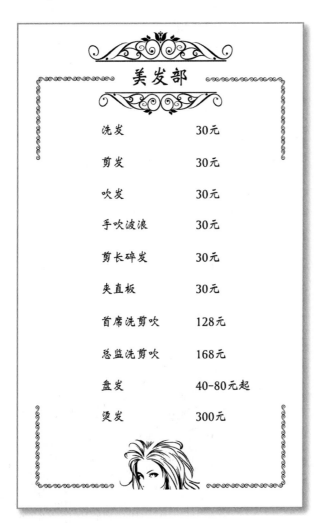

美发部

洗发	30元
剪发	30元
吹发	30元
手吹波浪	30元
剪长碎发	30元
夹直板	30元
首席洗剪吹	128元
总监洗剪吹	168元
盘发	40-80元起
烫发	300元

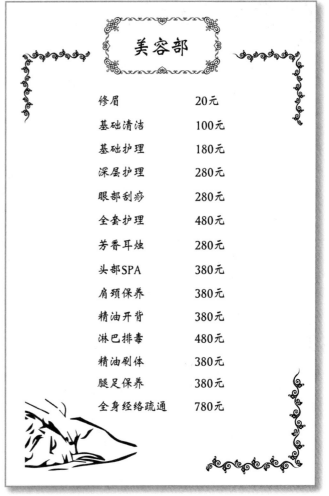

美容部

修眉	20元
基础清洁	100元
基础护理	180元
深层护理	280元
眼部刮痧	280元
全套护理	480元
芳香耳烛	280元
头部SPA	380元
肩颈保养	380元
精油开背	380元
淋巴排毒	480元
精油刷体	380元
腿足保养	380元
全身经络疏通	780元

_____

_____

_____

e *A poster on the wall of the salon identifies one of the lead stylists.* 用英文跟拼音填空。

jìshù zǒngjiān
Méi Qiángqiáng

Gōnghào: 823
Xǐ jiǎn chuī 168 yuán
Yùyuē diànhuà
18600785080

Bìyè yú Shànghǎi Shāxuān Měifà Xuéyuàn
Jìnxiū Níngbō Qiānshǒu zàoxíng yǔ sùxíng
2011 nián cānjiā Měitāo quánguó zhuānyè dàshī bǐsài rónghuò guànjūn

skilled supervisor
Mei Qiangqiang

Employee number: 823
_____ ¥168
Appointment _____
18600785080

_____ from the Shanghai Shaxuan Hair Styling Academy
Further trained at the Ningbo Qianshou Academy in styling and modeling
Participated in the _____ Maestro All-China Competition for professional stylists and won first place

f *If you have a complaint, you can call this number. Arrange the order of the pinyin below (by writing 1–4 in the blanks) to obtain the phrase "Complaint telephone (#)":*

huà   sù   tóu   diàn

_____   _____   _____   _____

▶ Reading a story

24.11 故事：小紅去做足療。　*Work with a partner or in a small group to read the story below.*

小紅剛到北京。她坐了一天的飛機，很累很累。她北京的一個好朋友跟她說，"我們去洗腳吧。會讓你感覺好多了，精神一點。"小紅問，"甚麼叫洗腳？"她朋友回答，"就是足療，也叫腳底按摩。特別特別舒服。我們到店裡去，他們先用熱水和中醫草藥給我們泡腳，然後給我們的腳底做按摩。我們去試試看吧！"小紅同意了。

在足療店裡，兩位按摩師先給小紅和她的朋友端來兩盆熱水。他們兩個人把腳放進去，在熱水裡頭泡著。小紅累得快睡著了。過了十分鐘，按摩師來開始按摩了。

哇，哇，哇！小紅覺得好疼啊！她的腳很敏感，按摩師一按，她就疼。按摩師說，要是疼，就要多按摩。越疼越得按摩。所以按摩師很用力，給小紅做了很久的按摩。小紅疼得快流眼淚了。不過她起碼不想睡覺了！

第二天早上，小紅的另外一個朋友來找她了。她朋友說，"今天我給你準備了一個驚喜。走！"

結果沒想到，他們又到了另一家足療店。小紅的朋友很高興地說，"我請你做一次足療！好舒服哦！"　小紅嚇了一跳，可是不好意思跟她朋友說她不喜歡足療，不要做。只好又做了一次。

可是真奇怪，這次比昨天晚上好多了，沒那麼疼。甚至真的有一點舒服。怎麼回事？她朋友說，"足療這種事，越做越舒服。要不要明天再來？"

小紅趕緊說，"不了，謝謝！暫時試一次就夠了，非常感謝！我暫時先不想再讓任何人碰我的腳了！"

24.12 *Write a short story about a visit to a salon. Have it edited by your teacher or someone else who is fluent in Chinese. Illustrate your story as best as you can before sharing it with your classmates.*

Encounter 3 | Extension: Cultural mini-documentary

 View the cultural mini-documentary for this unit and complete the exercises below.

24.13 *In the first part of the video (00:00–00:59), you'll see interview footage with a hair stylist. The stylist says that the hair of Chinese and Westerners—he actually says "foreigners"* (wàiguórén 外國人／外国人)—*is different* (fàzhì bù yíyàng 髮質不一樣／发质不一样). *For each of the following descriptors, write a* C *if the term is used to describe Chinese hair or a* W *if it is used to describe Western (non-Chinese) hair.*

____ xìruǎn 細軟／细软 *fine and soft*

____ jiǎnchūlai de xiàoguǒ, chuīfēng yì chuī, dōu hěn hǎo 剪出來的效果，吹風一吹，都很好／剪出来的效果，吹风一吹，都很好 *the result of the cut is great as soon as you blow-dry it*

____ tóufa yìng 頭髮硬／头发硬 *the hair is stiff*

____ rúguǒ tóufa hòu, dǎbáojiǎn qù dǎ 如果頭髮厚，打薄剪去打／如果头发厚，打薄剪去打 *if the hair is dense, we use thinning shears on it*

24.14 *The stylist points out differences between two kinds of scissors and their associated functions.* 請把中文跟英文對上。／请把中文跟英文对上。

____ a. dài chǐ de jiǎndāo 帶齒的剪刀／带齿的剪刀

____ b. dǎbáojiǎn 打薄剪

____ c. dānchún de jiǎndāo 單純的剪刀／单纯的剪刀

____ d. jiǎn yuántóu 剪圓頭／剪圆头

____ e. jiǎn cùntóu 剪寸頭／剪寸头

1. *give a crew cut*
2. *serrated scissors*
3. *give a bowl cut*
4. *thinning shears*
5. *plain scissors*

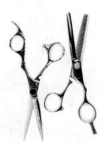

24.15 *In the next part of the video (01:00–01:45), a costuming and makeup specialist talks about styling hair. Since actors wear hairstyles they don't usually wear in their daily life, she does not give them perms. She therefore prefers to use a styling iron.* 請用拼音填空。／请用拼音填空。

_____ 燙頭髮／烫头发 *perm the hair*

_____ 做頭髮／做头发 *style the hair*

24.16 *Here are illustrations that represent three different ways the specialist uses a styling iron. Match each phrase to the corresponding picture by writing the appropriate letter in the blank.*

1. _____   2. _____   3. _____

a. shùnzhe tóufa zhèyàng jiā, jiù shì zhí le
順著頭髮這樣夾，就是直了／
順着头发这样夾，就是直了

b. wǎng lǐ jiā, jiù wǎng lǐ juǎn
往裡夾，就往裡捲／
往里夾，就往里卷

c. wǎng wài jiā, jiù wǎng wài juǎn
往外夾，就往外捲／
往外夾，就往外卷

24.17 *The specialist says the look will stay the same as long as the hair is not* _____. （用英文填空。）

Hint: 如果不洗頭髮的情況下,它就會一直是這樣的。／
如果不洗头发的情況下,它就会一直是这样的。

24.18 *In the next part of the video (01:46–02:26), the topic is dyeing, tinting, and highlighting hair.* 請把中文跟英文對上。／请把中文跟英文对上。

_____ a. piànrǎn 片染   1. *highlighting*

_____ b. tiǎorǎn 挑染   2. *whole-head dyeing*

_____ c. quánrǎn 全染   3. *patch dyeing*

24.19 *Here are illustrations that represent several effects described in the video. Match each phrase to the corresponding picture by writing the appropriate letter in the blank. (More than one statement may describe the same picture.) The phrases are summarized below in English.*

  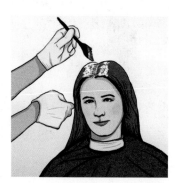

1. _____   2. _____   3. _____

a. quánbù rǎn yí ge yánsè
　全部染一個顏色／全部染一个颜色
　dye it all one color

b. rǎn tóng yí ge fàsè
　染同一個髮色／染同一个发色
　dye it the same color

c. yǒu liǎng jié, wǒ xiǎng bǎ tā rǎnchéng tóng yí ge yánsè
　有兩截，我想把它染成同一個顏色／有兩截，我想把它染成
　同一个颜色
　there are two sections along the length; I want to dye them the same color

d. zhěngtǐ de yí ge yánsè
　整體的一個顏色／整体的一个颜色
　one entire color

e. wàiguórén huì gèng xǐhuan yìxiē, Zhōngguórén huì bǐjiào shǎo
　外國人會更喜歡一些，中國人會比較少／外国人会更喜欢一
　些，中国人会比较少
　foreigners like it more than Chinese people do

f. céngcìgǎn huì fēicháng fēnmíng
　層次感會非常分明／层次感会非常分明
　a very obvious "layered" feel

g. yǒu hēisè, yǒu zōngsè, zhèyàng yìdiǎn yìdiǎn de
　有黑色，有棕色，這樣一點一點的／有黑色，有棕色，这样
　一点一点的
　there's black, there's brown, here and here like this

24.20 *The next section of the video (starting at 2:30) gives advice about how to get the haircut you want. Female hairstyles are addressed first, which are followed by male hairstyles. Based on the phrases given, match the Chinese and English words.* 請把中文跟英文對上。／请把中文跟英文对上。

■ **duì nǚxìng lái shuō** 對女性來說／对女性来说:

tóufa de chángduǎn 頭髮的長短／头发的长短

jí duǎn, bú yào gàizhù ěrduo 極短，不要蓋住耳朵／极短，不要盖住耳朵
chāoguò ěrduo, bú yào dào jiānbǎng 超過耳朵，不要到肩膀／超过耳朵，不要到肩膀
yào kàndào bózi 要看到脖子
dào jiānbǎng 到肩膀
wǒ yào (bǐ jiānbǎng) gèng cháng 我要（比肩膀）更長／我要（比肩膀）更长

____ 1. chángduǎn 長短／长短   A. *cover up*

____ 2. gàizhù 蓋住／盖住   B. *neck*

____ 3. chāoguò 超過／超过   C. *ears*

____ 4. ěrduo 耳朵   D. *shoulders*

____ 5. bózi 脖子   E. *length ("long-short")*

____ 6. jiānbǎng 肩膀   F. *go beyond*

b

liúhǎir 劉海兒／刘海儿

wǒ bù xiǎngyào liúhǎir, wǒ xiǎng lòuchū étóu 我不想要劉海兒，我想露出額頭／我不想要刘海儿，我想露出额头
wǒ xiǎngyào liúhǎir, kěshì yào gàizhù méimao 我想要劉海兒，可是要蓋住眉毛／我想要刘海儿，可是要盖住眉毛
wǒ yào duǎn yìdiǎnr de liúhǎir, yào bǎ méimao lòuchūlai 我要短一點兒的劉海兒，要把眉毛露出來／我要短一点儿的刘海儿，要把眉毛露出来

____ 1. liúhǎir 劉海兒／刘海儿   A. *eyebrows*

____ 2. lòuchū(lai) 露出(來)／露出(来)   B. *forehead*

____ 3. duǎn yìdiǎnr de 短一點兒的／短一点儿的   C. *reveal, show*

____ 4. étóu 額頭／额头   D. *on the shorter side*

____ 5. méimao 眉毛   E. *bangs, fringe*

c

fēn tóufa 分頭髮／分头发
piānfēn, sān-qī fēn 偏分，三七分 zhōngfēn, wǔ-wǔ fēn 中分，五五分
céngcì 層次／层次
hòumian shì píng de, zhěngqí yì diǎn 後面是平的，整齊一點／后面是平的，整齐一点 jiǎn de suì yì diǎn, yǒu céngcì yì diǎn 剪得碎一點，有層次一點／剪得碎一点，有层次一点
tàng tóufa 燙頭髮／烫头发
wǎng lǐmian juǎn 往裡面捲／往里面卷 wǎng wàimian juǎn 往外面捲／往外面卷

____ 1. fēn tóufa 分頭髮／分头发   A. *layers, layering*

____ 2. piānfēn 偏分   B. *part the hair*

____ 3. céngcì 層次／层次   C. *tidier, more even*

____ 4. zhěngqí yì diǎn 整齊一點／整齐一点   D. *perm the hair*

____ 5. suì yì diǎn 碎一點／碎一点   E. *flat, smooth*

____ 6. píng de 平的   F. *side part, uneven part*

____ 7. tàng tóufa 燙頭髮／烫头发   G. *choppier, less even*

■ **duì nánxìng lái shuō** 對男性來說／对男性来说:

d

zěnme jiǎn 怎麼剪／怎么剪
duō duǎn 多短
shénmeyàng de xíngzhuàng, shénmeyàng de xiàoguǒ 甚麼樣的形狀，甚麼樣的效果／什么样的形狀，什么样的效果
Jiǎnchūlai de xiàoguǒ huì gèng ràng tā mǎnyì. 剪出來的效果會更讓他滿意。／剪出来的效果会更让他满意。
Zuì hǎo de bànfǎ shì tā ná yí ge túpiàn gěi tā kàn. 最好的辦法是他拿一個圖片給他看。／最好的办法是他拿一个图片给他看。

____ 1. jiǎnchūlai de 剪出來的／剪出来的   A. *method, solution*

____ 2. xiàoguǒ 效果   B. *satisfied, happy*

____ 3. mǎnyì 滿意／满意   C. *obtained by the cut*

____ 4. duō duǎn 多短   D. *picture, diagram*

____ 5. xíngzhuàng 形狀／形状   E. *effect*

____ 6. bànfǎ 辦法／办法   F. *shape, form*

____ 7. túpiàn 圖片／图片   G. *how short*

▶ Grammar

A little about "a little" or 說 "一點兒"

The little word *yìdiǎnr* 一點兒／一点儿 (a little) pops up constantly in Chinese—just as it does in English. It is often used in comparative constructions expressing degree. However, its placement in a sentence often varies, so a little bit of practice might be in order. Consider the following instances drawn from this unit.

Wǒ bùxiǎng zuò Spa, wǒ xiǎng bǎ tóufa jiǎn duǎn **yìdiǎnr**.

我不想做 Spa，我想把頭髮剪短一點兒。／我不想做 Spa，我想把头发剪短一点儿。

Běijīng zhème gānzào, yě kěyǐ gěi pífū hē **yìdiǎn** shuǐ.

北京這麼乾燥，也可以給皮膚喝一點水。／北京这么干燥，也可以给皮肤喝一点水。

Shìbushì **yǒudiǎnr** zhòng le ya?

是不是有點兒重了呀？／是不是有点儿重了呀？

Rúguǒ nǐ juéde tòng jiù ràng tā qīng **yìdiǎnr**.

如果你覺得痛就讓她輕一點兒。／如果你觉得痛就让她轻一点儿。

Let's discover patterns in the examples.

1. Verb + *yìdiǎnr* + object: Drink a little water. *Hē yìdiǎnr shuǐ.* 喝一點兒水。／喝一点儿水。

2. Verb + stative verb + *yìdiǎnr*: Cut it a little shorter. *Jiǎn duǎn yìdiǎnr.* 剪短一點兒。／剪短一点儿。

3. Stative verb + *yìdiǎnr* + verb: Do a lighter massage. *Qīng yìdiǎnr ànmó.* 輕一點兒按摩。／轻一点儿按摩。

Exercise: Here are a few sentences with *yìdiǎnr* based on the patterns above. Of course, other structures are also involved, so take care. Work with a partner and try to express the thoughts in Chinese. You can check your work with the answers provided on the next page.

1. The food is getting cold; hurry up and come eat.
2. Come out quickly and see who's here.
3. The characters are too small; write a little larger.
4. It's a bit hot; open the window wider.
5. If you're thirsty, drink some water.
6. I'm too fat; the doctor says I ought to eat a little less.
7. I asked the teacher to speak slower, but she still speaks too fast.
8. If we go a little early, then we can come back a little early.

....

Keep in mind that expressions of degree can, of course, involve expressions other than *yìdiǎnr*. So:

Shǎo huā jǐ kuài qián.

少花幾塊錢。／少花几块钱。
Spend a little less money.

Míngtiān zǎo lái jǐ fēnzhōng, kěyǐ ma?

明天早來幾分鐘，可以嗎？／明天早来几分钟，可以吗？
Can you come a few minutes earlier tomorrow?

Answers:

1. Cài dōu liángle, kuài yìdiǎnr lái chī.
菜都凉了，快一点儿来吃。

2. Kuài yìdiǎnr chūlai kàn shuí lái le.
快一点儿出来看谁来了。

3. Zì tài xiǎole, xiě dà yìdiǎnr.
字太小了，写大一点儿。

4. Yǒu yìdiǎnr rè, bǎ chuānghu kāi dà yìdiǎnr.
有一点儿热，把窗户开大一点儿。

5. Yàoshi nǐ kǒu kě, hē yìdiǎnr shuǐ.
要是你口渴，喝一点儿水。

6. Wǒ tài pàngle, yīshēng shuō wǒ yīnggāi shǎo chī yìdiǎnr.
我太胖了，医生说我应该少吃一点儿。

7. Wǒ qǐng lǎoshī shuō màn yìdiǎnr, kěshì tā háishì shuō de tài kuài.
我请老师说慢一点儿，可是他还是说得太快。

8. Wǒmen yàoshi zǎo yìdiǎnr qù, jiù kěyǐ zǎo yìdiǎnr huílai.
我们要是早一点儿去，就可以早一点儿回来。

▶ Vocabulary

Please refer to page R-2 for a list of grammatical abbreviations used throughout this book.

ànmó 按摩 massage V/N

bǎobèi(r) 寶貝(兒)／宝贝(儿) darling N

chuīgān 吹乾／吹干 blow-dry V

dāndān 單單／单单 only; alone A

…dehuà ⋯⋯的話／⋯⋯的话 X if X C

dì 遞／递 hand to/over; pass to V

diàn qìng 店慶／店庆 anniversary of (our) store N

fàngsōng 放鬆／放松 relax V

fàzhì 髮質／发质 hair quality N

fūliǎn 敷臉／敷脸 facial N

gān 乾／干 dry SV

gānzào 乾燥／干燥 dry/arid SV

gēnjù 根據／根据 according to; on the basis of C; basis; grounds N

huódòng 活動／活动 activity; program N

jiǎn tóufa 剪頭髮／剪头发 get a haircut VO

jièshào 介紹／介绍 introduction/guide (to service, contents, etc.) N

jiéshù 結束／结束 end; conclude; close V

kǎolù 考慮／考虑 consider; think about; think over V

lìdù 力度 strength; pressure; intensity N

liú 留 (let) grow V

mǎi yī zèng yī 買一贈一／买一赠一 buy one, get one free N

měibái 美白 skin toning N

měiróng 美容 improve one's looks VO; cosmetology N

miànbù hùlǐ 面部護理／面部护理 facial; skin protection N

miǎnfèi 免費／免费 be free of charge VO

mìnglìng 命令 order; command V/N

mùlù 目錄／目录 list; table of contents; list of services N

nánzǐhàn 男子漢／男子汉 a real man *(in the macho sense)* N

péi 陪 accompany; keep somebody company V

piàn 騙／骗 deceive; fool V

pífū 皮膚／皮肤 skin N

qīn'ài de 親愛的／亲爱的 dear; beloved IE

qīng 輕／轻 gentle; light; soft SV

quē 缺 be short of; lack V

rǎnfà 染髮／染发 to dye/tint/color the hair VO

rěn 忍 bear; endure V

ruǎn 軟／软 soft *(to the touch)* SV

rùnfū 潤膚／润肤 skin toning N

shǎguā 傻瓜 fool N

shēncéng qīngjié 深層清潔／深层清洁 deep (skin) cleansing N

shīfu 師傅／师傅 *(general term of address or title for service workers)* N

shǐyòng 使用 use; utilize; employ V

shuàigē 帥哥／帅哥 handsome young man N

shuāngrénjiān 雙人間／双人间 double room N

tàng 燙／烫 perm V

tàocān 套餐 set package *(of food, services, etc.)* N

tiǎorǎn 挑染 give hair tinted highlights VO

tīng 聽／听 heed; obey V

tòng 痛 painful SV

tóngshí 同時／同时 at the same time A

wèile 為了／为了 for the sake of; for C

xǐ jiǎn chuī 洗剪吹 wash, cut, and blow-dry IE

xiàng 項／项 *(for itemized things)* item M

xiǎngshòu 享受 enjoy V; enjoyment; treat N

xǐtóu 洗頭／洗头 wash hair VO

yánggāng zhī qì 陽剛之氣／阳刚之气 manliness; virility N

yàome … yàome … 要麼……要麼……／要么……要么…… ~V1 (~ V2) either … or … C

yàoshuǐ 藥水／药水 medicinal liquid; lotion N

yìng 硬 hard; stiff *(to the touch)* SV

yōuhuì 優惠／优惠 preferential treatment; discount N

yuánlái 原來／原来 so …; so, after all N

zhǐjia hùlǐ 指甲護理／指甲护理 manicure/pedicure N

zhōunián 週年／周年 anniversary N

zuòliǎn 做臉／做脸 have a facial VO

❱ Checklist of "can do" statements

After completing this unit, you should be able to perform each of the following tasks:

Listening and speaking

- ☐ Ask at the counter of a salon what personal-care items are available.
- ☐ Specify what services you want.
- ☐ Ask about the prices of various services.
- ☐ Give instructions for specific services (shorter, longer, harder, lighter, etc.).
- ☐ Request adjustments as necessary.

Reading and writing

- ☐ Read some short notes about personal care.
- ☐ Decipher some signs in a salon.
- ☐ Read a short story about salon services, and write one of your own.

Understanding culture

- ☐ Make one or more accurate statements in English about Chinese perceptions of "foreign" versus Chinese hair.
- ☐ State your opinion in English about the availability of personal-care services in China, what you might want to try when you are there, and what Chinese customers generally ask for.

"Something new every day"

25

日新月異

Rìxīnyuèyì

Communication technology

In this unit, you will learn how to:

- state your needs, and ask for help regarding cell phone services.
- ask for more information, and respond with details when queried.
- correct someone when he/she doesn't understand your meaning.

- comprehend brief notes describing cell phones.
- describe the phone you want (or have) in writing.
- decipher some signs in a cell phone store.
- comprehend a short story about a cell phone, and write one of your own.
- interpret the cultural significance of some numbers.

Encounter 1   Shopping for cell phones

25.1 *Fang Lan, Emma, and one of their friends are shopping for a cell phone for Emma. What vocabulary do you think they will be using on their quest? Add to the list below, and see if you already know the Chinese equivalents of the first three terms.* 請寫漢字或者拼音。／请写汉字或者拼音。

cell phone: _____

price: _____

service: _____

_____ : _____

_____ : _____

25.2 *View Episode 25, Vignette 1. Put the following events in the order in which they occur.*

_____ The friend tells Emma she can buy a fake phone online.

_____ Emma says how much she's willing to pay.

_____ Emma picks a phone number.

_____ Emma says she needs to be able to watch video on her phone.

_____ The salesperson describes service packages.

25.3 *View Episode 25, Vignette 1 again. Identify who makes each of the following statements (presented in the order in which they are made).*

> a. Fang Lan   b. Emma   c. Friend   d. Salesperson

_____ I think you should buy a smartphone, such as a Samsung, Apple, Sony, or the like.

_____ Hey! You can get a counterfeit phone on Taobao, but the quality won't be great.

_____ Is there a style that appeals to you?

_____ You have to first think about what you want a cell phone for. Are receiving calls and sending text messages good enough, or do you need to look things up in a dictionary, play games, listen to music, or watch videos and stuff?

_____ Ooh, video is good. Our teacher just reminded us that we can use our cell phones to watch the video that comes with our textbook!

_____ These two styles are a little more expensive than that one, but they also fall within your price range.

_____ See, in Chinese the word "four" is homophonous with death. And "seven", if you're superstitious, means "rites of seven" [post-funerary rites]. In any case, this number is unlucky.

_____ 1-8-8-6: "six-six" is fortunate, and "eight" means "prosperity."

 25.4 *View Episode 25, Vignette 1 again. In the end, what did Emma decide to do about each of the following issues?* 圈選正確的項目。／圈选正确的项目。 Quānxuǎn zhèngquè de xiàngmù. *(Circle the correct answer.)*

a. Does she decide to buy a smartphone?   yes   no
b. How much can she afford to spend?   ¥100   ¥1,000
c. What about the service package?   She picked #66.   She will decide later.
d. Which phone number does she pick?   18641077431   18806686221
e. Why did she pick the phone she did?   value-price ratio   color

FYI 供你参考

What's in a number?

Much of it is about punning. Except for the tone, *liù* 六 (six) sounds the same as *liú* 流 (flow) and *liū* 溜 (slide along)—positive conditions as expressed in the saying *liūliūdàshùn* 溜溜大順／溜溜大順 (everything working in one's favor). Since "six" puns with "flow" and "slide," it implies good fortune. There is also an older, classical referent of *liùliùdàshùn* 六六大順／六六大顺 (literally, "six of six: the greatest good fortunes") that derives from the historical text *Zuǒzhuàn* 左傳／左传. In it, 六六大順／六六大顺 refers to the following: *jūn yì* 君義／君义 (a just overlord), *chén xíng* 臣行 (a minister-follower who carries out policies), *fù cí* 父慈 (a benevolent father), *zǐ xiào* 子孝 (a filial son), *xiōng ài* 兄愛／兄爱 (a loving older brother), and *dì jìng* 弟敬 (a respectful younger brother).

These six propensities of the six key figures in your life would bring you the best possible fortune! It is understood, of course, that the feminine is reflected by the masculine: mothers, daughters, and sisters can be held to the same ideals as their male counterparts.

Another propitious number is *bā* 八 (eight), which in this case sounds like *fā* 發／发 (prosper)—the tone and the final sounds match, although the initial sounds do not. The Chinese term for to "strike it rich" is *fācái* 發財／发财, so a pair of eights (*fā-fā*) would mean double prosperity! Not to mention that the numeral 88 looks something like *shuāngxǐ* 囍 (double happiness), which is why it's a popular blessing at weddings.

The number three—*sān* 三—is sometimes considered lucky since it sounds like *shēng* 生 (life) (or "sēng" in some regional pronunciations). By contrast, it is also sometimes considered to be unlucky since 三 also sounds like *sàn* 散 (to separate). When giving a gift, for example, one shouldn't give three of something (e.g., three flowers), since that might imply a wish that the friendship will break up. The number seven—*qī* 七—also has multiple values. It is sometimes considered lucky because it sounds like *qǐ* 起 (rise up, take off) and *qì* 氣／气, the universal life force. However, another referent of

七 is *zuòqī* 坐七—keeping the seven-day vigil for the dead. By this connotation, the number would be considered unlucky.

As for the number four—*sì* 四—there is no doubt. It is widely feared as a harbinger of misfortune since it sounds like *sǐ* 死 (death, to die). Some East Asian buildings avoid a fourth floor (or even floors that contain the numeral 4) for this reason.

Wǔ 五 (five) sounds like *wǒ* 我 (I; me), so the numeral 5 is often used to mean "I, me" in text messages. Further, since the five elements (*jīn* 金 metal, *mù* 木 wood, *shuǐ* 水 water, *huǒ* 火 fire, *tǔ* 土 earth) are fundamental to Chinese philosophy, 5 tends to be a well-liked numeral.

Similarly, since *jiǔ* 九 (nine) is entirely homophonous with *jiǔ* 久 (long-lasting, eternal), nine is another highly respected number. As the highest single-digit number, nine indicates power. The Forbidden City, seat of imperial power, is riddled with multiples of nine. For example, nine rows of nine golden knobs on vermilion doors and nine figures on a roofline reflect imperial might.

The number two—*èr* 二— has not been so fortunate. On the one hand, it is considered lucky because mating (forming pairs) brings happiness. However, the number 250 (read *èrbǎiwǔ*) has unfortunately, for obscure reasons, come to mean "slovenly, stupid." In modern parlance, even the number two by itself indicates someone who is off the mark or slow, as in the put-down *Tā nèige rén zhēn èr* 他那個人真二／他那个人真二 (That guy is pretty stupid).

25.5 *Guess the meaning of each of the terms below (presented in the order in which they appear).* 圈選正確的英文。／圈选正确的英文。

a. huānyíng guānglín 歡迎光臨／欢迎光临
   (Welcome [to the store]. / Welcome [to my home].)

b. shénmeyàng de shǒujī 甚麼樣的手機／什么样的手机
   (what kind of cell phone / which cell phone)

c. zhìnéng (shǒu)jī 智能(手)機／智能(手)机
   (camera phone / smartphone)

d. shānzhài bǎn de 山寨版的
   (name brand / knockoff)

e. bù néng mǎi jiǎ de 不能買假的／不能买假的
   (can't buy a fake / can't buy a name brand)

f. zìjǐ xǐhuan de kuǎnxíng 自己喜歡的款型／自己喜欢的款型
   (a store you like / a style you like)

g. tuījiàn 推薦／推荐
   (recommend / demonstrate)

h. jiē diànhuà fā duǎnxìn 接電話發短信／接电话发短信
   (receive calls, write letters / receive calls, send texts)

i. kàn shìpín 看視頻／看视频
   (watch video / watch TV)

j. kèběn pèitào de shìpín 課本配套的視頻／课本配套的视频
   (video of TV shows / the video that goes along with the textbook)

k. jiàgé bǐjiào gāo 價格比較高／价格比较高
   (price is relatively higher / quality is relatively higher)

l. píngmù bǐjiào dà 屏幕比較大／屏幕比较大
   (screen is relatively bigger / size is relatively bigger)

m. pāizhào qīngchu 拍照清楚
   (voice quality is clear / picture quality is clear)

n. diànchí kàngshǐ 電池抗使／电池抗使
   (battery is rechargeable / battery is long-lasting)

o. bié de xuǎnzé 別的選擇／别的选择
   (other choices / other styles)

p. gāng hǎo shìhé nǐ 剛好適合你／刚好适合你
   (suits you just right / is just the right price)

q. fúwù tàocān 服務套餐／服务套餐
   (restaurant service / service package)

r. sānbǎi zhào 三百兆
   (300 megabytes / 300 megahertz)

s. xiān xuǎn hào 先選號／先选号
   (first write a number / first pick a number)

t. míxìn 迷信
   (superstitious / knowledgeable)

u. bù jílì 不吉利
   (unlucky / not useful)

v. wǒ gǎi(biàn) zhǔyi le 我改(變)主意了／我改(变)主意了
   (I've changed my mind / I've made a decision)

w. huàn 換／换
   (return / exchange)

25.6 *There are many brand names mentioned in the conversation.* 請把中文跟英文對上。／请把中文跟英文对上。

____ a. Sānxīng 三星   1. *Sony*

____ b. Píngguǒ 蘋果／苹果   2. *Jinli*

____ c. Suǒní 索尼   3. *Motorola*

____ d. Táobǎo 淘寶／淘宝   4. *Samsung*

____ e. Mótuōluólā 摩托羅拉／摩托罗拉   5. *Taobao Net*

____ f. Jīnlì 金立   6. *Apple*

25.7 *What do you use your cell phone for? Check the activities below. Write in any that are missing.* 請寫漢字或者拼音。／请写汉字或者拼音。

☐ dǎ diànhuà 打電話／打电话

☐ fā duǎnxìn 發短信／发短信

☐ shàngwǎng 上網／上网

☐ kàn shìpín 看視頻／看视频

☐ jiē diànhuà 接電話／接电话

☐ shōu duǎnxìn 收短信

☐ chá zīliào 查資料／查资料

☐ wán diànzǐ yóuxì 玩電子遊戲／玩电子游戏

_____

_____

_____

25.8 *Pretend that you, like Emma, are shopping for a cell phone. Answer the following questions about your ideal phone. (You can base your answers on the cell phone you have, if you'd like.)*

Shì shénme páizi de? 是甚麼牌子的？／是什么牌子的？ *(What brand is it?)*

_____

Shì zhìnéng shǒujī ma? 是智能手機嗎？／是智能手机吗？

_____

Néng fā duǎnxìn ma? 能發短信嗎？／能发短信吗？

_____

Néng shàngwǎng ma? 能上網嗎？／能上网吗？

_____

Pāizhào qīngchu ma? 拍照清楚嗎？／拍照清楚吗？

_____

Néng lùxiàng ma? 能錄像嗎？／能录像吗？ *(Can it make video recordings?)*

_____

Néng kàn shìpín ma? 能看視頻嗎？／能看视频吗？

_____

Píngmù dà ma? 屏幕大嗎？／屏幕大吗？

_____

Néng dǎ Zhōngwén ma? 能打中文嗎？／能打中文吗？

_____

Fúwù tàocān shì něige gōngsī de? 服務套餐是哪個公司的？／服務套餐是哪个公司的？ *(Which company provides a service plan?)*

_____

Jiàgé duōshaoqián? 價格多少錢？／价格多少钱？

_____

25.9 *Mingling:* *Have conversations with several of your classmates about the cell phone you want (e.g., 我要的手機……／我要的手机……), or currently have (e.g., 我現在的手機……／我现在的手机……). Find out as much as you can about your classmates' phones, taking notes below. Report back to the whole class what you have learned.*

25.10 *View Episode 25, Vignette 2. It features Emma trying out her new phone and making a series of mistakes that turn into a compounding joke. Fill in the blanks to figure out the joke.*
請填英文。／请填英文。

a. *What Emma wants to text to Xiao Cui:*

Wǒ mǎi le xīn shǒujī. 我買了新手機。／我买了新手机。   *I bought a new cell phone.*

b. *What she actually texts:*

Wǒ mǎi le xīn shòujī. 我買了新瘦雞。／我买了新瘦鸡。   *I bought a new* _____.

c. *What Xiao Cui texts back:*

Nǐ wèishénme mǎi shòujī, bù mǎi féijī? 你為甚麼買瘦雞, 不買肥雞?／你为什么买瘦鸡, 不买肥鸡?   *Why did you buy a* _____ *and not a* _____?

d. *What Emma understands* féijī *to mean:*

肥雞／肥鸡 ➝ 飛機／飞机 _____

Do you get it? Did you ever try to say or write something in Chinese that turned out to be completely different? If so, make notes here and then tell the story to one or more of your classmates. 請寫拼音、漢字或者英語。／请写拼音、汉字或者英语。

Encounter 2   Reading and writing

25.11 *Following are notes written by Chinese friends about their cell phones. Highlight the parts you can understand.*

a 我的手机是白色的。很便宜可是很好用。是智能手机，所以又可以照相又可以上网。

b 我的手機是蘋果6。它是白色的，背面是金色的。我的手機是2015年2月買的。我非常喜歡我的手機，因為它不僅可以打電話、發短信，還可以收發郵件甚麼的，總之有很多的功能！

c 我用苹果公司生产的 iPhone 5S 快两年了，很喜欢它的许多应用软件和功能，可是不习惯它的键盘。我不是果粉，但是我觉得 iPhone 的确是比其它牌子的手机更实用一些。

Label each of the following sentences a, b, or c, depending on the note to which it corresponds.

____ I've used an Apple iPhone 5S for almost two years.

____ It's white with gold on the back.

____ It's a smartphone, so I can take photos and go online.

____ I love its many apps and functions, but I don't like its keyboard.

____ I am not an Apple fan, but I think the iPhone is really easier to use than other brands.

____ My phone is an iPhone 6.

____ In sum, it has a lot of functions!

____ It's cheap and easy to use.

25.12 *Write a note like the ones in 25.11, briefly describing your own cell phone.*

▶ **Reading real-life texts**

25.13 *Here are some signs Fang Lan, Emma, and their friend saw in the cell phone store.*

a 把中文跟英文對上。／把中文跟英文对上。

1. 迪信通 díxìntōng   A. *chain (store)*

2. 手机 shǒujī   B. *D. phone (a brand name)*

3. 连锁 liánsuǒ   C. *cell phone*

b 中国移动 = _____ _____
（用拼音填空）

c *These two signs appear on a display rack of cell phones.* 用漢字填空。／用汉字填空。

1. special price = _____

2. Buy the phone for 0 yuan =
_____

d *This handwritten sign reads:* 两年不交钱，打的 high。4 核 5 寸大屏智能机，用的 high！！！ *Complete the English translation.* 用英文填空。

With no payments for _____, get high* making _____. A quad-core 5-inch _____ _____, get high using it!"

* get high = have fun (*colloquial*)

e *Match each phrase with its English translation. Write the number of the Chinese phrase in the blank.*

_____ *Write intelligently.* (zhìnéng shūxiě)

_____ *[It's] a pad from which you can make phone calls.* (kě dǎdiànhuà de píngbǎn)

_____ *micro 6D card supports storage and expansion* (micro 6D kǎ cúnchǔ kuòzhǎn)

_____ *quad-core processor* (sìhé chǔlǐqì)

_____ *multiscreen, multifunction* (duō píng duō rènwù)

f

1. *Fill in the blanks in the pinyin below, based on the text within the circle.*

   a. _____ qiú tōng

   b. Jíxiáng _____ _____

   c. Yùcún _____ _____ _____ jīngxǐ

   d. _____ jiǎn _____ jiǎn

2. *Label the English below following this same text.*

   _____ *Connects worldwide*

   _____ *Cut once and reduce again*

   _____ *Prepaid telephone fees bring joy*

   _____ *Lucky telephone numbers*

3. *Can you explain this pun?* 一剪再减

   _____

   _____

4. *Make a list of all the "lucky numbers" included in this picture; then reread the "What's in a number?" FYI cultural note on pages 89–90.*

25.14 *Pretend you work in a cell phone store. On a separate sheet of paper, design an ad for the phone you currently have or would like to have. Make sure you include at least three statements in Chinese.*

▶ **Reading a story**

25.15 故事：小貓找手機 。 *Work with a partner or in a small group to read the story below.*

小貓住在城的北邊。它最要好的朋友是小狗。小狗住在城的南邊。

小貓和小狗上同一所學校。它們的學校在城的中間。放學以後，小貓和小狗一起花一個鐘頭左右的時間在一起寫作業。寫完作業以後，小貓和小狗各自回自己的家。小貓很想念它的好朋友，小狗。

小貓跟它媽媽說，"媽，請給我買一個手機，好嗎？"貓媽媽說，"你為甚麼要手機？"

小貓說，"我的朋友小狗它家離我們家太遠了。我想找它聊天的時候只能用手機給它打電話，所以一定要有手機。"

貓媽媽說，"小貓，咱們家是貓，不是狗。你不應該跟狗交朋友。"

小貓回答說，"可是我不是普通的小貓。我是受過教育的小貓。小狗是我的同學，我們一起讀書。媽媽，你不能不讓我跟我的同學交朋友吧？"

貓媽媽想了想，然後說，"你說得對。只要你們能把書讀好，貓和狗當朋友也沒甚麼不好。我明天就給你買手機去。"

第二天，小貓在學校的時候，很高興地告訴了小狗買手機的事，然後叫小狗也趕快去買手機。小狗回家以後跟它爸爸說，"爸爸，我需要一個手機，因為我要跟我的好朋友小貓聊天。"

狗爸爸說，"我們家是狗，不是貓。你最好不要和貓交朋友。" 小狗說，"可是我不是普通的小狗，我是受過教育的小狗……"

最後，小貓和小狗都有了手機，它們放學以後還可以很高興地聊天、發短信。

25.16 *Write a short story about a cell phone. Have it edited by your teacher or someone else who is fluent in Chinese. Illustrate your story as best as you can before sharing it with your classmates.*

Encounter 3   Extension: Cultural mini-documentary

View the cultural mini-documentary for this unit and complete the exercises below.

25.17 *In the first part of the video (00:00–1:17), two women share their reasons for choosing their current cell phones. Using the following key words to support your understanding, fill in the blanks with the correct numbers.*

wǒ wèishénme xuǎnzé . . . shì yīnwèi . . . 我為甚麼選擇……是因為……／我为什么选择……是因为…… *the reason I use . . . is because . . .*	wàixíng 外形 *external appearance*
	gōngyì 工藝／工艺 *craftsmanship*
quán chùpíng 全觸屏／全触屏 *touch screen*	bèimian 背面 *back surface, reverse*
	chōngdiànqì 充電器／充电器 *battery charger*
chéngxù 程序 *programs; apps*	nándé 難得／难得 *rare; precious; hard to achieve*
ruǎnjiànr 軟件兒／软件儿 *software*	
xiàzǎi 下載／下载 *download*	gèxìng 個性／个性 *individual(ity); unique(ness)*

Reasons:

1. There are lots of apps that are helpful to me after I download them.
2. Everyone on the street has Apple phones, so my phone makes me stand out as an individual.
3. They have a pretty exterior, the craftsmanship is really good, and the shell comes in purple.
4. The screen is big enough, which makes it convenient to use.
5. It's super convenient with the touch screen.
6. My family members all use Apple products, and we can share the same battery charger when we go on trips. That's a rare thing.

The reasons why I use an iPhone 5: _____ _____ _____

The reasons why I use a Sony phone: _____ _____ _____

25.18 *In the next part of the video (1:19–1:55), users explain what kind of cell phone plan they have chosen. For each speaker's plan profile, add the missing pinyin and the number of the corresponding English summary.*

a.

Wǒ yòng de tàocān xiànzài shì Yídòng de tàocān… Yídòng tàocān _____ hěn duō de liúliàng, yīnwèi xiànzài yòng _____ jīběnshang huā de dōu shì liúliàng, _____ yě bù zěnme dǎ, yīnwèi wǒmen dōu yòng Wēixìn lái jìnxíng gōutōng, duǎnxìn yě yòng de bú shì hěn duō le.

我用的套餐现在是移动的套餐⋯⋯移动套餐包括很多的流量，因为现在用手机基本上花的都是流量，电话也不怎么打，因为我们都用微信来进行沟通，短信也用得不是很多了。

Summary: ____

b.

Wǒ yòng de jiù shì Liántōng de… miǎn _____, shèngxià de jiù méi le.

我用的就是联通的⋯⋯ 免接听，剩下的就没了。

Summary: ____

c.

Wǒ xiànzài yòng de _____ ne, shì Liántōng de, shì _____ kuài qián yí ge yuè, tā shì yǒu _____ zhào liúliàng, hái yǒu èrbǎi sìshí fēnzhōng de zhèi ge diànhuà de shíjiān… zhèi ge tàocān ne, tā jiētīng háishi _____ de.

我现在用的套餐呢，是联通的，是九十六块钱一个月，它是有三百兆流量，还有二百四十分钟的这个电话的时间⋯⋯ 这个套餐呢，它接听还是免费的。

Summary: ____

1. No charge to receive calls . . . there's really nothing else.
2. The plan I'm using now is from China Unicom. It's ¥96 a month and has 300 MB of data and 240 minutes of talk time. . . . With this plan, received calls are free.
3. The plan I use is from China Mobile. Their plan includes a lot of data because nowadays basically everything we use is data. We don't really make phone calls because we use WeChat to communicate. We don't send many texts either.

25.19 *Next (1:58–2:15), users briefly discuss how often they change phones. Add the missing pinyin for the first speaker and fill in the blanks for the second speaker.*

_____

_____

我大概是一年或者到两年换一次手机。

Summary: I change my cell phone once every year or two.

_____ hěn zhuīcóng zhèyàng de chǎnpǐn, nèi ge, gēngxīn huàndài, chūlai yì kuǎn xīn de tā jiù huì . . . huàn yì xiē, zhè shì yí dà bùfen rén. Dàn wǒ jiù shǔyú . . . _____ zhèi ge shǒujī tā jiùshì kěyǐ _____ jiù kěyǐ le, yì kāishǐ, zhèyàng shì . . . wǒ jiù yìzhí _____.

年轻人很追从这样的产品，那个，更新换代，出来一款新的他就会……换一些，这是一大部分人。但我就属于……我觉得这个手机它就是可以通话就可以了，一开始，这样是……我就一直没有换。

Summary: Young people really go after these products. They, you know, chase the trends. As soon as a new model comes out, they'll just . . . replace . . . that's most people. But I'm the kind of person who . . . I think as long as you can talk on the cell phone, that's enough. So from the beginning, it was like . . . I've just never replaced it.

25.20 *In the last part (2:16 to the end), users talk about whether they use cell phones or computers to go online. Using the list below as a guide, can you figure out what the speakers are saying? Fill in the following table with the letters for the English summaries that follow, and then check the results with your classmates. Several of the boxes will be blank.*

wǎngluò fùgàilǜ　網絡覆蓋率／网络覆盖率　*Internet coverage*

kuāndài　寬帶／宽带　*broadband*

kuàisù　快速　*high-speed*

biànjié　便捷　*quick and convenient*

yídòng　移動／移动　*on the move, mobile*

qīngxī　清晰　*clear, high-resolution*

wénzì cāozuò　文字操作　*text manipulation*

shùjù cāozuò　數據操作／数据操作　*data manipulation*

liáotiān gōngjù　聊天工具　*tool for chatting*

jiēshōu, fāsòng　接收，發送／接收，发送　*receiving and sending*

júxiànxìng　局限性　*limitations ("limitedness")*

	When and why I use the computer . . .	When and why I use my cell phone . . .

a. When I'm shopping or watching films

b. When I'm out and about

c. For simple things, such as looking up the translation of a word or maps when driving

d. For looking at images; I like photography, and it's convenient

e. For manipulating text and data

f. For going on Weibo, sending data, and searching resources

g. When I'm on the move, because China's Internet coverage is high, and I can get on the Web at any time and at any place

h. For chatting and receiving and sending simple e-mails

i. For going on the Web, playing games, watching films, and chatting with friends while at home

j. When I'm at home, because the broadband is faster and more convenient and the screen is bigger

Recap

▶ Grammar

Verbal extensions

As you have already learned, Chinese verbs do not change form; they do not conjugate to match number, tense, or anything else. Verbs in Chinese use "add-ons"—that is, there is a wide variety of words added (or subtracted) to indicate location, duration, direction, possibility, fulfillment, and so on. What follows are some sentences adapted from Units 21 through 25 that illustrate many of these variations. Go over these examples carefully with a classmate, and make sure you can work out the full meaning of the "add-ons."

- Xiao Mao suggests they go into the hutong and take a look:

  Wǒmen jìnqu kànkan.

  我們進去看看。／我们进去看看。

- Xiao Mao says he was attracted to come to the hutong by an ad:

  bèi guǎnggào xīyǐn guòlai de

  被廣告吸引過來的／被广告吸引过来的

- Mike asks Xiao Mao to leave behind his e-mail address:

  liú xiàlai yóuxiāng dìzhǐ

  留下來郵箱地址／留下来邮箱地址

- Mike has received the text message:

  duǎnxìn shōudào le

  短信收到了

- Professor Mao asked students to do their exercises:

  bǎ sīkǎotí dōu zuòxiàlai

  把思考題都做下來／把思考题都做下来

- Professor Mao hopes that everyone will go back and review thoroughly:

  Máo lǎoshī xīwàng dàjiā huíqu hǎohāo fùxí

  毛老師希望大家回去好好複習／毛老师希望大家回去好好复习

- Professor Mao says the scope of the test has already been narrowed down as much as it can be:

  cèyàn suō dào zuìxiǎo le

  測驗縮到最小了／测验缩到最小了

- Fang Lan has a foreign student living at her home:

  Yí ge liúxuéshēng zhù zài wǒ jiā.

  一個留學生住在我家。／一个留学生住在我家。

- Emma is sick but couldn't throw up:

  Bìng le, kěshì tù bù chūlai.

  病了，可是吐不出來。／病了，可是吐不出来。

- The doctor asks Emma if she caught a chill after eating:

  Chīwán yǐhòu yǒu méiyǒu shòuliáng a?

  吃完以後有沒有受涼啊？／吃完以后有没有受凉啊？

- Fang Lan probably can't remember:

  Fāng Lán kěnéng jìbudé.

  方蘭可能記不得。／方兰可能记不得。

- The doctor asks Emma to roll up her sleeve:

  bǎ yīfu nòng shàngqu

  把衣服弄上去

- Zhang Suyun thinks the bank's procedures sound convenient:

  Yínháng de shǒuxù tīng qǐlai tǐng fāngbiàn.

  銀行的手續聽起來挺方便。／银行的手续听起来挺方便。

- Fang Lan and Emma put their backpacks on the sofa:

  bǎ bēibāo fàng zài shāfā shang

  把背包放在沙發上／把背包放在沙发上

- Emma recalls that her teacher mentioned the Beijing opera:

  lǎoshī tídào le jīngjù

  老師提到了京劇／老师提到了京剧

- Emma did not misremember her bank password:

  Àimǎ méi jìcuò yínháng mìmǎ.

  艾瑪沒記錯銀行密碼。／艾玛没记错银行密码。

- Emma's bank card will be ejected (after use):

  kǎ jiù huì tuì chūlai

  卡就會退出來／卡就会退出来

- Aima has not thought through buying her cell phone:

  Àimǎ hái méi xiǎnghǎo mǎi shǒujī de shìqing.

  艾瑪還沒想好買手機的事情。／艾玛还没想好买手机的事情。

- She also has not selected (to her satisfaction) which kind to buy:

  Yě méiyǒu xuǎnhǎo mǎi shénme yàngzi de shǒujī.

  也沒有選好買甚麼樣子的手機。／也没有选好买什么样子的手机。

▶ Vocabulary

Please refer to page R-2 for a list of grammatical abbreviations used throughout this book.

ànzhào 按照 according to; on the basis of   PREP

bǎn 版 version, type, kind (literally, "edition of book, newspaper")   N

chéngshòu 承受 bear; endure   V

dà shùn 大順／大顺 auspicious (literally, "greatly favorable")   IE

dài huài 帶壞／带坏 lead astray; corrupt   RV

diànchí 電池／电池 (electric) battery   N

fǎngzhì 仿製／仿制 copy; imitate   V

fǎnzhèng 反正 in any case; anyway; anyhow   A

gǎi zhǔyi 改主意 change one's mind   VO

gānghǎo 剛好／刚好 just; exactly   A

guóchǎn 國產／国产 product of a country; domestic product   N

jiǎ 假 false; phony; fake; artificial   SV

jiàwèi 價位／价位 price range   N

jílì 吉利 lucky; fortuitous; auspicious   SV; good luck   N

jīngdiǎn 經典／经典 classic; "best of the lot"   ATTR

jīzi 機子／机子 small machine   N

kàngshǐ 抗使 stands up to use (long-lasting)   VO

kěbù zěnmeyàng 可不怎麼樣／可不怎么样 nothing to speak of; not very good   IE

kěndìng 肯定 definitely; surely; for sure   A

kuǎn 款 type; style   N

kuǎnxíng 款型 style; pattern; design   N

liúliàng 流量 data usage   N

míxìn 迷信 superstition   N; have blind faith in   V

pāizhào 拍照 take (a picture); shoot (a film)   VO

pèitào 配套 form a set   VO

píngmù 屏幕 screen   N

pǐnpái 品牌 trademark; brand   N

qiángzhì 強制／强制 force; compel; coerce   V

rényuán 人員／人员 staff   N

shàngwǎng 上網／上网 go online; be on the Internet   VO

shānzhài 山寨 phony; fake; knockoff (literally, "mountain fastness")   N

shāowēi 稍微 slightly; a bit   A

shìhé X yòng 適合X用／适合X用 appropriate/good for X   IE

shìpín 視頻／视频 video   N

shǒujīhào 手機號／手机号 cell phone number   N

tiāohuāyǎn 挑花眼 eyes blur with so many choices *(literally, "cross (stitch) the eyes")*   VO

tíxǐng 提醒 remind; alert to   V

tuī 推 push; promote   V

tuījiàn 推薦／推荐 recommend   V

wánle 完了 and then   VP

xiāoshòu 銷售／销售 sell; market   V

xiéyīn 諧音／谐音 homophonic   N

xìngjiàbǐ 性價比／性价比 quality/price ratio   N

yāo 幺 one *(used when saying the number 1 in phone numbers, etc.)*   NU

yóuxì 遊戲／游戏 game *(for recreation)*   N; play   V

zài X zhī nèi 在 X 之内 within   IE

zhào 兆 *(computer)* mega; million   NU

zhìliàng 質量／质量 quality   N

zhìnéngjī 智能機／智能机 smartphone *(literally, "intelligent machine")*   N

▶ Checklist of "can do" statements

After completing this unit, you should be able to perform each of the following tasks:

Listening and speaking

☐ State your needs and ask for help regarding cell phone services.

☐ Press for more information and respond with details when queried.

☐ Correct someone when he or she doesn't understand your meaning.

Reading and writing

☐ Understand brief notes describing cell phones.

☐ Write a brief description of the phone you have/want.

☐ Decipher some signs in a cell phone store.

☐ Read a short story about a cell phone, and write one of your own.

Understanding culture

☐ Correctly describe the cultural significance of some numbers.

☐ Make an accurate statement about cell phone usage in China.

"The rarer an item, the more valuable it becomes"

物以稀為貴

Wù yǐ xī wéi guì

Shopping in malls and stores

In this unit, you will learn how to:

- comment on the types of retail stores available in upscale shopping malls.

- ask about the locations of specific stores.

- compare prices and quality of different products.

- compare an upscale mall with other kinds of stores.

- decipher some signs in stores and malls.

- comprehend a short story about shopping, and write one of your own.

Encounter 1   Shopping in a mall

26.1 *A-Juan and Tang Yuan are browsing at an upscale shopping mall in Beijing. To prepare for their conversation as they wander through the mall, match the vocabulary below.* 請把中文跟英文對上。／请把中文跟英文对上。

_____ a. shāngchǎng 商場／商场

_____ b. gāodàng shāngshà 高檔商廈／高档商厦

_____ c. guàngguang 逛逛

_____ d. shāngdiàn 商店

_____ e. fúzhuāng zhuānmàidiàn 服裝專賣店／服装专卖店

_____ f. yīfu 衣服

_____ g. jiàqián 價錢／价钱

1. *store*
2. *clothes*
3. *upscale commercial building*
4. *prices*
5. *shopping mall*
6. *walk around, window shop*
7. *clothing specialty store*

26.2 *View Episode 26, Vignette 1. Put the following events in the order in which they occur.*

_____ Tang Yuan describes some of the stores in the shopping mall.

_____ A-Juan describes a very expensive skirt.

_____ Tang Yuan talks about moving to Beijing.

_____ A-Juan tells Tang Yuan to buy a suit.

_____ A-Juan and Tang Yuan go into a baby goods store.

26.3 *View Episode 26, Vignette 1 again. Identify who makes each of the following statements (presented in the order in which they are made).*

> a. A-Juan   b. Tang Yuan

_____ This is so much bigger than the malls in Yangshuo.

_____ This is a new upscale commercial building.

_____ After we move to Beijing, we can come often.

_____ On the left is menswear.

_____ There is a big electronic goods store.

_____ The supermarket is on the basement floor.

_____ Items like these can't be cheap.

_____ Don't worry about the price.

_____ For menswear such as suits, quality is the most important thing.

_____ It's meaningless to spend money for myself.

_____ What's worth seeing here?

_____ A little hat—it's so cute!

26.4 *View Episode 26, Vignette 1 again.* 請把中文跟英文對上。／请把中文跟英文对上。

_____ a. miànshì 面試／面试

_____ b. bān lái Běijīng 搬來北京／搬来北京

_____ c. duì zìjǐ hěn yǒu xìnxīn 對自己很有信心／对自己很有信心

_____ d. shāngdiàn tǐng duō 商店挺多

_____ e. nánzhuāng 男裝／男装

_____ f. nǚzhuāng 女裝／女装

_____ g. lǐpǐndiàn 禮品店／礼品店

_____ h. diànzǐ chǎnpǐn shāngdiàn 電子產品商店／电子产品商店

_____ i. xiǎoxīn 小心

_____ j. rìyòngpǐn 日用品

_____ k. shípǐn 食品

_____ l. língshí hé yǐnliào 零食和飲料／零食和饮料

_____ m. tiāo yí tào xīfú 挑一套西服

_____ n. zhìliàng 質量／质量

_____ o. zhídé 值得

1. *move to Beijing*
2. *men's fashion*
3. *snacks and drinks*
4. *be careful*
5. *gift store*
6. *interview*
7. *daily-use products*
8. *have confidence in oneself*
9. *women's fashion*
10. *be worth it*
11. *there are many stores*
12. *quality*
13. *food products*
14. *electronic goods store*
15. *pick out a suit*

26.5 *Pretend you need to buy several specific items. Use the measure words from the word bank to fill in the blanks.* 請填漢字。／请填汉字。

件	條/条	套	家
jiàn	tiáo	tào	jiā

我想買／我想买……

_____ 衣服 yīfu *clothing*

_____ 裙子 qúnzi *skirt*

_____ 西服 xīfú *suit*

我們去那 _____ 商店看看吧！／我们去那 _____ 商店看看吧！

26.6 *Tang Yuan uses a special measure word in the sentence below. Remember that shēn* 身 *means "body." What do you think this measure word means here?* 圈選正確的項目。／圈选正确的项目。

Zǒu, zánmen gěi nǐ tiāo liǎng **shēn** piàoliang de yīfu qù!

走，咱們給你挑兩身漂亮的衣服去！／走，咱们给你挑两身漂亮的衣服去！

(two pretty outfits / two pretty dresses)

 26.7 *Since Tang Yuan has been to this shopping mall before and A-Juan has not, he describes its layout to her as they stroll along the first floor. View Episode 26, Vignette 1 again. Label the location of each kind of store by writing the appropriate letters from the list that follows.*

三樓／三楼	
二樓／二楼	
一樓／一楼	
地下一層／地下一层	

a. nánzhuāng diàn 男裝店／男装店

b. nǚzhuāng diàn 女裝店／女装店

c. tóngzhuāng diàn 童裝店／童装店

d. lǐpǐn diàn 禮品店／礼品店

e. xié diàn 鞋店

f. diànzǐ chǎnpǐn shāngdiàn 電子產品商店／电子产品商店

g. chāoshì 超市

h. rìyòngpǐn diàn 日用品店　*(included as part of* 超市)

i. shípǐn diàn 食品店　*(included as part of* 超市)

j. língshí diàn 零食店

k. yǐnliào diàn 飲料店／饮料店

26.8 *Think about your community. What are your favorite stores? Write their names in the blanks provided.* 請寫英文。／请写英文。

我最喜欢的 _____ 的名字叫 _____。

男裝店／男装店：_____　　女裝店／女装店：_____

童裝店／童装店：_____　　禮品店／礼品店：_____

鞋店：_____　　電子產品商店／电子产品商店：_____

日用品店：＿＿＿＿＿＿＿＿   食品店：＿＿＿＿＿＿＿＿

超市：＿＿＿＿＿＿＿＿   零食店：＿＿＿＿＿＿＿＿

飲料店／饮料店：＿＿＿＿＿＿＿＿   藥店／药店 (yào diàn *drugstore*)：＿＿＿＿＿＿

26.9 *Pair work: Chat with your partner for three minutes (or until your teacher signals time)—IN CHINESE ONLY—about where you like to shop, why those stores are your favorites, and what you shop for. If necessary, tell your partner where your favorite stores are and how to get there. Talk about the locations of specific stores in malls. Jot down some vocabulary items here to get started.*

26.10 *In Episode 26, Vignette 2, A-Juan and Tang Yuan browse a modest neighborhood store. To prepare for their conversation, match the vocabulary below.* 請把中文跟英文對上。／请把中文跟英文对上。

_____ a. jiàgé piányi hěn duō
　　價格便宜很多／价格便宜很多

_____ b. jiàgé xiāngchà zhème dà
　　價格相差這麼大／价格相差这么大

_____ c. gāngcái yě shì zhè ge biāozhì
　　剛才也是這個標誌／刚才也是这个标志

_____ d. gēnběn méishénme qūbié
　　根本沒甚麼區別／根本没什么区别

_____ e. xìnghǎo méi mǎi
　　幸好沒買／幸好没买

_____ f. gāodàng hé pǔtōng shāngdiàn de qūbié
　　高檔和普通商店的區別／高档和普通商店的区别

_____ g. bǎihuò shāngdiàn zài nǎr
　　百貨商店在哪兒／百货商店在哪儿

_____ h. chūqu xiàng zuǒ yǒu yí ge Wò'ěrmǎ
　　出去向左有一個沃爾瑪／出去向左有一个沃尔玛

1. *this is the same brand as what we just saw*

2. *it's a good thing we didn't buy (it)*

3. *the price is much cheaper*

4. *where's the department store*

5. *turn left after you go out, and there's a Walmart*

6. *there's no difference at all*

7. *the difference between an upscale and an ordinary store*

8. *there's such a big difference in price*

26.11 *View Episode 26, Vignette 2. Identify who makes each of the following statements (presented in the order in which they are made).*

> a. A-Juan   b. Tang Yuan   c. Clerk

_____ 1. Look! This outfit is the same as the one we just saw in the mall, but there's such a big difference in price!

_____ 2. Was the one just now also this brand? Did it have these pants as well?

_____ 3. It did. There's absolutely no difference.

_____ 4. Good thing we didn't buy it.

_____ 5. Wow! It's almost five times more!

_____ 6. That's the difference between an upscale store and an ordinary store!

_____ 7. Boys' clothes are generally light blue, and girls generally wear pink.

_____ 8. You got it backwards!

_____ 9. Where is the department store here?

_____ 10. You can go out and turn left, and there's a Walmart.

_____ 11. Well then, should we go look around a department store?

26.12 *Match the pinyin with the English in 26.11.* 請把下面的拼音跟上面的英文對上。／请把下面的拼音跟上面的英文对上。

_____ a. Wa, chà le kuài wǔ bèi la!

_____ b. Yǒu a, gēnběn méishénme qūbié.

_____ c. Nǐ shuō fǎn le!

_____ d. Nín kěyǐ chūqu xiàng zuǒ guǎi, nàlǐ yǒu yí ge Wò'ěrmǎ.

_____ e. Gāngcái nà jiàn yě shì zhè ge biāozhì? Hái yǒu zhè kùzi a?

_____ f. Zhè jiùshì gāodàng shāngdiàn hé pǔtōng shāngdiàn de qūbié!

_____ g. Xìnghǎo méi mǎi.

_____ h. Yào bù zánmen qù yìjiā bǎihuòdiàn guàngguang?

_____ i. Nǐ kàn, zhè jiàn yīfu hé gāngcái wǒmen zài shāngchǎng lǐ kànjiàn de yíyàng, dànshì jiàgé què xiāngchà zhème dà!

_____ j. Nánháizi de yīfu tōngcháng chuān dàn lán sè, nǚháizi tōngcháng chuān fěnhóng sè.

_____ k. Nà zhèlǐ bǎihuò shāngdiàn zài nǎr?

26.13 *Read the following sentences out loud. Use the previous two exercises as a guide.*

a. 你看，這件衣服和剛才我們在商場裡看見的一樣，但是價格卻相差這麼大！／你看，这件衣服和刚才我们在商场里看见的一样，但是价格却相差这么大！

b. 剛才那件也是這個標誌？還有這褲子啊？／刚才那件也是这个标志？还有这裤子啊？

c. 有啊，根本沒甚麼區別。／有啊，根本没什么区别。

d. 幸好沒買。／幸好没买。

e. 哇，差了快5倍啦！

f. 這就是高檔商店和普通商店的區別！／这就是高档商店和普通商店的区别！

g. 男孩子的衣服通常穿淡藍色，女孩子通常穿粉紅色。／男孩子的衣服通常穿淡蓝色，女孩子通常穿粉红色。

h. 你說反了！／你说反了！

i. 那這裡百貨商店在哪兒？／那这里百货商店在哪儿？

j. 您可以出去向左拐，那裡有一個沃爾瑪。／您可以出去向左拐，那里有一个沃尔玛。

k. 要不咱們去一家百貨店逛逛？／要不咱们去一家百货店逛逛？

26.14 Pair work: *Work with a partner. Compare and contrast shopping at a superstore such as Walmart with shopping at an upscale store such as Neiman Marcus. Make a list of similarities and differences and when you might shop at each. Some useful vocabulary is provided for your convenience.*

gāodàng shāngdiàn   高檔商店／高档商店   *upscale store*

pǔtōng shāngdiàn   普通商店   *ordinary store*

zhìliàng hǎo   質量好／质量好   *good quality*

zhìliàng chà   質量差／质量差   *poor quality*

zhídé   值得   *be worth it*

bù zhídé   不值得   *not worth it*

kěyǐ mǎidào míngpái   可以買到名牌／可以买到名牌   *be able to buy name brands*

méishénme qūbié   没甚麼區別／没什么区别   *there's no difference*

chà le kuài X bèi   差了快 X 倍   *the difference is almost X-fold*

děng dào jiǎnjià cái mǎi   等到減價才買／等到减价才买   *buy only when there's a sale*

Encounter 2   Reading and writing

26.15 *Following is a chain of e-mail correspondence. Fill in the chart based on the notes.* 請寫拼音。／请写拼音。

誰寫的？／谁写的？	寫給誰的？／写给谁的？	主要内容 (zhǔyào nèiróng *key content; main points*)
a.		
b.		
c.		

a 小张：

你明天一定要和我一起去新唐百货大楼逛逛。我今天已经去过了，所有的店都起码打六折，有的甚至打五折、四折。我买了两条裙子，一条裤子。我明天想再去一趟。今天看到了几件衬衫，可是时间不够，没来得及试穿。你明天下午有空陪我一起去吗？请回话。
旦旦

b 旦旦：

你还在买衣服！你的柜子都装不下了，你还想买！我可以陪你去逛，也愿意陪你去逛，可是我对服装实在不感兴趣。不知道电脑店里也打折扣吗？我可以去电脑店里转转，看有什么新的配套设备。还有，我们班上来了一位新的留学生，台湾来的。我明天把她也叫上，没问题吧？她叫刘若水。我这也抄送给她。
张华

c 張華：

收到你的來信了。謝謝你邀請我明天和你們一起去逛商場。其實人多的地方我有一點不敢 (bù gǎn *don't dare*) 去，可是因為有你和你的同學陪同，我就大膽 (dàdǎn *courageous*) 一點吧！我們明天不是一起吃午飯嗎？完了以後我就跟你一起去找旦旦，好嗎？旦旦：很高興在網上認識你。張華常提起你。盼望著明天見面！
若水

26.16 *Now write a note to one of your classmates, suggesting a shopping excursion of some sort.* 請寫漢字。／请写汉字。 *When you're done, have it checked, and then pass it to your classmate for a written response.*

▶ **Reading real-life texts**

26.17 *These are some signs A-Juan and Tang Yuan saw on their shopping excursion.*

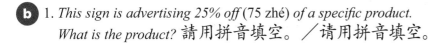

a *The Chinese for Indigo (a mall) is* 颐堤港 *Yídīgǎng. What does the sign say you will find in this mall? Check three.*

☐ gòuwù *shopping*

☐ yúlè *entertainment*

☐ tíngchē *parking*

☐ měishí *fine foods*

b 1. *This sign is advertising 25% off (75 zhé) of a specific product. What is the product?* 請用拼音填空。／请用拼音填空。

男式 POLO 衫

____ ____ POLO shān

men's style polo shirt

2. *The white print at the bottom of the sign (beneath* 男式 POLO 衫*) provides a clarification.* 請用英文填空。／请用英文填空。

购满两件或以上即可享受

Gòu mǎn liǎng jiàn huò yǐshàng jí kě xiǎngshòu

If you buy _____ or more, you can enjoy this discount.

c *What is the discount being offered? Check one.* 然後填空。／然后填空。

☐ 30%

☐ 70%

全场3折，一件不留

Quán chǎng sān zhé, yí jiàn bù liú

Entire stock _____ % off; not one shirt withheld

d *This sign appears in the window of a clothing store. Using the English equivalent as a guide, add the missing pinyin.* 请用拼音填空。／请用拼音填空。

Set out from here
Begin a professional career in fashion

We currently seek to hire:
Sales consultants
(Full-time / part-time students)

____ ____ ____ chūfā

____ ____ shíshàng de ____ ____ shēngyá

Wǒmen xiàn zhèng zhāopìn:

xiāoshòu gùwèn

(quánzhí / _____ jiānzhí)

e *What do these signs say?* 請把中文跟英文對上。／请把中文跟英文对上。

1. 新店 xīn diàn   A. *open for business*

2. 开业 kāiyè   B. *about to; will soon*

3. 即将 jíjiāng   C. *new store*

---

f *The escalators lead downstairs to the supermarket. When you turn around to go back upstairs, you see this sign posted on the glass doors of the supermarket. What is the warning? Match the columns below, and then figure out what the sign says.* 請把拼音跟英文對上，然後用英文填空。／请把拼音跟英文对上，然后用英文填空。

1. gòuwùchē   A. *escalator*

2. jìnzhǐ   B. *prohibited*

3. chéngzuò   C. *shopping cart*

4. fútī   D. *ride on, take on*

购物车禁止乘坐扶梯 ＝ _____

g *Inside the supermarket is this display of health foods.* 請用拼音和英文填空。／请用拼音和英文填空。

Jiànkāng — _____ _____ _____ de zhuīqiú

Jiànkāng — shíshàng de xuǎnzé

_____ — wǒmen kěyǐ _____ _____ dǎzào de

Health — what everyone seeks
Health — the _____ choice
Health — what we can create for you

h

1. *There is a food court in this mall. Write out the pinyin for this sign.*

_____ _____ _____ _____

2. *Number the English below (from 1 to 4) to match the order of the characters from left to right.*

   drink   cold   product   hot

   ____   ____   ____   ____

i *There are many vendors selling food. This one offers snacks of a particular variety. Write out the English to match the pinyin.* 請用英文填空／请用英文填空。

Lǎo Běijīng _____

hútòng _____

xiǎochī _____

j *Finally, remember that this mall promises entertainment* (yúlè 娛樂／娱乐) *in addition to shopping* (gòuwù 購物／购物) *and food* (měishí 美食). *This sign advertises a movie night. What does the Chinese tell you that the English does not? Guess the meanings of these three phrases.* 請用英文填空／请用英文填空。

星空下 xīngkōng xià   *beneath the _____*

夏日 xiàrì   *during the _____*

电影节 diànyǐngjié   *_____ festival*

▶ **Reading a story**

26.18 故事： 王明和李南去逛街。 *Work with a partner or in a small group to read the story below.*

王明和李南是高中同學。他們剛畢業，過幾個月就要上大學了。今年夏天比較輕鬆，所以他們找個時間一起去逛街。

他們先去一個高檔購物中心去逛。上下有十層，裡面各種各樣的店都有。最多的是女裝店，其次是男裝店。書店、電子產品店、鞋店，甚麼都有。這些店裡賣的產品都是名牌，質量都很好，可是價錢也非常貴，比外面要貴好幾倍。

王明和李南在購物中心裡逛了很久，一層一層地從上逛到下，可是没找到一樣自己喜歡而且買得起的東西。

逛了三個鐘頭，他們逛累了，覺得又渴又餓，想起這個購物中心裡有很多賣飲料和小吃的店，就決定去找一點吃的、喝的，順便休息一會兒。他們看了看商場指南，發現在三樓有美食廣場，就坐扶梯到三樓去看看。

三樓有各種各樣的小吃，真豐富！中國東西南北的菜都有，還有歐美洲的風味。王明和李南注意到有一家賣老北京胡同小吃，像各種各樣的餅還有麵食，他們就決定喝一壺茶，吃幾樣小吃。這樣又過了兩個鐘頭。

等到他們吃好了，休息夠了，離開美食廣場的時候，發現有一場很流行的電影快開始了。主角都是明星，故事介紹看起來也很有趣。他們兩個人買了票就進了電影院了。

電影結束以後，小王和小李出來一看，天已經黑了，該回家了！逛了一天的商場，甚麼也没買，倒覺得玩得很過癮 (guòyǐn *enjoy oneself to the fullest*)。改天真的要買東西的時候再來吧！

26.19 *Write a short story about shopping. Have it edited by your teacher or someone else who is fluent in Chinese. Illustrate your story as best as you can before sharing it with your classmates.*

Encounter 3　Extension: Cultural mini-documentary

 View the cultural mini-documentary for this unit and complete the exercises below.

26.20 *In the first part of this video, we see some footage of Beijing's famous Silk Street. A few decades ago, this market was a real street market with temporary stalls, located on Xiushui Street. In recent years, it has been housed in a specially constructed building. Starting at about 0:24 in the video, one of the merchants shares information about her small business. For the items that the merchant mentions, match the pictures with the text. Write the correct letters in the blanks.*

_____　　_____　　_____　　_____

_____　　_____　　_____　　_____

a. tiānrán de zhēnzhū 天然的珍珠　　　　e. xiàngliàn 項鍊／项链

b. shítou, záshí 石頭／石头，雜石／杂石　　f. ěrhuán 耳環／耳环

c. yù 玉　　　　　　　　　　　　　　　　g. shǒuliàn, shǒuzhuó 手鍊／手链，手鐲／手镯

d. shuǐjīng 水晶　　　　　　　　　　　　h. jièzhi 戒指

26.21 *Starting at 0:41, the merchant is asked what's different about selling at Silk Street. Fill in the blanks in English to reflect her answers during the conversation.* 用英文填空。

a. Here there are more _____ customers; at other places there are more _____.

b. Customers' nationalities at the Silk Market include _____, _____, and Russian.

c. I can speak _____, _____, and _____, but not any other languages.

26.22 *Starting at about 1:18, the merchant responds with several possible answers to the question, "How do you interact with customers?" Add numbers in the blanks to indicate the order in which she responds.*

_____ There are many styles of pearls. I could show them to you.

_____ For example, we could give your wife (*xifur* 媳婦兒／媳妇儿) a pearl necklace.

_____ Are you looking for gifts? For how old a person?

_____ What do you need?

_____ What pearls does she have already? If she doesn't have any, the first strand should be white.

26.23 *Starting at about 1:46, the merchant responds with several possible answers to the question, "How can you tell what jewelry would be appropriate for each customer?" Add numbers in the blanks to indicate the order in which she responds.*

_____ If she is fashionable, I would suggest a long necklace.

_____ If it's a woman, for example, look at her clothes. Are they fashionable or simple?

_____ First I ask; I go by my feelings.

_____ If she is a motherly type, I'd offer one like this.

_____ If she is a large person—a heavy person—I would suggest large pearls or long necklaces.

_____ If she is wearing a T-shirt, she likes simplicity. I would not suggest a necklace like this. I'd offer a very simple necklace—a very fine one.

_____ If she is thin, I would offer a choker that grips the neck tightly.

26.24 *Starting at about 2:31, the merchant talks about how she would advise a new shopper.* 請用拼音填空。／请用拼音填空。

Nǐ shì shuō kǎnjià de wèntí shì ba? Jiùshì, e, gāng lái de shíhou, tāmen kěnéng bù zhīdao Xiùshuǐ, yīnwèi Xiùshuǐ shìchǎng shì yào kǎnjià. Dànshì xiànzài wǒmen de yuánzé jiùshì, hěn shízài de _____, ránhòu tā kěyǐ kǎn yìdiǎn, yīnwèi zánmen zuò mǎimài de, kěndìng shì nǐ yào _____ cái zìjǐ xīnlǐ shūfu, ránhòu wǒmen ne, mài yuè gāo yuè hǎo. Háishi yào kàn dōngxi la. Bǐrú shuō, wǒ zhè ge _____ tǐng hǎo de, nǐ xǐhuan, nǐ kěyǐ mǎi de guì yìdiǎn. Rúguǒ nǐ bù xǐhuan, wǒ gěi nǐ zài _____ le, yě méiyǒu yòng, shì ba?

Wǒmen _____, yǒuxiē rén háishi xǐhuan dài yí ge hǎo de, yào shōucáng. Shōucáng de huà, nǐ yào mǎi Nányáng zhū, jiù hǎo de, yào fēicháng yuán, ránhòu guāngzé hǎo, ránhòu háiyào wúxiá de. Xiàng guówài de, tāmen zuì zhǔyào shì zhuīqiú _____, yīnwèi yǒu shénme party a, tāmen dōu yào bù yíyàng de kuǎnshì, ránhòu bù xūyào hěn hǎo de, jiù yìbān de jiù kěyǐ le ma. Zuì zhǔyào háishi

_____.

你是说砍价的问题是吧？就是，哦，刚来的时候，他们可能不知道秀水，因为秀水市场是要砍价。但是现在我们的原则就是，很实在的价钱，然后他可以砍一点，因为咱们做买卖的，肯定是你要砍价才自己心里舒服，然后我们呢，卖越高越好。还是要看东西啦。比如说，我这个项链挺好的，你喜欢，你可以买的贵一点。如果你不喜欢，我给你再便宜了，也没有用，是吧？

我们中国人，有些人还是喜欢戴一个好的，要收藏。收藏的话，你要买南洋珠，就好的，要非常圆，然后光泽好，然后还要无瑕的。像国外的，他们最主要是追求款式，因为有什么party 啊，他们都要不一样的款式，然后不需要很好的，就一般的就可以了嘛。最主要还是装饰。

*You mean about haggling? When they first arrive, they might not know that you have to bargain at Xiushui. But our principle is that our **prices** are fair, and they can bargain them down a little. We merchants know that buyers won't feel good unless they can **bargain down**. We of course want the price to be as high as possible. Of course it depends on the item. This **necklace**, for example, is pretty good. If you like it, you won't mind paying more. If you don't like it, no matter how **cheap** I make it, it won't help.*

*We **Chinese**, some of us like to wear something good, something collectible. As a collectible, you have to buy Southeast Asian pearls. The good ones have to be very round, with good luster and no flaws. Foreigners generally look for **style**. If they are going to a party, they want to wear a distinctive style. And the items don't need to be very good—an average piece would do. It's all about **adornment**.*

26.25 *Starting at about 3:53, the merchant mentions four basic characteristics in response to the question, "How can you tell a good pearl from a bad one?"* 請把中文跟英文對上。／请把中文跟英文对上。

____ a. yuán dù 圓度／圆度   1. *purity*

____ b. dàxiǎo 大小   2. *luster*

____ c. chúnjìng dù 純淨度／纯净度   3. *size*

____ d. guāngzé 光澤／光泽   4. *roundness*

Recap

▶ Grammar

Comparing this and that

The comparison structure in Chinese is further proof that Chinese is a "fill-in" language—that is, instead of changing words (as is the case for other languages) Chinese rearranges words to convey meaning. This is not as simple as it sounds, and it demands practice. Therefore, let's have a review of this pattern and take a look at how Chinese compares things.

Just as in English, you can make comparisons in Chinese a number of different ways. Most commonly, it is with a key word—in this case, the coverb *bǐ* 比 (compared with). Take a look at how the people in this unit flex the pattern to compare various things.

Zhèr zhēn dà! Bǐ Yángshuò de shāngchǎng kě dà duō le.

這兒真大！比陽朔的商場可大多了。／
这儿真大！比阳朔的商场可大多了。

(It's big here! It's certainly much bigger than the markets of Yangshuo.)

Wǒ fāxiàn nánzhuāng bǐ nǚzhuāng hái guì.

我發現男裝比女裝還貴。／我发现男装比女装还贵。

(I found out that clothes for men are even more expensive than [those] for women.)

Běijīng de xīfú suīrán guì, dànshì zhìliàng bǐ zánmen nàr hǎo hěn duō.

北京的西服雖然貴，但是質量比咱們那兒好很多。／北京的西服虽然贵，但是质量比咱们那儿好很多。

(Although Beijing's suits are expensive, their quality is much better than [those] where we are.)

Nàr huòwù bǐ zhè xiē xiǎo diàn qíquán.

那兒貨物比這些小店齊全。／那儿货物比这些小店齐全。

(There the merchandise is more complete than in these small stores.)

This structure is basically A *bǐ* B + stative verb / adjective (+ *yìdiǎnr, de duō, hěn duō, duō le*, etc.). Here are some variations of this pattern, all worth your close attention.

Zhōngwén bǐ Yīngwén nán. *(harder)*

中文比英文難。／中文比英文难。

Zhōngwén bǐ Yīngwén hái yào nán. *("still more hard" = even harder)*

中文比英文還要難。／中文比英文还要难。

Zhōngwén bǐ Yīngwén gèng nán. *("even more hard" = even harder)*

中文比英文更難。／中文比英文更难。

Zhōngwén bǐ Yīngwén nán yìdiǎnr. *(harder by a little)*

中文比英文難一點兒。／中文比英文难一点儿。

Zhōngwén bǐ Yīngwén nán de duō. *(harder by a lot)*

中文比英文難得多。／中文比英文难得多。

Zhōngwén bǐ Yīngwén nán duō le. *(harder by a lot)*

中文比英文難多了。／中文比英文难多了。

Zhōngwén bǐ Yīngwén nán yìqiān bèi. *(a thousand times harder)*

中文比英文難一千倍。／中文比英文难一千倍。

Now take a look at the negative forms.

> Zhōngwén bù bǐ Yīngwén nán. Liǎng ge dōu yíyàng
> nán. *(not more difficult)*

中文不比英文難。兩個都一樣難。／
中文不比英文难。两个都一样难。

> Zhōngwén méiyǒu Yīngwén nàme nán. Yīngwén
> fēicháng nán. *(not as difficult)*

中文沒有英文那麼難。英文非常難。／
中文没有英文那么难。英文非常难。

Exercise: Let's now try to apply this grammar to your life. Make comparative statements to your classmates about some of the following topics. Agree or disagree with your classmates' statements.

- the Yankees (*Yángjī* 洋基), the Mets (*Dàdūhuì* 大都會／大都会), and baseball (*bàngqiú* 棒球)
- shopping at Walmart (*Wò'ěrmǎ* 沃爾瑪／沃尔玛) compared to shopping at Macy's (*Méixī* 梅西)
- French and Chinese cuisines
- American and Japanese cars

▶ Vocabulary

Please refer to page R-2 for a list of grammatical abbreviations used throughout this book.

bèi 倍 times; -fold M

bèi 備／备 prepare; get (something) ready V

biāozhì 標誌／标志 sign; mark; brand N

bú zhìyú 不至於／不至于 not necessarily IE

chāoshì 超市 supermarket N

chuānzhuó 穿著／穿着 apparel; dress; attire N

dàjiē 大街 main street; avenue N

dàn 淡 light; pale SV

dānxīn 擔心／担心 worry; feel anxious SV/V/VO

déyì 得意 be proud of oneself; smug VO

diànzǐ chǎnpǐn 電子產品／电子产品 electronic products N

dìxià 地下 underground; basement N

dòngbudòng 動不動／动不动 *(usually followed by* jiù 就, *indicating an act or situation occurring frequently and often unwished for)* frequently; easily; at every turn; apt to A

éi 誒／诶 *(expressing surprise, realization)* I

fúzhuāng 服裝／服装 clothing N

gāodàng 高檔／高档 top-quality; superior grade SV

guàng 逛 stroll; ramble; roam V

huā 花 spend; expend V

huòwù 貨物／货物 goods; commodities; merchandise N

jiǎngjiu 講究／讲究 be particular/fussy about SV

jiǔdiàn 酒店 hotel N

jùnnán měinǚ 俊男美女 handsome man and beautiful woman N

kě 可 actually; remarkably A

kě'ài 可愛／可爱 loveable; lovely; cute SV

kěshì 可是 be indeed C

kǒudàir 口袋兒／口袋儿 pocket N

kùzi 褲子／裤子 pants; trousers N

lǎogōng 老公 husband N

língshí 零食 snacks N

lǐpǐn 禮品／礼品 gifts N

měiyuàn 美院 (= *měishù xuéyuàn* 美術學院／美术学院); school of arts N

miànshì 面試／面试 interview; audition VO/N

mùjiàng 木匠 carpenter N

mǔyīng 母嬰／母婴 mother and baby N

nánzhuāng 男裝／男装 men's clothing N

nuó 喏 look; see; there *(dialect) (used to call attention to sth)*

nǚzhuāng 女裝／女装 women's clothing N

pǐnzhì 品質／品质 quality N

qiānxū 謙虛／谦虚 modest; unassuming SV

qiáo 瞧 look at V

qíquán 齊全／齐全 complete; all in readiness SV

qūbié 區別／区别 difference; distinction N; distinguish; differentiate V

qúnzi 裙子 skirt N

rénjiā 人家 (somebody) else; people (in general) PR

rìyòngpǐn 日用品 daily-use items N

shàng 上 + number up to *(preceding numbers)* BF; **shàngwàn** 上萬／上万 more than 10,000

shāngchǎng 商場／商场 market; bazaar; mall N

shāngdiàn 商店 shop; store N

shāngshà 商廈／商厦 high-rise commercial building N

shēn 身 *(for an outfit, suit of clothing)* M

shípǐn 食品 foods N

shìzhōng 適中／适中 moderate; appropriate; just right VP

shuō fǎn le 説反了／说反了 get it backward RV

tǎngxià 躺下 lie down RV

tǎnzi 毯子 blanket N

tiāo 挑 choose; select V

tóngzhuāng 童裝／童装 children's clothing N

Wángfǔjǐng 王府井 *(major shopping area in Beijing)* PW

wánjù 玩具 toy; plaything N

wànyī 萬一／万一 just in case; supposing; if by any chance C

Wò'ěrmǎ 沃爾瑪／沃尔玛 Walmart N

xiàng 像 be like; resemble V

xiāngchà 相差 difference N; differ (by) V

xiǎoqū 小區／小区 city/town district; residential area PW

xiē 歇 have a rest V

xiédiàn 鞋店 shoe store N

xīfú 西服 Western-style suit/clothes N

xìnghǎo 幸好 fortunately; luckily IE

xīnjiàn 新建 newly built ATTR

xìnxīn 信心 confidence; faith; belief N

Yángshuò 陽朔／阳朔 *(a popular tourist town in southwest China's Guangxi Province, famous for its spectacular mountain scenery of karst topography)* PW

yǐ 椅 chair BF; **yǐzi** 椅子 chair

yī fēn jiàqián yī fēn huò 一分價錢一分貨／一分价钱一分货 "You get what you pay for" IE

yīng'ér 嬰兒／婴儿 baby; infant N

yǐnliào 飲料／饮料 drinks; beverages N

yìshùjiā 藝術家／艺术家 artist N

yìshùpǐn 藝術品／艺术品 work of art N

yòngpǐn 用品 articles for use; appliances N

yǒu shénme hǎo ne 有甚麼好呢／有什么好呢 what's so good about that PH

yǒudeshì 有的是 have plenty of; no lack of IE

yūn 暈／晕 dizzy SV

zán liǎ 咱倆／咱俩 we two; you and I PR

zánmen 咱們／咱们 we; you and I PR

zhǎng 長／长 grow; grow up; increase V

zhèngqián 掙錢／挣钱 earn/make money VO

zhèngshì 正式 formal *(of actions, speeches, etc.)* SV

zhídé 值得 merit; deserve; (be) worth it SV/AV

zhuàn 轉／转 turn; shift; rotate; revolve; stroll around V

zhuānmàidiàn 專賣店／专卖店 specialty store N

zìjǐ shēnshang 自己身上 one's own self PH

zuòpǐn 作品 works *(of literature, art)* N

zuòyǐ 座椅 chair; seat N

❱ Checklist of "can do" statements

After completing this unit, you should be able to perform each of the following tasks:

Listening and speaking

☐ Comment on the retail stores available in an upscale mall.

☐ Ask and tell about the locations of specific stores.

☐ Compare prices and quality of different products.

☐ Compare an upscale mall with other stores you frequent.

Reading and writing

☐ Read some short notes about going shopping, and write one of your own.

☐ Decipher some signs in stores and malls.

☐ Read a short story about shopping, and write one of your own.

Understanding culture

☐ Make some accurate introductory statements about Beijing's famous Silk Street.

☐ Give some reliable advice to a tourist about shopping for jewelry on Silk Street.

"Even the cleverest wife cannot cook without rice"

巧婦難為無米之炊

Qiǎo fù nánwéi wúmǐzhīchuī

Grocery shopping and cooking

In this unit, you will learn how to:

- shop for cooking ingredients.
- understand and name some common ingredients in Chinese cooking.
- understand amounts used in cooking.

- understand the basic steps in making gongbao chicken.
- decipher some signs and labels relating to groceries.
- comprehend a short story about food, and write one of your own.

Encounter 1 **Shopping for and cooking a Chinese dish**

27.1 *Xiao Mao and Luo Xueting go shopping for ingredients for an upcoming class. To prepare for their conversation as they shop, match the vocabulary below.* 請把中文跟英文對上。／请把中文跟英文对上。

_____ a. gòuwù dānzi 購物單子／购物单子

_____ b. (dà)cōng (大)蔥／(大)葱

_____ c. (shēng)jiāng (生)薑／(生)姜

_____ d. gōngbǎo jīdīng 宮保雞丁／宫保鸡丁

_____ e. húluóbo 胡蘿蔔／胡萝卜

_____ f. huánggua 黃瓜

_____ g. tiáowèipǐn 調味品／调味品

1. *green onion; scallion*

2. *gongbao chicken*

3. *seasoning*

4. *cucumber*

5. *shopping list*

6. *ginger*

7. *carrot*

 27.2 *View Episode 27, Vignette 1. Mark the following statements* Zhēnde 真的 *(true) or* Jiǎde 假的 *(false).*

	Zhēnde 真的	Jiǎde 假的
a. Xiao Mao and Luo Xueting are shopping for ingredients to make a Chinese dish.	☐	☐
b. The cooking teacher has given them a list of things to buy.	☐	☐
c. Xiao Mao wants to stick to buying the items on the list.	☐	☐
d. Luo Xueting wants to buy carrots and cucumbers.	☐	☐
e. Xiao Mao says that Chinese cooking allows for creativity.	☐	☐

27.3 *View Episode 27, Vignette 1 again. Identify who makes each of the following statements (presented in the order in which they are made).*

> a. Xiao Mao   b. Luo Xueting

____ 1. You go buy the green onions and ginger, and I'll get everything else.

____ 2. Aren't we only learning (to cook) gongbao chicken?

____ 3. This isn't much; I haven't bought much at all.

____ 4. Cucumbers, carrots . . . er . . . sesame oil, enoki mushrooms, shiitake mushrooms.

____ 5. This is 13-spice (powder), and then these are star anise, cinnamon, orange rind, and oyster sauce.

____ 6. I just want to learn the basics now.

____ 7. No, no, no. You can be creative at any time.

____ 8. Look at a Chinese cuisine recipe.

____ 9. I'm not a foreigner!

____ 10. I'll admit your cooking is delicious.

____ 11. Cucumbers and carrots—these aren't on the list either.

____ 12. This is my secret weapon!

____ 13. Let's go.

27.4 *Match the Chinese with the English in 27.3.* 請把底下的中文跟上面的英文對上。／请把底下的中文跟上面的英文对上。

____ a. Huánggua, húluóbo, e, máyóu, jīnzhēngū, xiānggū.
黃瓜、胡蘿蔔，呃，麻油、金針菇、香菇。／黄瓜、胡萝卜，呃，麻油、金针菇、香菇。

____ b. Bù bù bù, nǐ rènhé shíhou dōu kěyǐ chuàngzào.
不不不，你任何時候都可以創造。／不不不，你任何时候都可以创造。

____ c. Wǒ jiù xiǎng xué zuì jīběn de dōngxi.
我就想學最基本的東西。／我就想学最基本的东西。

____ d. Nǐ kàn Zhōngcān de càipǔ.
你看中餐的菜譜。／你看中餐的菜谱。

____ e. Nǐ qù mǎi dàcōng hé shēngjiāng, qíyú de wǒ lái mǎi.
你去買大蔥和生薑，其餘的我來買。／你去买大葱和生姜，其余的我来买。

____ f. Wǒ chéngrèn nǐ zuò de cài hǎochī.
我承認你做的菜好吃。／我承认你做的菜好吃。

____ g. Zhè ge shì shísān xiāng, ránhòu zhè ge shì bājiǎo, guìpí, chénpí, háiyǒu háoyóu.
這個是十三香，然後這個是八角、桂皮、陳皮、還有蠔油。／这个是十三香，然后这个是八角、桂皮、陈皮、还有蚝油。

_____ h. Wǒmen bú shì jiù xué gōngbǎo jīdīng ma?

我們不是就學宮保雞丁嗎？／我们不是就学宫保鸡丁吗？

_____ i. Wǒ bú shì wàiguórén!

我不是外國人！／我不是外国人！

_____ j. Zhè nǎr duō ya, mǎi de yìdiǎnr dōu bù duō.

這哪兒多呀，買的一點兒都不多。／这哪儿多呀，买的一点儿都不多。

_____ k. Zhè kě shì wǒ de mìmì wǔqì!

這可是我的秘密武器！／这可是我的秘密武器！

_____ l. Huánggua, nà ge húluóbo ne, yě bú zài dānzi shang.

黃瓜，那個胡蘿蔔呢，也不在單子上。／黄瓜，那个胡萝卜呢，也不在单子上。

_____ m. Zǒu.

走。

27.5 _Put the pinyin and characters from the word bank in the chart to make an organized shopping list._

cù	huājiāo	jiàngyóu	liàojiǔ	xiānggū
dàcōng	huánggua	jītuǐ ròu	máyóu	yán
dàsuàn	huāshēngmǐ	jīxiōng ròu	shēngjiāng	yóu
háoyóu	húluóbo	làjiāo	táng	

雞胸肉／鸡胸肉	花生米	胡蘿蔔／胡萝卜	辣椒	蠔油／蚝油
生薑／生姜	花椒	雞腿肉／鸡腿肉	大蔥／大葱	鹽／盐
油	黃瓜	麻油	醬油／酱油	糖
大蒜	料酒	香菇	醋	

	拼音	漢字／汉字
tiáowèipǐn 調味品／调味品		
green onions		
chili peppers		
Sichuan peppers		
salt		
sugar		
vinegar		
soy sauce		
cooking wine		

garlic		
oyster sauce		
ginger		
sesame oil		
shūcài 蔬菜		
carrots		
cucumbers		
mushrooms		
ròu 肉		
chicken breast		
chicken legs		
qítā 其他		
oil		
peanuts		

27.6 *Xiao Mao and Luo Xueting are learning how to make gongbao chicken. What is your favorite Chinese dish other than gongbao chicken? Pretend you are going to make that dish (or use one of the dishes below). Do some research to find out what is in it, and make a list of the ingredients in Chinese.* 請寫拼音或者漢字。／请写拼音或者汉字。 *Then think about what is currently available in your kitchen, and place a check mark in the appropriate column to indicate what you already have versus what you need to buy.*

咕咾肉
gūlǎoròu
sweet-and-sour pork

乾煸四季豆／干煸四季豆
gānbiān sìjìdòu
dry-cooked string beans

素什錦／素什锦
sùshíjǐn
mixed vegetables

餃子／饺子
jiǎozi
gyoza

炸醬麵／炸酱面
zhájiàngmiàn
noodles with bean sauce

家常豆腐
jiāchángdòufu
homestyle tofu

需要甚麼？／需要什么？	已經有了／已经有了	還得買／还得买
	☐	☐
	☐	☐
	☐	☐
	☐	☐
	☐	☐
	☐	☐
	☐	☐
	☐	☐
	☐	☐
	☐	☐
	☐	☐
	☐	☐
	☐	☐
	☐	☐

27.7 Pair work: *Chat with your partner for three minutes (or until your teacher signals time)—IN CHINESE ONLY—about the dish you identified for 27.6, what you like about it, and what is in it. Jot down any additional vocabulary and expressions you need.*

27.8 *In Episode 27, Vignette 2, Xiao Mao and Luo Xueting learn how to make gongbao chicken. To prepare to view this vignette, match the expressions below.* 請把中文跟英文對上。／请把中文跟英文对上。

_____ a. láizì Sìchuān
　　　　來自四川／来自四川

_____ b. yuánliào fēicháng jiǎndān
　　　　原料非常簡單／原料非常简单

_____ c. fēicháng shòu dàjiā de xǐhuan
　　　　非常受大家的喜歡／非常受大家的喜欢

_____ d. yóuqí shì zài xīfāng guójiā
　　　　尤其是在西方國家／尤其是在西方国家

_____ e. dàjiā dōu chīdaoguo zhè dào cài
　　　　大家都吃到過這道菜／大家都吃到过这道菜

_____ f. jiāo dàjiā zuòfǎ
　　　　教大家做法

_____ g. zhè dào zhèngzōng de "gōngbǎo jīdīng"
　　　　這道正宗的"宮保雞丁"／这道正宗的"宫保鸡丁"

_____ h. sè-xiāng-wèi jùquán
　　　　色香味俱全

1. *it is very well liked by everyone*

2. *everyone has tried this dish*

3. *teach everyone how to cook it*

4. *the ingredients are very simple*

5. *comes from Sichuan*

6. *appearance, fragrance, taste—it's all there*

7. *especially in Western countries*

8. *this authentic "gongbao chicken"*

27.9 *View Episode 27, Vignette 2. Put the following steps in the order in which the chef does them.*

_____ a. Cut the chicken into 1.5-centimeter strips.

_____ b. Cut the skin off the ginger.

_____ c. Cut the skin off the chicken.

_____ d. Put the chicken into a container with soy sauce, cooking wine, and cornstarch.

_____ e. Add peanuts and stir fry.

_____ f. Cut the washed green onions into segments.

_____ g. Cut the chicken into 1.5-centimeter cubes.

_____ h. Massage the chicken.

_____ i. Add chili pepper and Sichuan pepper and stir fry.

_____ j. Marinate it for 20 minutes.

_____ k. Add green onions and stir fry.

_____ l. Add some cornstarch in water.

_____ m. Add just a little garlic.

_____ n. Add chicken and stir fry.

_____ o. Add peanut oil to the pan, and heat to about 40 to 50 degrees.

27.10 *Match the pinyin with the English in 27.9.* 請把底下的拼音跟上面的英文對上。／请把底下的拼音跟上面的英文对上。

_____ 1. Gěi jīròu zuò ànmó.

_____ 2. Bǎ jīròu qiēchéng 1.5 límǐ de xiǎo duàn.

_____ 3. Jiārù jīròu, jìnxíng biānchǎo.

_____ 4. Bǎ xǐhǎo de cōng qiēchéng duàn.

_____ 5. Jiārù huāshēngmǐ, chǎoyichǎo.

_____ 6. Bǎ jiāng de pí qùdiào.

_____ 7. Jiārù cōng duànr, chǎoyichǎo.

_____ 8. Qùdiào jīpí.

_____ 9. Jiārù yìdiǎndiǎn suàn.

_____ 10. Bǎ huāshēngyóu jiārù yóuguō, shāo dào dàyuē sìshí zhì wǔshí dù.

_____ 11. Jiārù yìdiǎnr shuǐ diànfěn.

_____ 12. Yānzhì 20 fēnzhōng.

_____ 13. Bǎ jīròu fàngrù jiārùhǎo jiàngyóu, liàojiǔ hé diànfěn de róngqì lǐ.

_____ 14. Bǎ jīròu qiēchéng 1.5 límǐ de xiǎo dīngr.

_____ 15. Jiārù làjiāo, huājiāo, chǎoyichǎo.

27.11 *Read the following sentences out loud. Use the previous two exercises as a guide.*

a. 把洗好的葱切成段。

b. 把姜的皮去掉。

c. 去掉鸡皮。

d. 把鸡肉切成1.5厘米的小段。

e. 把鸡肉切成1.5厘米的小丁儿。

f. 把鸡肉放入加入好酱油、料酒和淀粉的容器里。

g. 给鸡肉做按摩。

h. 腌制20分钟。

i. 把花生油加入油锅，烧到大约四十至五十度。

j. 加入辣椒、花椒，炒一炒。

k. 加入一点点蒜。

l. 加入鸡肉，进行煸炒。

m. 加入花生米，炒一炒。

n. 加入葱段儿，炒一炒。

o. 加入一点儿水淀粉。

27.12 *Match each of the following sentences with a picture.*

____　　____　　____　　____　　____

____　　____　　____　　____　　____

____　　____　　____　　____　　____

a. 把花生油加入油鍋，燒到大約四十至五十度。

b. 加入一點點蒜。

c. 給雞肉做按摩。

d. 把雞肉放入加入好醬油，料酒和澱粉的容器裡。

e. 加入蔥段，炒一炒。

f. 把雞肉切成1.5厘米的小段。

g. 醃製20分鐘。

h. 加入雞肉，進行煸炒。

i. 把洗好的蔥切成段。

j. 加入辣椒、花椒，炒一炒。

k. 去掉雞皮。

l. 加入花生米，炒一炒。

m. 把薑的皮去掉。

n. 加入一點兒水澱粉。

o. 把雞肉切成1.5厘米的小丁兒。

27.13 *Pair work: Work with a partner. Together, retell the steps involved in making gongbao chicken—either in your own words or as the chef tells it.*

27.14 *Now look at the Chinese dish you researched for 27.6 and 27.7. How would you describe the steps required to make this dish? Write some notes in Chinese to help you.*

27.15 *Pair work: Tell your partner the steps involved in making your dish. Try to follow along as your partner tells you how to make his or her dish. Take notes about these instructions.*

Encounter 2   Reading and writing

▶ Reading real-life texts

27.16 *These are some signs from around* The Hutong *kitchen that the chef, Xiao Mao, and Luo Xueting saw.*

ⓐ *This is a clever ad for* The Hutong *that plays on multiple meanings of the word* tōng 通, *which can mean "go through," "connect to," or "be knowledgeable about." See what sense you can make of the ad, and fill in the blanks in the English equivalent.* 用英文填空。

> Tōng Hútòng, tōng Zhōngguó.
> Hútòng tōng, Zhōngguó tōng.

Go through the _____ *to connect to* _____.
If you become knowledgeable in all the _____ *has to offer, you will be a* _____ *expert.*

ⓑ *What are these two products? Check below.*

1. Golden Dragon Fish . . .
   ☐ peanut oil
   ☐ soybean oil

2. Muslim . . .
   ☐ chili paste
   ☐ sesame paste

3. 請寫漢字。／请写汉字。
   dàdòuyóu _____
   qīngzhēn (*Muslim*) _____
   chún (*pure*) zhīmajiàng _____

c *1. Match the pictures with the following.*

_____ millet from Shanxi Province
_____ the newest green (mung) beans
_____ the best new glutinous rice

2. 請寫拼音。／请写拼音。

A. _____
B. _____
C. _____

d *Match the pictures with the captions.*

_____ yùmǐ ¥5/pén
_____ yóucàimiáo (*rapeseed sprouts*)
_____ tǔdòu ¥2/jīn (1 jīn = *1.1 lbs*)
_____ xiǎo xīhóngshì ¥2/jīn

e *Match the pictures with the captions.* 然後寫拼音。／然后写拼音。

_____ *fresh chicken eggs*
_____ *salted duck eggs*

咸鴨蛋 _____
鲜鸡蛋 _____

f *What does the message on the cake say?* 請寫拼音。／请写拼音。

_____

g *These are the names of some stores in a market. Match the pictures with the captions.* 然後寫拼音。／然后写拼音。

___ handmade generously filled flash-frozen jiaozi

___ The Fragrant Bean tofu house with onsite production

___ Longquan Delicatessen

___ Fatty's Meat Store

A. 豆豆香豆腐坊 (fáng) 现场制作

_____

B. 胖子肉店

_____

C. 手工大馅 (xiàn) 速冻 (sùdòng) 饺子

_____

D. 隆泉 (Lóngquán) 熟食店

_____

h *In this sign,* liáng 粮 *means "grain" or "feed." What do you think* 猫粮·狗粮 *means?* 請寫英文。／请写英文。

_____ · _____

(new product on the market)

27.17 *You've invited several friends over to cook a meal, and you've offered to go shopping for everyone. Three of them have left you notes specifying what they need. Read the notes, and then make a shopping list for yourself on a separate sheet of paper..*

a 非常感謝你幫大家去買菜！我準備做一道最簡單的菜：番茄炒雞蛋。我只需要六個新鮮的雞蛋，兩個大一點的熟番茄。我想你家裡大概油、鹽、糖都有，不用買。沒有的話請發個短信告訴我，我可以帶一些來，你不用買。

b 不知道你吃过红烧肉没有？我想试着做这道菜。请帮买一块猪肉，要带点儿肥肉的那种。大概2斤就够了。我还需要生姜、大蒜、酱油、料酒、还有盐和糖。谢谢！

c 我要做一道素菜。请给我买一块豆腐，两根胡萝卜，一个西兰花，一块姜，一头大蒜。这样就够了。别忘了买米，我们也得煮一锅饭。

27.18 *Pretend it's a different day and a different circumstance. Write a short note in characters, asking a friend to to buy four or five of the items indicated at the stores depicted in 27.16. Include a few sentences about why you want these items.*

▶ Reading a story

27.19 故事：你為甚麼不吃素？ *Work with a partner or in a small group to read the story below.*

大偉是美國人。他學了幾年的中文，說得不錯，可以用中文聊天。他有好幾個中國朋友，他常常跟他們在一起玩遊戲啊、打牌打球啊、出去逛街甚麼的。大家相處得很好，都感覺在一起很愉快。

只有一點讓大偉不滿意。他一直很愛動物，所以捨不得吃肉。他看見他的好朋友們買豬肉、牛肉，吃炸雞、烤鴨、蒸魚，心裡很難過，老想這些可憐的動物被殺的時候有多痛苦。

大偉不吃肉，只吃素。他最喜歡的蔬菜是綠菜花，他認為綠菜花又有營養味道又好。他每天吃很多各種顏色的蔬菜：紅色的西紅柿和胡蘿蔔，紫色的茄子，綠色的青菜、包菜、菠菜等。所有的水果他都喜歡，尤其是西瓜和芒果。他還吃很多糧食：大米飯、小米粥、綠豆粥。

他的中國朋友問他，"你不覺得沒意思嗎？光吃蔬菜水果不吃肉？"他回答，"一點都不。我聞到肉的味道就覺得噁心。"但有很多人說，"不行。我們一定要吃肉，要不然總覺得吃不飽。"大偉說，"這只是習慣而已，你習慣了吃素也就完全可以靠蔬菜水果糧食填飽肚子。"

有一個朋友叫安東，特別聽不慣，他說，"你主要可憐動物而不吃肉。那麼你為甚麼不可憐蔬菜？蔬菜也有生命啊。我們把它們吃了，它們也會覺得痛苦，不是嗎？"

大偉說，"蔬菜水果糧食沒有眼睛，叫不出聲音。我沒辦法看著動物的眼睛還去吃他們的肉。"

他的中國朋友們說，"那你在中國的時候會有困難的。中國也有吃素的人，可是大多數的中國菜裡有菜，也有肉。如果你一定不吃肉的話會有很多很多的菜都不能吃。"

大偉想了想，回答，"我知道了。好在中國有豆腐。雖然光吃豆腐炒青菜也不夠吧，但是我在中國的時候可以常常吃花生醬塗麵包！還有，我特別喜歡吃甜點。我要是飯吃完還不飽的話，我就可以去吃冰淇淋呀、蛋糕呀、餅乾呀，那樣就能飽！"

他的朋友們笑了，說，"怪不得你不吃肉也不瘦！"

27.20 *Write a short story about food. Have it edited by your teacher or someone else who is fluent in Chinese. Illustrate your story as best as you can before sharing it with your classmates.*

Encounter 3   Extension: Cultural mini-documentary

 View the cultural mini-documentary for this unit and complete the exercises that follow.

27.21 *In the first part of this video (0:00–1:10), a cooking instructor introduces cooking utensils (gōngjù 工具) for Chinese cooking. In this segment, the instructor is a little nervous, so she may not notice that she calls her wok or frying pan by two different names. Both names are OK! Match the names and descriptions of the cooking utensils to the pictures. Write the letters and numbers in the correct place.*

	漢字／汉字	拼音	Description

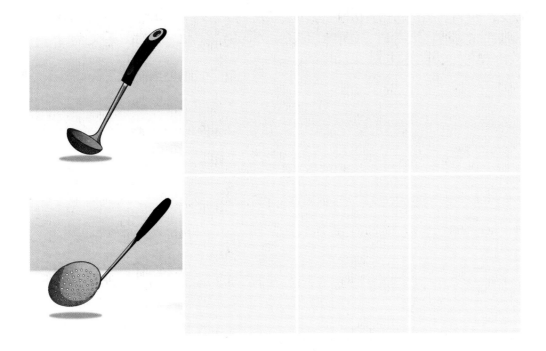

a. 炒鏟／炒铲
b. 炒鍋／炒锅
c. 炒勺
d. 勺子
e. 漏勺
f. 菜刀
g. 菜板

1. chǎosháo
2. chǎochǎn
3. chǎoguō
4. lòusháo
5. sháozi
6. càibǎn
7. càidāo

A. Xiàng hěn dà [de] yí ge sháozi. Tā bǐjiào shēn. *(It looks like a giant spoon. It's fairly deep.)*

B. Zhè shì wǒmen zuì jīběn yào xūyào de. *(This is a very basic thing we will need.)*

C. Tā shì píng de, kěyǐ yòng tā liáng hěn duō, yì xiē, yóu zhī lèi de, jiàngyóu zhī lèi de cáiliào. *(It's flat; you can use it to measure a lot of ingredients, such as oil, soy sauce, and so on.)*

D. Zuò jiǎozi de shíhou yòng de bǐjiào duō, kěyǐ lāo jiǎozi chūlai, jiùshì bǎ shuǐ lǜdiào. *(It's used more often when making dumplings; you can scoop the dumplings out with it and drain the water through a sieve.)*

E. Yòng tā lái qiē hěn duō dōngxi, kěyǐ qiē shūcài, kěyǐ qiē yú, kěyǐ qiē gǔtou zhī lèi de dōngxi. *(Use it to cut up a lot of things—you can cut up vegetables, fish, bones, and so on.)*

F. Zuò tāng de shíhou, kěyǐ chéngchū tāng chūlai. *(When you make soup, you can ladle out the soup with it.)*

27.22 *In the next part (1:10–3:52), the instructor talks about seasonings (tiáoliào, tiáowèipǐn 調料／调料、調味品／调味品).* 請把中文跟英文對上。／请把中文跟英文对上。

____ a. yán 鹽／盐

____ b. hújiāofěn 胡椒粉

____ c. miánbáitáng 綿白糖／绵白糖

____ d. làjiāofěn 辣椒粉

____ e. làjiāoyóu 辣椒油

____ f. jiàngyóu 醬油／酱油 (shēngchōu 生抽, lǎochōu 老抽)

____ g. cù 醋

____ h. liàojiǔ 料酒

1. *chili pepper oil*

2. *soft white sugar*

3. *cooking wine*

4. *salt*

5. *vinegar*

6. *chili pepper powder*

7. *ground pepper*

8. *soy sauce (light and dark)*

27.23 *Mark the following statements as* Zhēnde 真的 *(true) or* Jiǎde 假的 *(false), based on the content of the video. If you need a hint, check the modified transcript that follows.*

	Zhēnde 真的	Jiǎde 假的
a. Some salt in China comes from lakes.	☐	☐
b. Chinese white pepper is fermented to soften the flavor.	☐	☐
c. "Soft white sugar" is soft due to the addition of sugar syrup.	☐	☐
d. "Soft white sugar" melts more slowly than other sugars.	☐	☐
e. Chili pepper powder is used universally in China.	☐	☐
f. The most common use for chili pepper powder is as an ingredient in chili pepper oil.	☐	☐
g. Sugar is one of the basic ingredients from which soy sauce is produced through fermentation.	☐	☐
h. Chinese vinegar always has a dark color.	☐	☐
i. Chinese cooking wine is made from grapes.	☐	☐
j. The addition of cooking wine can counteract unpleasant "fishy" notes in the flavor of meat.	☐	☐

- Zhōngguó de yán dōu shì hǎiyán, huòzhě shì húyán. 中國的鹽都是海鹽，或者是湖鹽。／中国的盐都是海盐，或者是湖盐。

- Zhōngguó de báihújiāo shāowēi fāxiào (fājiào) le yìxiē, tā de wèidao bǐjiào nóng. 中國的白胡椒稍微發酵了一些，它的味道比較濃。／中国的白胡椒稍微发酵了一些，它的味道比较浓。

- Zhōngguó de táng jiā le yìxiē tángjiāng, suǒyǐ jiào miánbáitáng. Zhōngguócài xūyào hěn gāo de huǒ, kuài chǎo, xūyào táng huà de sùdù bǐjiào kuài. 中國的糖加了一些糖漿，所以叫綿白糖。中國菜需要很高的火，快炒，需要糖化的速度比較快。／中国的糖加了一些糖浆，所以叫绵白糖。中国菜需要很高的火，快炒，需要糖化的速度比较快。

- Làjiāofěn bú shì suǒyǒu de rénjiā dōu yòng. Wǒmen yòng làjiāofěn yòngde zuì duō de shíhou wǒmen bǎ tā zuòchéng làjiāoyóu. 辣椒粉不是所有的人家都用。我們用辣椒粉用得最多的時候我們把它做成辣椒油。／辣椒粉不是所有的人家都用。我们用辣椒粉用得最多的时候我们把它做成辣椒油。

- Jiàngyóu zuì kāishǐ de yuánliào jiùshì huángdòu, xiǎomàifěn, táng hé yán, yìqǐ fāxiào (fājiào). 醬油最開始的原料就是黃豆、小麥粉、糖和鹽，一起發酵。／酱油最开始的原料就是黄豆、小麦粉、糖和盐，一起发酵。

- Zhōngguórén xǐhuan chī mǐcù. Wǒmen yǒu bái mǐcù, yǒu hóng mǐcù, hái yǒu chéncù. 中國人喜歡吃米醋。我們有白米醋，有紅米醋，還有陳醋。／中国人喜欢吃米醋。我们有白米醋，有红米醋，还有陈醋。

- Liàojiǔ yě shì yòng liángshi fāxiào (fājiào) chūlai de. Jīběnshang shì yòng zuò ròucài, yīnwèi kěyǐ qùdiào ròu de xīngwèir. 料酒也是用糧食發酵出來的。基本上是用做肉菜，因為可以去掉肉的腥味兒。／料酒也是用粮食发酵出来的。基本上是用做肉菜，因为可以去掉肉的腥味儿。

27.24 *Watch the last part of the video (3:52 to the end). Add tone marks to the pinyin names for the following ingredients.*

a. huajiao   花椒 *Sichuan peppercorns*

b. gan lajiao   乾辣椒／干辣椒 *dried chili peppers*

c. bajiao, daliao   八角（大料）*star anise*

d. cong   蔥／葱 *green onions; scallions*

e. jiang   薑／姜 *ginger*

f. suan   蒜 *garlic*

g. chaocaiyou   炒菜油 *cooking oil*

h. xiangyou   香油 *sesame oil*

Recap

▶ Grammar

Bǎ-ing your way to delicious gongbao chicken

Carefully review the eleven steps (somewhat simplified) to make gongbao chicken, each of which uses the *bǎ* pattern. Here again are the main features of the *bǎ* 把 construction:

把 + noun (or noun phrase) + verb phrase ("do the verb phrase to the noun or noun phrase")

Consult these key words as you review the eleven steps. In the first three examples, the nouns and verb phrases have been identified for you. For the remaining steps, circle the nouns and underline the verbs.

biānchǎo	煸炒	*stir fry*
chǔlǐ	處理／处理	*process*
cōng	蔥／葱	*green onion; scallion*
diǎnrán	點燃／点燃	*light the fire*
gōuqiàn	勾芡	*thicken with cornstarch*
jiājìnqu	加進去／加进去	*add in*
jiāng	薑／姜	*ginger*
jìnxíng	進行／进行	*carry on/forth*
jīròu	雞肉／鸡肉	*chicken meat*
pí	皮	*skin*
qí	齊／齐	*even*
qiēchéng	切成	*slice into*
qùdiào	去掉	*get rid of*
shāorè	燒熱／烧热	*heat (V)*
shǒuxiān	首先	*first; first of all*
shuǐ diànfěn	水澱粉／水淀粉	*cornstarch in water*
suàn	蒜	*garlic*
xiǎodīngr	小丁兒／小丁儿	*cube*
zhuāngpán	裝盤／装盘	*put on a plate*

1. Shǒuxiān ne, bǎ xǐhǎo de cōng, jiāng, háiyǒu jīròu zuò yí ge jiǎndān de chǔlǐ.

首先呢，把洗好的蔥、薑，還有雞肉做一個簡單的處理。／

首先呢，把洗好的葱、姜，还有鸡肉做一个简单的处理。

2. Cōng ne, bǎ liǎng tóu qiē zhěngqí diǎnr, hái yào bǎ cōng qiēchéng cùn duànr.

蔥呢，把兩頭切整齊點兒，還要把蔥切成寸段兒。／

葱呢，把两头切整齐点儿，还要把葱切成寸段儿。

3. Jiāng ne, xiān bǎ pí qùdiào, ránhòu qiēchéng sī.

薑呢，先把皮去掉，然後切成絲。／

姜呢，先把皮去掉，然后切成丝。

4. Jīròu ne, xiān bǎ tā qiēchéng duànr, ránhòu zài bǎ duànr qiēchéng dīngr.

雞肉呢，先把它切成段兒，然後再把段兒切成丁兒。／

鸡肉呢，先把它切成段儿，然后再把段儿切成丁儿。

5. Wán le yǐhòu, yào bǎ huǒ diǎnrán.

完了以後，要把火點燃。／

完了以后，要把火点燃。

6. Bǎ huāshēngyóu jiājìnqu, shāorè le yǐhòu, bǎ suàn jiājìnqu, biānchǎo.

把花生油加進去，燒熱了以後，把蒜加進去，煸炒。／

把花生油加进去，烧热了以后，把蒜加进去，煸炒。

7. Chū xiāngwèi yǐhòu, bǎ jīròu jiājìnqu, jìnxíng biānchǎo.

出香味以後，把雞肉加進去，進行煸炒。／

出香味以后，把鸡肉加进去，进行煸炒。

8. Shāoshāo děng yìhuǐr, zài bǎ huāshēngmǐ dàojìnqu, jìnxíng biānchǎo.

稍稍等一會兒，再把花生米倒進去，進行煸炒。／

稍稍等一会儿，再把花生米倒进去，进行煸炒。

9. Chǎo jǐ fēnzhōng jiù bǎ cōng duànr jiājìnqu.

炒幾分鐘就把蔥段兒加進去。／

炒几分钟就把葱段儿加进去。

10. Zuìhòu bǎ shuǐ diànfěn dàojìnqu gōuqiàn.

最後把水澱粉倒進去勾芡。／

最后把水淀粉倒进去勾芡。

11. Wán le, bǎ cài zhuāngpán, bǎ huǒ guānshang. Gāogāoxìngxìng de chī!

完了，把菜裝盤，把火關上。高高興興地吃！／

完了，把菜装盘，把火关上。高高兴兴地吃！

Exercise: With a classmate, write instructions on how to make a cup of coffee or tea, using the *bǎ* construction.

▶ Vocabulary

Please refer to page R-2 for a list of grammatical abbreviations used throughout this book.

bājiǎo 八角 (star) anise N

biānchǎo 煸炒 stir fry V

càipǔ 菜譜／菜谱 recipe; menu N

chǎo 炒 stir fry; sauté V

chénpí 陳皮／陈皮 dried tangerine/orange peel N

cōng 蔥／葱 green onion; scallion N

cù 醋 vinegar N

dào 道 (for course or dish of food) M

dàyuē 大約／大约 about; around; approximately A

diànfěn 澱粉／淀粉 starch N

dīngr 丁兒／丁儿 cube N

dù 度 (for angles; degrees; temperature) M

duàn 段 sections; strips N

fàngrù 放入 put into VP

gōngbǎo jīdīng 宮保雞丁／宫保鸡丁 spicy diced chicken; gongbao chicken N

gòuwù 購物／购物 go shopping VO; shopping N

guìpí 桂皮 Chinese cinnamon N

háoyóu 蠔油／蚝油 oyster sauce N

huājiāo 花椒 Sichuan peppers; peppercorns N

huánggua 黃瓜 cucumber N

huāshēngmǐ 花生米 shelled peanuts N

huāshēngyóu 花生油 peanut oil N

húluóbo 胡蘿蔔／胡萝卜 carrot(s) N

jiāng 薑／姜 ginger N

jiàngyóu 醬油／酱油 soy sauce N

jiārù 加入 add; mix; put in VP

jīnzhēngū 金針菇／金针菇 enoki mushrooms N

jīpí 雞皮／鸡皮 chicken skin N

jīròu 雞肉／鸡肉 chicken meat N

jītuǐ ròu 雞腿肉／鸡腿肉 chicken leg (meat) N

jīxiōng ròu 雞胸肉／鸡胸肉 chicken breast (meat) N

láizì 來自／来自 come/originate/stem from VP

làjiāo 辣椒 hot pepper; chili N

lǎochōu 老抽 thick soy sauce N

liàojiǔ 料酒 cooking wine N

límǐ 厘米 centimeter M

máyóu 麻油 sesame oil N

pí 皮 skin N

qiēchéng 切成 cut into pieces; slice; dice RV

qítā 其他 others; the rest PR

qíyú 其餘／其余 others; the rest PR

qùdiào 去掉 get rid of RV

rènhé 任何 any; whatever ATTR

róngqì 容器 container N

ròu 肉 meat N

sè-xiāng-wèi jùquán 色香味俱全 look, smell, and taste great IE

shāo 燒／烧 heat; cook V

shēngchōu 生抽 thin soy sauce N

shēngjiāng 生薑／生姜 fresh ginger N

shísān xiāng 十三香 13-spice (powder) N

shòu dàjiā de xǐhuan/huānyíng 受大家的喜歡｜歡迎／受大家的喜欢｜欢迎 well liked/welcomed by all

shūcài 蔬菜 vegetable N

suàn 蒜 garlic N

táng 糖 sugar N

tiáowèipǐn 調味品／调味品 flavoring; seasoning; condiment N

xiānggū 香菇 shiitake mushrooms N

xīfāng 西方 west; the West; the Occident; Western world N

xǐhǎo 洗好 washed (fully) RV

yán 鹽／盐 salt N

yānzhì 醃製／腌制 soak; marinate; cure V

yóuguō 油鍋／油锅 frying pan N

yóuqíshì 尤其是 especially A

yuánliào 原料 material; raw material N

zhèngzōng 正宗 authentic; genuine; authoritative SV

zhì 至 to; until; till CV

Zhōngcān 中餐 Chinese cuisine/meal/food N

zuòfǎ 做法 way of doing something N

▶ Checklist of "can do" statements

After completing this unit, you should be able to perform each of the following tasks:

Listening and speaking

☐ Shop for cooking ingredients.

☐ Understand the names of common ingredients in Chinese cooking.

☐ Understand some amounts used in cooking.

☐ Understand the basic steps in making gongbao chicken.

☐ Understand some basic steps in making other common dishes.

Reading and writing

☐ Comprehend some notes about grocery shopping, and write some of your own.

☐ Decipher some signs and labels related to groceries.

☐ Read a short story about food, and write one of your own.

Understanding culture

☐ Have a sense of the basic cooking utensils used in a Chinese kitchen.

☐ Have a sense of which ingredients are "must haves" in a Chinese kitchen.

"The Eight Immortals display their personal magic"*

八仙過海，各顯神通

Bāxiānguòhǎi, gèxiǎnshéntōng

Personalities and appearances

In this unit, you will learn how to:

- describe some aspects of people's physical appearances.
- describe some aspects of people's personalities.
- make a persuasive oral statement about your strengths.
- make a persuasive written statement about your strengths.
- decipher some signs in a media production studio.
- comprehend a short story about an interesting personality, and write one of your own.

* This idiom literally refers to the Eight Chinese Immortals—each with his or her own supernatural ability and all of which are on display when they cross the seas. Figuratively, this saying refers to the great diversity among people.

Encounter 1   Discussing personalities and appearances

28.1 *Xiao Mao and Chen Feng discuss the sort of person they're looking for to star in a public service commercial. Chen Feng feels that looks are key, whereas Xiao Mao argues that personality is more important. Before you listen to their conversation, look over the vocabulary below.* 請把中文跟英文對上。／请把中文跟英文对上。

_____ a. xiàngmào píngpíng 相貌平平   1. *click rate*

_____ b. pāi guǎnggào 拍廣告／拍广告   2. *ordinary appearance*

_____ c. shìxì 試戲／试戏   3. *audition*

_____ d. guānzhòng 觀眾／观众   4. *shoot a commercial*

_____ e. yǎnyuán 演員／演员   5. *have life experience*

_____ f. yǒu shēnghuó jīnglì 有生活經歷／有生活经历   6. *audience*

_____ g. diǎnjīlǜ 點擊率／点击率   7. *actor*

 28.2 *View Episode 28, Vignette 1. Mark the following statements* Zhēnde 真的 *(true)* or Jiǎde 假的 *(false).*

	Zhēnde 真的	Jiǎde 假的
a. The audience for this public service commercial is young.	☐	☐
b. The commercial seeks volunteers to teach in impoverished regions.	☐	☐
c. The production company seeks a big-name personality.	☐	☐
d. Chen Feng and Xiao Mao are collaborating for the first time.	☐	☐
e. They decide to call up two groups of actors to audition.	☐	☐

28.3 *View Episode 28, Vignette 1 again. Identify who makes each of the following statements (presented in the order in which they are made).*

> a. Xiao Mao   b. Chen Feng

_____ 1. What's most important is to attract an audience.

_____ 2. We must have the audience identify with the people on screen.

_____ 3. The actors have to be young, because the audience we are looking at is made up of young people.

_____ 4. They of course can't be too tall or too short; they have to be good-looking.

_____ 5. They must have regular features and good skin.

_____ 6. They must have even teeth.

_____ 7. Common people are of all sorts—tall, short, heavy, thin.

_____ 8. A public service commercial is still a commercial.

_____ 9. The actors we pick must have personality, enthusiasm, and energy.

_____ 10. I see that I'm not going to be able to convince you.

_____ 11. OK, you go ahead and leave. Bye!

28.4 把下面的中文跟上面的英文對上。／把下面的中文跟上面的英文对上。

_____ a. Tāmen bù néng tài gāo dāngrán yě bù néng tài ǎi, zhǎngxiàng yào hǎo.

他們不能太高當然也不能太矮，長相要好。／他们不能太高当然也不能太矮，长相要好。

_____ b. Yáchǐ yídìng yào zhěngqí.

牙齒一定要整齊。／牙齿一定要整齐。

_____ c. Xíng, nǐ zǒu ba, báibái!

行，你走吧，拜拜！

_____ d. Zuì zhòngyào de shì xīyǐn guānzhòng.

最重要的是吸引觀眾。／最重要的是吸引观众。

_____ e. Wǒmen tiāoxuǎn de yǎnyuán yào yǒu gèxìng, yǒu rèqíng, yǒu huólì.

我們挑選的演員要有個性、有熱情、有活力。／我们挑选的演员要有个性、有热情、有活力。

_____ f. Pǔtōng lǎobǎixìng zhǎng shénmeyàngr de dōu yǒu: gāo de, ǎi de, pàng de, shòu de.

普通老百姓長甚麼樣兒的都有：高的、矮的、胖的、瘦的。／普通老百姓长什么样儿的都有：高的、矮的、胖的、瘦的。

_____ g. Yào ràng guānzhòng duì píngmùshang de rénwù yǒu yìzhǒng rèntónggǎn.

要讓觀眾對屏幕上的人物有一種認同感。／要让观众对屏幕上的人物有一种认同感。

_____ h. Gōngyì guǎnggào yěshì guǎnggào.

公益廣告也是廣告。／公益广告也是广告。

_____ i. Děi shì wǔguān-duānzhèng, pífū hǎo.

得是五官端正、皮膚好。／得是五官端正、皮肤好。

_____ j. Wǒ kàn wǒ shuōfú* bùliǎo nǐ.

我看我説服不了你。／我看我说服不了你。

*Shuōfú is also pronounced shuìfú, as Chen Feng says in the video.

_____ k. Yǎnyuán yào niánqīng, yīnwèi zánmen miànduì de guānzhòng jiùshì niánqīngrén.

演員要年輕，因為咱們面對的觀眾就是年輕人。／演员要年轻，因为咱们面对的观众就是年轻人。

28.5 _Following is a list of expressions used to describe people. Write the pinyin and characters in the appropriate places in the chart (to match the English), in preparation for expressing your own opinion about personal characteristics later._

bízi yǒudiǎn dà	hěn yǒu huólì	yáchǐ hěn zhěngqí	yǒudiǎn shòu
bú tài gāo yě bú tài ǎi	liǎn shang zhǎng diǎn qīngchūndòu	yǒu shēnghuó jīnglì	zhǎngxiàng hěn hǎo
hěn rèqíng	pífū hěn hǎo	yǒu yōumògǎn	zhǎngxiàng hěn pǔtōng
hěn yǒu gèxìng	wǔguān-duānzhèng	yǒudiǎn pàng	
有幽默感	有點胖／有点胖	皮膚很好／皮肤很好	臉上長點青春痘／脸上长点青春痘
長相很好／长相很好	很熱情／很热情	不太高也不太矮	長相很普通／长相很普通
五官端正	很有活力	很有個性／很有个性	牙齒很整齊／牙齿很整齐
有點瘦／有点瘦	鼻子有點大／鼻子有点大	有生活經歷／有生活经历	

	拼音	漢字／汉字
tán zhǎngxiàng 談長相／谈长相		
have nice facial features; be good-looking		
have a regular, symmetrical face		
have even teeth		
have good skin		
be ordinary looking		
be neither too tall nor too short		
have a somewhat large nose		
have some pimples on the face		
be a bit heavy		
be a bit thin		
tán gèxìng 談個性／谈个性		
have a sense of humor		
have great life experiences		
be very passionate		
be very energetic		
have a great personality		

28.6 Synonyms and antonyms: *Indicate whether the terms in each set below have the same or opposite meanings. Write = or ≠ in the blank between the terms.*

a. xiàngmào 相貌 ____ zhǎngxiàng 長相／长相

b. zhǎngxiàng pǔtōng 長相普通／长相普通 ____ xiàngmào píngpíng 相貌平平

c. zhǎngxiàng hǎo 長相好／长相好 ____ zhǎngxiàng bù zěnmeyàng 長相不怎麼樣／长相不怎么样

d. wàixíng tiáojiàn hěn búcuò 外形條件很不錯／外形条件很不错 ____ xiàngmào bǐjiào hǎo 相貌比較好／相貌比较好

28.7 *The following terms represent additional vocabulary related to personalities and appearances.* 把中文跟英文對上。／把中文跟英文对上。

____ a. piàoliang 漂亮	1. *smart*
____ b. yīngjùn 英俊	2. *bad-tempered*
____ c. nénggàn 能幹／能干	3. *hardworking*
____ d. cōngming 聰明／聪明	4. *friendly*
____ e. yònggōng 用功	5. *cool*
____ f. píqi hǎo 脾氣好／脾气好	6. *pretty*
____ g. píqi huài 脾氣壞／脾气坏	7. *good-tempered*
____ h. rén hǎo 人好	8. *considerate*
____ i. zhōudào 周到	9. *handsome*
____ j. yǒushàn 友善	10. *kindhearted*
____ k. shànliáng 善良	11. *nice*
____ l. kù 酷	12. *capable*

28.8 *Pair work: Chat with your partner for five minutes (or until your teacher signals time)—IN CHINESE ONLY—about the appearance and personality of the characters depicted below.*

28.9 *Pair work: What are some nice things that people who like you might say about you? Write at least three statements.* 請寫漢字或者拼音。／请写汉字或者拼音。 *Then make these statements to a partner (e.g., "Biérén shuō wǒ . . .").* *Take some notes about what your partner says about himself or herself.*

我：_____

我：_____

我：_____

他／她：_____

他／她：_____

他／她：_____

28.10 *Pair work: Write something about yourself that you don't really like. Tell your partner about it. Your partner should tell you that he or she doesn't agree and then say something nice about you. Do the same for your partner. Use the space below the example dialogue to take notes.*

例如：

我：Wǒ juéde wǒ yǒudiǎn pàng. 我覺得我有點胖。／我觉得我有点胖。

他／她：Búhuì ba, wǒ juéde hái hǎo a. Érqiě nǐde pífū hěnhǎo. 不會吧，我覺得還好啊。而且你的皮膚很好。／不会吧，我觉得还好啊。而且你的皮肤很好。

_____

我 (–): _____

我 (+ supplied by your partner): _____

他／她 (–): _____

他／她 (+ supplied by you): _____

28.11 *Practice four-character terms. You already know the following:*

wǔguānduānzhèng   五官端正   *regular features (literally, five features [on face] + regular)*

xiàngmào píngpíng   相貌平平   *ordinary appearance (literally, appearance + ordinary)*

See if you can work out the meanings of the following expressions that Chen Feng and Xiao Mao use. Match each term with its English meaning. 把中文跟英文對上。／把中文跟英文对上。

____ a. yángguāngshuàiqì 陽光帥氣／阳光帅气 (sunlight + handsome air)

____ b. qīngchūnliànglì 青春靚麗／青春靓丽 (youthful + bright beauty)

____ c. quánránfùchū 全然付出 (completely + put out)

____ d. wújīngdǎcǎi 無精打采／无精打采 (no spirit + beaten air)

____ e. mòbùguānxīn 漠不關心／漠不关心 (absolutely not + caring)

____ f. mǎnbúzàihu 滿不在乎／满不在乎 (fully not + concerned)

1. *fully engaged*

2. *lackadaisical*

3. *handsome and vigorous*

4. *completely uncaring*

5. *fresh-faced and beautiful*

6. *absolutely uninterested*

28.12 *Complete each statement with a four-character expression from 28.11.* 用拼音和漢字填空。／用拼音和汉字填空。

a. Luó Xuětíng zuò shénme shìqing dōu fēicháng tóurù. Tā zuò mápódòufu de shíhou yě shì _____.

羅雪婷做甚麼事情都非常投入。她做麻婆豆腐的時候也是_____。／罗雪婷做什么事情都非常投入。她做麻婆豆腐的时候也是_____。

b. Xiǎo Fēi gāng kāishǐ de shíhou shénme dōu búhuì, yě bù xiǎng hǎohāo de xué, zhěngtiān zhǐ xiǎng chīhē-wánlè, duìyú gōngzuò _____.

小飛剛開始的時候甚麼都不會，也不想好好地學，整天只想吃喝玩樂，對於工作_____。／小飞刚开始的时候什么都不会，也不想好好地学，整天只想吃喝玩乐，对于工作_____。

c. Ā-Juān shì ge _____ de měinǚ.

阿娟是個 _____ 的美女。／阿娟是个_____ 的美女。

d. Táng Yuǎn zhēn shì hěn yīngjùn, chōngmǎn le _____.

唐遠真是很英俊，充滿了 _____。／唐远真是很英俊，充满了 _____。

e. Táng Yuǎn hái méi jiéhūn, tā fùmǔ jísǐ le, kěshì Táng Yuǎn zhǐ duì yìshù yǒu xìngqù, duìyú jiéhūn de shì, wánquán _____.

唐遠還沒結婚，他父母急死了，可是唐遠只對藝術有興趣，對於結婚的事，完全_____。／唐远还没结婚，他父母急死了，可是唐远只对艺术有兴趣，对于结婚的事，完全_____。

f. Fāng Lán zuótiān wǎnshang qù chàng kǎlā OK, chàng de hěn wǎn. Jīntiān zǎoshang shàngkè de shíhou yìzhí hěn xiǎng shuì, _____.

方蘭昨天晚上去唱卡拉OK，唱得很晚。今天早上上課的時候一直很想睡，_____。／方兰昨天晚上去唱卡拉OK，唱得很晚。今天早上上课的时候一直很想睡，_____。

28.13 *Mingling: Of the eight four-character expressions in 28.11, select one as your favorite and memorize it. Identify someone you know and apply this expression to him or her. Depending on the expression you choose, use one of these patterns and fill in the blanks.* 用漢字填空。／用汉字填空。

我的 ＿＿＿＿＿＿ 長得／长得＿＿＿＿＿＿＿＿。
（長相／长相）

我的 ＿＿＿＿＿＿ 做甚麼事都／做什么事都
＿＿＿＿＿＿＿＿＿。（個性／个性）

Walk around the room and say your sentence to your classmates. Try to understand what your classmates tell you. If you want to challenge yourself, follow up by asking your classmates, 怎麼說呢／怎么说呢？ *(What do you mean?) See if they can provide a sentence of explanation.*

28.14 *In Episode 28, Vignette 2, Xiao Mao and Chen Feng listen to audition tapes. To prepare for this vignette, match the expressions below.* 請把中文跟英文對上。
／请把中文跟英文对上。

____ a. biǎoyǎn jīnglì 表演經歷／表演经历　　　1. *a positive personality*

____ b. zhèngmiàn rénwù 正面人物　　　　　　2. *narcissistic; be full of oneself*

____ c. fǎnmiàn de juésè 反面的角色　　　　　3. *actor; performer*

____ d. dǎoyǎn 導演／导演　　　　　　　　4. *performance experience*

____ e. zìliàn 自戀／自恋　　　　　　　　　5. *negative role*

____ f. yǎnyuán 演員／演员　　　　　　　　6. *public service activity*

____ g. gōngyì huódòng 公益活動／公益活动　　7. *earthquake*

____ h. zhìyuànzhě 志願者／志愿者　　　　　8. *earnest*

____ i. dìzhèn 地震　　　　　　　　　　　9. *director*

____ j. zhēnchéng 真誠／真诚　　　　　　　10. *volunteer*

28.15 *View Episode 28, Vignette 2. Chen Feng and Xiao Mao view two applicants' self-introductory videos for the leading role in a public service ad seeking volunteer teachers for a poor region. The first is the "good-looking actor" who impressed Chen Feng, and the other the "earnest candidate" who impressed Xiao Mao. Identify who makes each of these statements (presented in the order in which they were made). Check the correct boxes.*

	陳峰／ 陈峰	小毛	漂亮	真誠／ 真诚	方蘭／ 方兰
a. Shēngāo 1 mǐ 8, zhǎng de yě suàn yángguāngshuàiqì.	☐	☐	☐	☐	☐
b. Kěndìng néng xīyǐn bù shǎo nǚguānzhòng.	☐	☐	☐	☐	☐
c. Wǒ shì xuéxí biǎoyǎn zhuānyè de.	☐	☐	☐	☐	☐
d. Wǒ yǎnguo zhèngmiàn rénwù, yě kěyǐ yǎn fǎnmiàn de juésè.	☐	☐	☐	☐	☐
e. Bǐrú shuō: Xǐ de, nù de, āi de, lè de.	☐	☐	☐	☐	☐
f. Jiùshì shuō dǎoyǎn nǐ xūyào shénmeyàng de dōngxi, wǒ jiù huì gěi nǐ chūlai shénmeyàng de dōngxi.	☐	☐	☐	☐	☐
g. Tài zìliàn le. Wǒ juéde.	☐	☐	☐	☐	☐
h. Yǎnyuán ma, zìliàn diǎnr shì zhèngcháng de.	☐	☐	☐	☐	☐
i. Jiēzhe zài kàn.	☐	☐	☐	☐	☐
j. Wǒ xiànzài shì zài xiào de dàxuéshēng.	☐	☐	☐	☐	☐
k. Wǒ de jiāxiāng fāshēngguo yícì tèdà de dìzhèn.	☐	☐	☐	☐	☐
l. Wǒ huí dào jiāxiāng zuò zhìyuànzhě de shíhou, yǒu hěnduō rén bāng wǒ.	☐	☐	☐	☐	☐
m. Wǒ gēn hěn duō rén tāmen chéngwéi le xiōngdì péngyou.	☐	☐	☐	☐	☐
n. Wǒ xiǎng yǐngxiǎng gèng duō de rén.	☐	☐	☐	☐	☐
o. Bùdé bù shuō, tā de zhēnchéng dǎdòng le wǒ.	☐	☐	☐	☐	☐
p. Tā zhè bú shì biǎoyǎn.	☐	☐	☐	☐	☐
q. Wǒ juéde zhè shì tā de zhēnshí jīnglì.	☐	☐	☐	☐	☐

28.16 請把下面的英文跟上面的拼音對上。／请把下面的英文跟上面的拼音对上。

_____ 1. For example, happiness, anger, sorrow, and joy.

_____ 2. I've played positive characters, and I could also play a negative role.

_____ 3. He's an actor, after all. Being full of himself is normal.

_____ 4. Which is to say, whatever you as the director want, I'll give you that.

_____ 5. I majored in acting.

_____ 6. I have to say, his sincerity moved me.

_____ 7. There was once an extremely big earthquake in my hometown.

_____ 8. He's too full of himself, I think.

_____ 9. I'd like to have an influence on more people.

_____ 10. With a height of a meter eight, he could be said to be handsome and vigorous.

_____ 11. He's not performing.

_____ 12. Let's keep watching.

_____ 13. When I went home as a volunteer, many people helped me.

_____ 14. He'll certainly attract quite a few female audience members.

_____ 15. I think this is his real experience.

_____ 16. I become friends, like brothers, with many people.

_____ 17. I'm currently enrolled as a college student.

28.17 _Read the following sentences out loud. Use the previous two exercises as a guide._

a. 我想影响更多的人。

b. 比如说：喜的、怒的、哀的、乐的。

c. 太自恋了。我觉得。

d. 我的家乡发生过一次特大的地震。

e. 肯定能吸引不少女观众。

f. 我现在是在校的大学生。

g. 他这不是表演。

h. 接着再看。

i. 我回到家乡做志愿者的时候，有很多人帮我。

j. 就是说导演你需要什么样的东西，我就会给你出来什么样的东西。

k. 我是学习表演专业的。

l. 不得不说，他的真诚打动了我。

m. 演员嘛，自恋点儿是正常的。

n. 我觉得这是他的真实经历。

o. 身高1米8，长得也算阳光帅气。

p. 我演过正面人物，也可以演反面的角色。

q. 我跟很多人他们成为了兄弟朋友。

28.18 *Pair work:* Work with a partner. Tell each other as much as you can about both of the people who applied for the public service ad.

28.19 *Pretend that you would like to be featured in the public service ad. Prepare a self-introduction. Begin by completing the sentences below.* 用拼音填空。

Dàjiā hǎo, wǒ jiào _____, láizì _____ xuéxiào _____ xì de xuéshng,
              (YOUR NAME)   (NAME OF YOUR SCHOOL)   (YOUR MAJOR DEPARTMENT)

wǒ shì _____ de xuéshng. Wǒ jīnnián _____ suì, shēngāo shì _____, tǐzhòng shì _____.
   (YEAR IN SCHOOL)   (AGE)   (HEIGHT)   (WEIGHT)

> yīngchǐ 英尺 *foot*   yīngcùn 英寸 *inch*   yīngbàng 英磅 *pound*

Continue to make at least five statements about why you would be well suited to this assignment.

_____

_____

_____

_____

_____

Have your teacher improve your statements, and then share them with as many classmates as you can. If you feel up to it, record your statements and submit your video to a "review committee" for feedback.

Encounter 2 | Reading and writing

28.20 *Following are brief notes written by the two applicants in Vignette 2. Read them as best as you can, and then write a similar statement (in characters) that would be part of an application to act in a public service ad. Have your composition checked by your teacher or other advisor, and share it with your classmates.*

ⓐ 我学习表演专业。我拍过一些电影。我认为我可以演正面的角色，也可以演反面的角色。导演需要什么，我都可以表现出来。比如说：喜的、怒的、哀的、乐的。我认为拍摄公益广告有很大的影响力。而且，对我想当演员来说，会是一个很有意义的经验。

ⓑ 我现在是在校的大学生，之前参加过一些学校组织的公益活动。我非常愿意参加这样一个公益活动。首先，我不是演员，而是志愿者。之前对我印象最深的一次，是我的家乡发生过一次特大的地震。我回到家乡做志愿者的时候，有很多人帮我。那一次环境非常艰苦，吃住行什么的。我跟很多人成为了兄弟朋友，所以让我希望能够参加公益活动，因为我想影响更多的人，一起去关注那些山区的孩子，帮助那些山区重新建立他们的家园。

▶ Reading real-life texts

28.21 *These are some signs around the studio at the Communications University of China, where Xiao Mao teaches and Chen Feng and Xiao Mao are meeting to review the application videos.*

ⓐ *This is the poster for the show that is being produced in the studio next door. The show is called "I Hear It's Great [to Watch]." Read the name out loud.*

b *This is the business card of someone who works at the Yishi Media Production Company. Whose card is it? What information can you obtain from this card?*

_____

_____

易勢媒體工作室

陳　峰

地址　北京朝陽區酒廠藝術區
郵箱　xiaoyu@bellsouth.net
電話　152-0138-9920

c *This bulletin board presents stills from programs that CUC TV has produced in the past. The characters state, "Programs Division."*
请用拼音填空。／请用拼音填空。

_____ _____ bù

---

d 1. *This warning is posted by the Communications University of China's TV station. Write the pinyin for the name of the TV station:* 中国传媒大学电视台.

_____ Chuánméi _____ _____

请 勿 吸 烟
远 离 火 灾

2. *What does the sign say? Read it out loud, and then write the English below.* (火灾 huǒzāi *fire disaster*)

_____

节约用水
www.ele.me

e *What is the name of the Web service that posted this sign, and what do they sell? What does the sign itself encourage people to do?* (节约 jiéyuē *conserve*)

饿了么网上订餐
www.ele.me

f *What is located to the right?* 請寫拼音和英文。／请写拼音和英文。

拼音: _____

英文: _____

g *This sign has been poorly translated. What would be a better translation?* 請寫英文。／请写英文。

_____

_____

h *This sign is posted by the security division of the Beijing Broadcast Academy. What does it say? Read it out loud.* 然後寫英文。／然后写英文。(电源 diànyuán *power source*)

_____

_____

i *The digital display at the entrance to the production department offers changing messages.*

1. *Read the first message out loud, and make sure you understand it.*

2. *The second message states, "Unify knowledge and action; learn and put (what you learn) into use." Read it out loud.* (致 zhì *implement; apply*)

3. *The third message is a four-part slogan. Number the phrases below in the order in which they appear, from left to right.*

____ bóxué *learn widely*

____ jìngyè *respect your work*

____ lìdé *establish virtue*

____ jìngxiān *strive to be first*

28.22 *Write a sign in characters that you could post in your classroom. It can be a warning, an instruction, or a slogan. Have it checked by your teacher, and then post the sign to share it with your classmates..*

▶ Reading a story

28.23 故事：　當女兒不容易 *Work with a partner or in a small group to read the story below.*

我認識一個人，剛滿四十歲。她是一個比較普通的人，相貌平平，不高也不矮，不胖也不瘦，可以說是五官端正，只是鼻子可能有一點偏大，嘴巴或許也有一點歪。好在她的牙齒很整齊，白白的，笑起來大家覺得很陽光亮麗。

她讀了快十二年的大學加上研究生，拿到了兩個碩士學位，已經工作十年了。她的工作不算太難，賺的錢也不特別多。每天下班以後一個人回家隨便做一點吃的，看一會兒電視，上一會兒網，然後洗了澡、刷了牙就上床睡覺了。天天都一樣。可是她自己覺得很滿意。

她一輩子都沒交過男朋友。她有幾個比較要好的女同學，經常介紹男生給她認識，可是不知道是因為她害羞，還是不夠自信，還是因為她懶得去社交，她就是很少同意和男的約會。她難得跟一個男的去吃一頓飯，或者看一場電影，完了以後她就等不及要回家，因為到底還是在家裡舒服，習慣些。

她父母看她這樣很著急。她又是獨生女，要是她不結婚生孩子，他們一輩子就不可能抱上孫子孫女了。急得他們常常罵女兒自私、不爭氣、對人生大事漠不關心。當初，他們勸她要找一個合適的男的，最好要有一個"長得好、背景好、賺錢多"的老公。可是時間久了以後，他們退了一步，說"面貌差一點、背景不怎麼樣、賺錢也不多"也沒關係，只要是男的就行了。

最後他們女兒帶了一個比自己小19歲的小男生回家，說他們兩個人相愛了。她父母非常驚訝，也不知道應該怎麼辦。是接受還是不接受這個"小女婿"？不接受的話將來還會有第二個嗎？

28.24 *Part 1: Write an ending to the story in 28.23, and share it with your classmates. Take a survey of all the different endings in your class, and see if there is a predominant one.*

Part 2: Now write a short story that touches on the personality of someone special you know. Have it edited by your teacher or someone else who is fluent in Chinese. Illustrate your story as best as you can before sharing it with your classmates.

 Encounter 3   **Extension: Cultural mini-documentary**

View the cultural mini-documentary for this unit and complete the exercises that follow.

■ **Part 1**

甚麼樣的人可稱為好看的人？／什么样的人可称为好看的人？

Shénmeyàng de rén kě chēngwéi hǎokàn de rén?

What kind of person can be called "good-looking"?

28.25 *In the first part of this video (0:00–1:20), four speakers offer observations about standards of physical appearance. Match each speaker's picture to the English summary of his or her comments on physical beauty. Note: The speakers' comments may reflect an understanding of societal norms—not necessarily their personal views.*

_____   _____   _____   _____

a. Whiter skin is more beautiful.

b. Darker skin is more beautiful, and plumpness helps too.

c. There are some characteristics that everyone considers beautiful.

d. What looks you prefer is very personal. What you find ugly I might find beautiful.

28.26 *Label each of the following groups of phrases according to which speaker used them.*

Speaker 1

Speaker 2

Speaker 3

Speaker 4

a. *Speaker* _____ *said the following:*

　Hànzúrén yǐ bái wéi měi.　漢族人以白為美。／汉族人以白为美。
　Ethnic Han Chinese equate "white" with "beautiful."

　yì bái zhē bǎi chǒu　一白遮百醜／一白遮百丑　*one "white" masks a hundred "ugly"; as long as the skin is fair, the looks don't matter*

b. *Speaker* _____ *said the following:*

　dàzhòng shěnměi　大眾審美／大众审美　*mass aesthetics, social aesthetics*

　Dàjiā dōu juéde zhèi ge rén hǎokàn.　大家都覺得這個人好看。／大家都觉得这个人好看。　*Everyone thinks this person is good-looking.*

　míngxīng　明星　*star, celebrity*

　mótèr　模特兒／模特儿　*fashion model*

　měinǚ　美女　*beautiful woman*

　jùnnán　俊男　*handsome man*

c. *Speaker* _____ *said the following:*

　Wǒmen kànlái gēn tā xiāngfǎn.　我們看來跟它相反。／我们看来跟它相反。　*It seems as if we're the opposite of that.*

　Wǒmen Wǎzú de fūsè bǐjiào yǒuhēi.　我們佤族的膚色比較黝黑。／我们佤族的肤色比较黝黑。　*We ethnic Wa have relatively dark skin.*

　yǐ pàng wéi měi　以胖為美／以胖为美　*consider plumpness beautiful*

　xīwàng xífu yòu hēi yòu pàng　希望媳婦又黑又胖／希望媳妇又黑又胖　*hope the bride has dark skin and is plump*

d. *Speaker* _____ *said the following:*

　zhǎngxiàng　長相／长相　*looks, physical appearance*

　Nǐ kàn tā bù hǎokàn de dōngxi bìng bú dàibiǎo wǒ kàn tā bù hǎokàn.　你看它不好看的東西並不代表我看它不好看。／你看它不好看的东西并不代表我看它不好看。　*The things you find unattractive aren't necessarily the things I find unattractive.*

　dà bízi shì quēdiǎn　大鼻子是缺點／大鼻子是缺点　*a big nose is a flaw*

　tèbié xīnshǎng　特別欣賞／特别欣赏　*really appreciate, very much enjoy*

　Wúsuǒwèi shénme měi hé chǒu.　無所謂甚麼美和醜。／无所谓什么美和丑。　*There is really no saying what is beauty and what is ugliness.*

■ **Part 2**

一個人的長相能反映他的性格嗎？／一个人的长相能反映他的性格吗？

Yí ge rén de zhǎngxiàng néng fǎnyìng tā de xìnggé ma?

Does a person's appearance reflect his or her character?

28.27 *In the next part of the video (1:21–2:11), three speakers discuss the relationship between character and appearance. After you watch, use some terms from the following list to express your own view on the subject in a group or class discussion. Alternatively, simply role-play one of the three speakers in the video.*

Zài wǒ kànlai . . . 在我看來……／在我看来…… *The way I see it . . .*

Wǒ (bú) rènwéi . . . 我（不）認為……／我（不）认为…… *I'm (not) of the opinion that . . .*

Wǒ (bù) tóngyì, yīnwèi . . . 我（不）同意，因為……／我（不）同意，因为…… *I (don't) agree, because . . .*

yǒu jù lǎo huà 有句老話／有句老话 *there is an old saying*

miàn yóu xīn shēng 面由心生 *the face originates in the mind/heart*

xīnxiōng kāikuò 心胸開闊／心胸开阔 *be open-minded and generous*

lìnsè xiǎoqì 吝嗇小氣／吝啬小气 *be stingy and ungenerous*

yí ge rén de shànliáng yǔ fǒu 一個人的善良與否／一个人的善良与否 *whether a person is good-hearted or not*

miànbù de fēnpèi 面部的分配 *distribution of facial features*

shì yǒu qiānlián de 是有牽連的／是有牵连的 *definitely has a connection*

kěyǐ kànde chūlai 可以看得出來／可以看得出来 *it is possible to discern*

tǐng yōumò de 挺幽默的 *good sense of humor*

hǎo shuōhuà 好說話／好说话 *easy to get along with*

xìnggé 性格 *personality; character*

shēntǐ zhuàngkuàng 身體狀況／身体状况 *state of one's health; health condition*

cóngshì yí ge hángyè 從事一個行業／从事一个行业 *engage in a profession; pursue a line of work*

shíjiān chángle 時間長了／时间长了 *after a length of time*

yǐngxiǎng 影響／影响 *influence; affect*

liǎn shang de yìxiē zǒuxiàng 臉上的一些走向／脸上的一些走向 *certain trends in the face/appearance*

lācháng liǎn 拉長臉／拉长脸 *lengthen one's face; look crestfallen*

zhòu méitou 皺眉頭／皱眉头 *crease one's brow; scowl*

liǎnshang shēng zhòuwén 臉上生皺紋／脸上生皱纹 *get wrinkles on one's face*

yángguāng 陽光／阳光 *be carefree; have a sunny disposition*

cháng dài xiàoróng 常帶笑容／常带笑容 *smile often*

pífū hěn guāngzé 皮膚很光澤／皮肤很光泽 *skin is smooth*

zhǎngpàng 長胖／长胖 *gain weight; become fat*

xiāoshòu 消瘦 *lose weight; waste away*

■ **Part 3**

什麼是 "五官端正" ？／什么是 "五官端正" ？

Shénme shì "wǔguānduānzhèng"?

What does it mean to have "regular features"?

28.28 *Traditionally, the placement of the eyes, ears, mouth, nose, and eyebrows is an important determiner of physical beauty. However, not everyone agrees on the exact meaning of the phrase* 五官端正, *or "regular features." In the next part of the video (2:12 to the end), nine different speakers tackle this question, and the variety of their answers is surprising. Based on the bits and pieces you can catch, match the English summaries to the appropriate speakers.*

a. We understand it as . . . maybe this person is relatively worth looking at. Like, with a woman, she might not actually have a "melon-seed face" or a pointed chin or "cherry lips"—those are [considered] the most beautiful—she might not be pretty, but you'll find that having looked one time, you want to go back for a second look. And after that second look, you're still not tired of looking and you want to look some more. These are the ones worth looking at, and they are the pretty ones. So in my understanding, that's the meaning of "regular features."

b. You have to look like—stuff like the eyes, nose, mouth, ears—they are all growing where they should be growing and in harmonious proportions.

c. I guess I could be considered basically to have "regular features." Nothing's crooked—the eyes are straight, the nose is straight, the mouth is straight. Taking them all together, I'm presentable.

d. It means maybe the eyes—the eyes are rather big, and the contours are clear-cut, and . . . it leaves you with a deep impression.

e. The way I understand it, it means that the eyes are not too big and not too small but have an animated appearance. The nose shouldn't be crooked. Overall, the person's appearance looks just right.

f. The most important thing is still the education one gets after birth—that can make a person's features . . . I don't know if regular is the right word to describe it, but it can fill a person's features with vitality.

g. This phrase means different things to different people. It gives you a clean and comfortable feeling, and that's enough. The eyes don't have to be large or small. Some people who have small eyes can also be good-looking, and you can call them "regular-featured." Whatever gives you a happy feeling, that's "regular features."

h. A face that is squarish and regular. The eyes should be large. The bridge of the nose should be tall. The lips should be somewhat full. This is what I think is called "regular features." And the ears can't be like big fans. The person has to be good-looking, haha.

i. Each person's understanding is different, right? Personally, I think it means that the eyebrows are relatively heavy, and the nose is high-bridged, and the eyes . . . shouldn't be too big and shouldn't be too small. Medium-sized is fine.

Recap

▶ Grammar

Saying a little but meaning a lot

Chinese speech and writings are often enlivened and colored by the frequent use of proverbs, concise sayings, and idioms that, in a few characters, say a great deal. These expressions provide us with an inside look at Chinese culture and allow us to compare it to our own. These set expressions are worth memorizing. They will add flavor to your own language. Remembering them will be easier with an understanding of the grammatical structure at their foundation. As you do the following exercises, notice the following points:

- Their length can vary from the very common four-character phrase to those that are somewhat longer.

- Most are written in classical or literary Chinese—not modern Chinese. Literary Chinese is a largely monosyllabic language in which every character is a word, unlike modern Chinese in which you might have noticed that most words are made up of one to three characters (e.g., *rén* 人 person, *nǚrén* 女人 woman, *Rìběnrén* 日本人 Japanese) and sometimes more than three characters (e.g., *Mòxīgērén* 墨西哥人 Mexican, *Mòsāngbǐkèrén* 莫桑比克人 Mozambican).

- Some are drawn from very famous literary, philosophical, or historical texts, recalling stories familiar to educated Chinese.

- Their internal makeup is structured around familiar grammatical patterns, such as verb + object, balanced phrases, and so on.

In the following exercise, look over the meaning and pronunciation of each word and then see how the English translation fits the Chinese version. Most, if not all, should be very familiar to you, at least in their English renditions.

騎／骑	虎	難／难	下
qí	hǔ	nán	xià
ride/astride	*tiger*	*hard (to)*	*(get) down*

(Have a tiger by the tail.)

玩	火	自	焚
wán	huǒ	zì	fén
play (with)	*fire*	*oneself*	*burn*

(He who plays with fire will get burned.)

愚	公	移	山
yú	gōng	yí	shān
foolish	*old man*	*move*	*mountain*

(God helps those who help themselves.)

The Foolish Old Man Who Moves Mountains is a famous story first told in *Liezi* 列子, a fifth-century Daoist book of Chinese mythology. The Foolish Old Man lived at the foot of two mountains that blocked his family's access, so he began to dig at them with a shovel. Ridiculed by the Wise Man for taking on this impossible task, he replied that, although he might not get the job done in his lifetime, his sons and grandsons would persevere, and in the fullness of time the mountains would be removed. The gods were impressed by his determination and selflessness, so they moved the mountains on his behalf. This tale has been interpreted as a testimonial to willpower, perseverance, and sacrifice.

Exercise: Work with a classmate to read the Chinese sayings that follow. Notice the meaning and pronunciation of each word, and then select the closest English equivalent from the list provided. For the sayings marked with asterisks, do an online search with the pinyin to help you figure out what they mean. Have fun!

a. *塞　　翁　　失　　馬／马
sài　　wēng　　shī　　mǎ
frontier　　*old man*　　*lose*　　*horse*

b. 活　　到　　老，　　學／学　　到　　老
huó　　dào　　lǎo,　　xué　　dào　　lǎo
live　　*reach*　　*old,*　　*study*　　*reach*　　*old*

c. 一　　回　　生，　　二　　回　　熟
yī　　huí　　shēng,　　èr　　huí　　shú
one　　*time*　　*unfamiliar,*　　*two*　　*time*　　*familiar*

d. 入　　鄉／乡　　隨／随　　俗
rù　　xiāng　　suí　　sú
enter　　*countryside*　　*follow*　　*customs*

e. *對／对　　牛　　彈／弹　　琴
duì　　niú　　tán　　qín
to　　*cow*　　*play*　　*lute*

f. 在 家　　千 日　　好，　　出 外　　時時／时时　　難／难.
zàijiā　　qiānrì　　hǎo,　　chūwài　　shíshí　　nán.
at home　　*1,000 days*　　*good,*　　*go abroad*　　*time after time*　　*difficult*

g. *説／说　　曹操，　　曹操　　到
shuō　　Cáo Cāo,　　Cáo Cāo　　dào
speak of　　*Cao Cao,*　　*Cao Cao*　　*arrive*
(*Cao Cao is a famous general from the second and third centuries.*)

h. 説一／说一　　是一，　　説二／说二　　是二
shuō yī　　shì yī,　　shuō’èr　　shì’èr
say one　　*be one,*　　*say two*　　*be two*

i. 一寸　　光陰／光阴,　　一寸　　金
yí cùn　　guāngyīn　　yí cùn　　jīn
one inch　　*time*　　*one inch*　　*gold*

j. *鐵／铁　　杵　　磨　　成　　針／针
tiě　　chǔ　　mó　　chéng　　zhēn
iron　　*pestle*　　*grind*　　*become*　　*needle*

____ 1. Every cloud has a silver lining.　　____ 6. There's no place like home.
____ 2. It's never too late to learn.　　____ 7. Time is money.
____ 3. Where there's a will, there's a way.　　____ 8. When in Rome, do as the Romans do.
____ 4. Say what you mean; mean what you say.　　____ 9. Cast pearls before swine.
____ 5. Speak of the devil and he appears.　　____ 10. Experience is the best teacher.

▶ Vocabulary

Please refer to page R-2 for a list of grammatical abbreviations used throughout this book.

biǎoyǎn 表演 perform; act; play V; performance N

bǐrú shuō 比如說／比如说 for example/ instance VP

bùdé bù 不得不 cannot but; have to VP

cōngming 聰明／聪明 smart SV

dǎdòng 打動／打动 move emotionally RV

dǎoyǎn 導演／导演 director N; direct (a film, play, etc.) V

diǎnjīlǜ 點擊率／点击率 click/strike rate (on a keyboard or other device) N

dìzhèn 地震 earthquake N

fǎnmiàn 反面 negative side; reverse/wrong side N

gǎn 感 feeling BF; **rèntónggǎn** 認同感／认同感 feeling/sense of identification

gèxìng 個性／个性 individual character; personality N

gōngyì 公益 public good; welfare; public service N

guānzhòng 觀眾／观众 spectator; audience N

huólì 活力 vigor; vitality; energy N

jí 急 anxious; worried SV

jiāxiāng 家鄉／家乡 hometown; native place N

jiēzhe 接著／接着 continue to; keep on VP

jīnglì 經歷／经历 experience N; go through; experience; undergo V

juésè 角色 role; part N

kù 酷 "cool" PL/SV

měinǚ 美女 beautiful woman; beauty N

miànduì 面對／面对 face; confront V

pāi 拍 take pictures; shoot film V

piàoliang 漂亮 pretty SV

píngpíng 平平 average; mediocre; so-so RF

píqi hǎo 脾氣好／脾气好 good-tempered SV

píqi huài 脾氣壞／脾气坏 bad-tempered SV

qīngchūndòu 青春痘 acne, pimple N

rén hǎo 人好 kind; nice (person) SV

rèntóng 認同／认同 identify V; identification N

rénwù 人物 character; personage; character in literature N

rèqíng 熱情／热情 enthusiastic; passionate SV

shànliáng 善良 kindhearted; decent SV

shēngāo 身高 height (of a person) N

shēnghuó jīnglì 生活經歷／生活经历 life experience N

shìxì 試戲／试戏 audition (for a performance) VO

shuōfú (shuìfú) 說服／说服 persuade; convince someone V

tèdà 特大 especially/exceptionally large VP

tiáojiàn 條件／条件 condition; factor; term N

tiāoxuǎn 挑選／挑选 choose; select; pick V

tǐzhòng 體重／体重 (body) weight N

tóurù 投入 absorbed; concentrated; devoted SV

wàixíng 外形 appearance; external form N

wǔguānduānzhèng 五官端正 have a regular, symmetrical face (with five facial features in the right places) VP

xǐ nù āi lè 喜怒哀樂／喜怒哀乐 happiness, anger, sorrow, joy IE

xiàngmào 相貌 looks; appearance N

xiōngdì péngyou 兄弟朋友 very close friends N

yáchǐ 牙齒／牙齿 tooth; teeth N

yǎnyuán 演員／演员 performer; actor N

yīngjùn 英俊 handsome SV

yǐngxiǎng 影響／影响 influence V/N

yònggōng 用功 hardworking; studious SV

yōumògǎn 幽默感 sense of humor N

yǒushàn 友善 friendly; amicable SV

zài xiào 在校 at school; currently enrolled VO

zhǎngxiàng 長相／长相 features (of a face) N

zhēnchéng 真誠／真诚 sincere; genuine; true SV; sincerity N

zhèngmiàn 正面 positive ATTR
zhěngqí 整齊／整齐 neat; tidy; in good order SV
zhìyuànzhě 志願者／志愿者 volunteer N
zhōudào 周到 thorough; attentive; considerate; thoughtful SV

zhuānyè 專業／专业 major *(in a university)* N
zìliàn 自戀／自恋 be full of oneself; narcissism; narcissistic N/SV

▶ Checklist of "can do" statements

After completing this unit, you should be able to perform each of the following tasks:

Listening and speaking

☐ Describe some aspects of people's physical appearance.

☐ Describe some aspects of people's personalities.

☐ Make a persuasive oral statement about your strengths.

Reading and writing

☐ Comprehend the gist of written statements about physical appearance and character.

☐ Make a persuasive written statement about your strengths.

☐ Decipher some signs in a media production studio.

☐ Read a short story about an interesting personality, and write one of your own.

Understanding culture

☐ Make several accurate statements about Chinese aesthetic standards regarding physical appearance.

☐ Make an accurate statement about the degree to which some Chinese people believe that appearance reflects character.

☐ Provide an accurate definition of what it means to have "regular features" (*wǔguānduānzhèng* 五官端正).

"Filial piety is the foundation of all virtues"

孝，德之本也

Xiào, dé zhī běn yě

Family relationships

In this unit, you will learn how to:

- describe your relationship with your parents (or guardians).
- understand aspects of Chinese filial piety.
- understand common activities during the Qingming Festival.

- decipher some notes describing Qingming activities.
- decipher some neighborhood signs.
- comprehend a short story about a teenager's relationship with his parents and write one about your own situation.

Encounter 1 Discussing parent-child relationships

29.1 *Emma and Fang Lan enjoy some "at home" time together and chat about their relationships with their parents.* 請把中文跟英文對上。／请把中文跟英文对上。

_____ a. chànggē 唱歌

_____ b. guānxi 關係／关系

_____ c. dúshēng zǐnǚ 獨生子女／独生子女

_____ d. guǎn 管

_____ e. xiǎoshíhou 小時候／小时候

_____ f. zhǎngdà yǐhòu 長大以後／长大以后

_____ g. gǎnqíng 感情

1. *relationship*

2. *during childhood*

3. *control, manage, bother with*

4. *sing*

5. *feelings*

6. *only child*

7. *after growing up*

FYI 供你參考

Songs and smiles

"Songs and smiles" (*Gēshēng yǔ wēixiào* 歌聲與微笑／歌声与微笑), by Gu Jianfen and Wang Jian, was first recorded in 1989 and has become a popular choral song in China. The verse that Fang Lan and Emma are singing is the following. You can hear the entire song by searching online (it is available on sites such as YouTube, Youku, and Tudou), and the complete lyrics are available on www.baidu.com.

請把我的歌帶回你的家,請把你的微笑留下。／请把我的歌带回你的家,请把你的微笑留下。 *(repeat)*

Qǐng bǎ wǒ de gē dài huí nǐ de jiā, qǐng bǎ nǐ de wēixiào liú xià.

Please take my song home with you, but leave your smile behind.

29.2 *View Episode 29, Vignette 1. Mark the following statements* Zhēnde 真的 *(true) or* Jiǎde 假的 *(false).*

	Zhēnde 真的	Jiǎde 假的
a. Fang Lan likes the picture of herself as a child.	☐	☐
b. The picture of Fang Lan's parents was taken when they were young.	☐	☐
c. Fang Lan likes the photo of her parents.	☐	☐

d. Fang Lan thinks that her mother hovers over her too much.	☐	☐
e. Fang Lan feels that her father tries to control the decisions she makes about her future.	☐	☐
f. Emma's father threatened to beat up any boy who didn't treat her well.	☐	☐
g. Emma feels particularly close to her mother.	☐	☐
h. Emma's parents put pressure on her to study in China.	☐	☐

29.3 *Rewatch the part of the video in which Emma and Fang Lan discuss Fang Lan's relationship with her parents.* 請選擇正確的答案來填空。／请选择正确的答案来填空。

Àimǎ: Kàn qǐlai nǐ gēn nǐ fùmǔ de _____ (guānxi / gǎnqíng) hěn hǎo.

Fāng Lán: Zhè jiùshì wǒmen dúshēng zǐnǚ de tèdiǎn le. Rúguǒ wǒ bù hé tāmen de guānxi hǎo, wǒ hé _____ (biéren / shéi) hǎo ne? Wǒ méiyǒu xiōngdì jiěmèi.

Àimǎ: Zhēn de, wǒ _____ (cónglái bù / cónglái méi) xiǎngdao zhè yìdiǎn.

Fāng Lán: Qíshí ya, wǒ mā duì wǒ tèbié de _____ (yánlì *strict* / yánzhòng *dire, serious*), zǒng shì _____ (děngzhe *waiting for* / dīngzhe *watching*) wǒ, lǎoshì zài wèn, nǐ shì zài gàn shénme ya? Nǐ dàodǐ shìbushì zài _____ (làngfèi *waste* / làngmàn *romantic*) shíjiān a? Zhēn de hǎo fán! Búguò hái hǎo, tā gōngzuò tǐng máng de, suǒyǐ ya méi shíjiān _____ (guài / guǎn) wǒ.

Àimǎ: Nǐ tài _____ (kuài / huài) le! Nà nǐ de bàba ne?

Fāng Lán: Wǒ bà jiù tèbié hǎo, cónglái dōu bù guǎn wǒ, wǒ xiǎng gàn shénme tā dōu suíbiàn, yīnwèi wǒ de wèilái wǒ _____ (zuòzhǔ *be the master* / zuòfèi *waste*) ma! Búguò, tā duì wǒ jiāo péngyou zhè jiàn shì kān de háishi hěn _____ (yán / xián) de.

Àimǎ: Tā pà nǐ jiāo dào _____ (kuài / huài) de nánhái.

Fāng Lán: _____ (Cái búshì ne / Hái búshì ma)!

Àimǎ: Wǒ jìde wǒ hái hěn xiǎo de shíhou, wǒ bàba jiù shuōguo yàoshi nǐ yǐhòu de nán péngyou duì nǐ bù hǎo, wǒ jiù bǎ tā _____ (zuò yí dùn *make a meal* / zòu yí dùn *beat up*)!

Fāng Lán: Duì duì duì, wǒ bà yě zhème _____ (shuōguo / zuòguo)! Jiù bù shuō xiǎoshíhou de shìr le ba, wǒ _____ (zhǎngdà / chángdǎ) yǐhòu, zhǐyào yǒu nán tóngxué lái wǒjiā, wèn wǒ ge wèntí, wǒ bà zǒng huì zài yí ge bùyuǎn-bújìn de dìfang zǒu lái zǒu qù zǒu lái zǒu qù, hǎoxiàng suíshí huì _____ (chōng *rush* / chàng *sing*) shànglai _____ (lǎohǔ *tiger* / bǎohù *protect*) wǒ yíyàng, _____ (tài fāngbiàn la / tài fánrén la)! Nǐ gēn nǐ māma de _____ (gānjìng / gǎnqíng) yídìng yě hěn hǎo ba?

Àimǎ: Zài jiāli wǒmen yě huì _____ (chǎojià *argue* / chǎocài *cook dishes*), dànshì dàduōshù shíjiān tā shì wǒ zuì hǎo de péngyou. Wǒ gēn tā shénme dōu kěyǐ shuō. Tā bú huì gàosu wǒ wǒ yào zuò shénme, bú zuò shénme, tā _____ (xìnrèn *trust* / xìngrén *almond*) wǒ de juédìng.

Fāng Lán: Zhēn hǎo, nà nǐ lái Běijīng dúshū yěshì nǐ zìjǐ de _____ (juédìng *decision* / juéwàng *despair*) ma? Nǐ bà mā bù _____ (dàngāo *cake* / dānxīn *worry*) nǐ dào zhème yuǎn de dìfang lái ya?

Àimǎ: Tāmen dāngrán hěn dānxīn wǒ. Dànshì yīnwèi wǒ hěn xiǎng lái, suǒyǐ tāmen zhǐhǎo _____ (zhīchí *support* / zhǐhuī *direct*) wǒ le.

Fāng Lán: Nǐ bà mā tài kù le! Yàoshi huàn chéng wǒ bà mā _____ (kěndìng *for sure* / kěnqiú *earnestly request*) bú huì tóngyì ràng wǒ qù nàme yuǎn de dìfang dúshū de, jiù hǎoxiàng shì qù Měiguó dú yánjiūshēng.

29.4 請把拼音跟漢字對上。／请把拼音跟汉字对上。

____ a. guānxi		1. 盯著／盯着
____ b. cónglái méi		2. 管
____ c. yánlì		3. 保護／保护
____ d. dīngzhe		4. 從來没／从来没
____ e. làngfèi		5. 長大／长大
____ f. guǎn		6. 嚴屬／严厉
____ g. huài		7. 太煩人了／太烦人了
____ h. zuòzhǔ		8. 浪費／浪费
____ i. yán		9. 壞／坏
____ j. cái búshì ne		10. 才不是呢
____ k. zòu yí dùn		11. 關係／关系
____ l. shuōguo		12. 衝／冲
____ m. zhǎngdà		13. 揍一頓／揍一顿
____ n. chōng		14. 做主
____ o. bǎohù		15. 説過／说过
____ p. tài fánrén le		16. 嚴／严
____ q. gǎnqíng		17. 支持
____ r. chǎojià		18. 擔心／担心
____ s. xìnrèn		19. 決定／决定
____ t. juédìng		20. 吵架
____ u. dānxīn		21. 肯定
____ v. zhīchí		22. 感情
____ w. kěndìng		23. 信任

29.5 *Pair work: Work with a partner to read the script of the conversation between Emma and Fang Lan. Switch roles and repeat when you are done.*

艾玛: 看起来你跟你父母的关系很好。

方兰: 这就是我们独生子女的特点了。如果我不和他们的关系好，我和谁好呢？我没有兄弟姐妹。

艾玛: 真的，我从来没想到这一点。

方兰: 其实啊，我妈对我特别的严厉，总是盯着我，老是在问，你是在干什么呀？你到底是不是在浪费时间啊？真的好烦！不过还好，她工作挺忙的，所以呀没时间管我。

艾玛: 你太坏了！那你的爸爸呢？

方兰: 我爸就特别好，从来都不管我，我想干什么他都随便，因为我的未来我做主嘛！不过，他对我交朋友这件事看得还是很严的。

艾玛: 他怕你交到坏的男孩。

方兰: 才不是呢！

艾玛: 我记得我还很小的时候，我爸爸就说过要是你以后的男朋友对你不好，我就把他揍一顿！

方兰: 对对对，我爸也这么说过！就不说小时候的事儿了吧，我长大以后，只要有男同学来我家，问我个问题，我爸总会在一个不远不近的地方走来走去走来走去，好像随时会冲上来保护我一样，太烦人啦！你跟你妈妈的感情一定也很好吧？

艾玛: 在家里我们也会吵架，但是大多数时间她是我最好的朋友。我跟她什么都可以说。她不会告诉我我要做什么，不做什么，她信任我的决定。

方兰: 真好，那你来北京读书也是你自己的决定吗？你爸妈不担心你到这么远的地方来呀？

艾玛: 他们当然很担心我。但是因为我很想来，所以他们只好支持我了。

方兰: 你爸爸妈妈太酷了！要是换成我爸妈肯定不会让我去那么远的地方读书的，就好像是去美国读研究生。

29.6 *Pair work: Follow up by talking for three to five minutes about your own relationship with your parent(s) or guardian(s). Take notes about your conversation below. If there is time, repeat with other people in your class.*

29.7 *Following are several commonly used expressions that appear in Vignette 2 of Episode 29.* 請把中文跟英文對上。／请把中文跟英文对上。

____ a. Nǐ lái le. 你來了。／你来了。

____ b. Zhè ge wǒ yě huì. 這個我也會。／这个我也会。

____ c. Nǐ zài gànmá? 你在幹嘛？／你在干嘛？

____ d. Wǒ jiù méi bànfǎ le. 我就没辦法了。／我就没办法了。

____ e. Nǐ hěn yǒu yùnqi. 你很有運氣。／你很有运气。

1. *What are you doing?*

2. *I had no way out.*

3. *Hi, there!*

4. *You're very lucky.*

5. *I can do that too.*

29.8 *Which of the expressions in 29.7 would you use in each of the following situations?* 寫拼音或漢字。／写拼音或汉字。

_____

_____

Now walk around the room and see if you can get your classmates to say each of these five statements by pantomiming or leading into the statements. (In return, try to guess which your classmate is angling for you to say.) You can stop when you've elicited all five statements at least once.

29.9 *View Episode 29, Vignette 2. Chen Feng and Xiao Mao are chatting about the upcoming Qingming (Tomb-Sweeping) Festival. Which of the following people will be doing each of the activities described?*

a. Li Wen   b. Xiao Mao   c. Chen Feng

_____ 1. Traveling to Yangshuo (陽朔／阳朔) to commemorate the anniversary of his/her grandmother's death.

_____ 2. Going to Babaoshan (八寶山／八宝山) Cemetery outside Beijing to sweep the tombs of his/her grandmother and grandfather.

_____ 3. Traveling to Tangshan (唐山) to clean the graves of his/her father and mother.

FYI 供你参考

The Tomb-Sweeping Festival

Qīngmíng (清明 "clear bright") is one of the major traditional Chinese holidays (*jiérì* 節日／节日 "node days"). The first and most important of these is *chūnjié* 春節／春节 (Spring Festival—Chinese New Year), followed by *qīngmíng* 清明, *duānwǔ* 端午 (Dragon Boat Festival), and *zhōngqiū* 中秋 (Mid-Autumn Festival). 清明 is also called *sǎomùjié* 掃墓節／扫墓节 (Tomb-Sweeping Festival). It occurs on the 15th day after the spring equinox and is an occasion for families to gather during springtime weather and make a trip to the family tombs, clean them, and pay respects to those who have passed. This day is a public holiday in Mainland China, Taiwan, Hong Kong, and Macau.

29.10 *Chen Feng mentions that, according to the customs of his hometown, people who visit the graves of their family members usually perform certain rituals. Match each term with a picture.*

_____   _____   _____   _____

_____   _____   _____

a. xiàn xiāngyān 獻香煙／献香烟

b. xiàn jiǔ 獻酒／献酒

c. xiàn chá 獻茶／献茶

d. shāoxiāng 燒香／烧香

e. xiàn huā 獻花／献花

f. shāo zhǐqián 燒紙錢／烧纸钱

g. xiàn shuǐguǒ 獻水果／献水果

Write the Chinese (漢字或拼音／汉字或拼音) for the following actions:

to burn = _____   *to offer* = _____

29.11 *View Episode 29, Vignette 2 again. Chen Feng and Xiao Mao mention many ways in which they can express their filial devotion to parents and other elders who are alive. Who names which action?*

> a. Chen Feng   b. Xiao Mao

_____ 1. Spend more time with them.

_____ 2. Take care of them when they can't move around anymore.

_____ 3. Care for them in their old age, and see them off when they die.

_____ 4. Don't leave Beijing.

_____ 5. The time has come to pay them back.

_____ 6. Bring them over to live with us.

_____ 7. Have a baby so they can have a grandson or granddaughter.

29.12 把上面的英語和下面的中文對上。／把上面的英语和下面的中文对上。

_____ a. Děng tāmen xíngdòng búbiàn de shíhou hǎohāo de zhàogu tāmen.

等他們行動不便的時候好好地照顧他們。／等他们行动不便的时候好好地照顾他们。

_____ b. Gěi tāmen yǎnglǎo sòngzhōng.

給他們養老送終。／给他们养老送终。

_____ c. Gāi dào le zánmen bàodá de shíhou le.

該到了咱們報答的時候了。／该到了咱们报答的时候了。

_____ d. Bǎ tāmen jiē guòlai, hé wǒmen yìqǐ zhù.

把他們接過來，和我們一起住。／把他们接过来，和我们一起住。

_____ e. Yǒu gèng duō de shíjiān qù péibàn tāmen.

有更多的時間去陪伴他們。／有更多的时间去陪伴他们。

_____ f. Yào ge háizi, ràng tāmen bào sūnzi bào sūnnǚ.

要個孩子，讓他們抱孫子抱孫女。／要个孩子，让他们抱孙子抱孙女。

_____ g. Bù líkāi Běijīng.

不離開北京。／不离开北京。

29.13 *Chen Feng and Xiao Mao talk about a circle in life. Fill in the missing step.* 請寫英文。／请写英文。

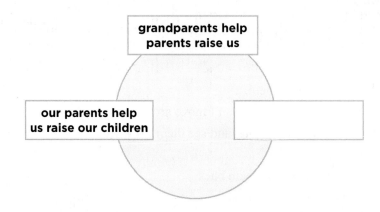

29.14 *Chen Feng and Xiao Mao talk about Confucius* (Kǒngzǐ 孔子) *and his notions about the duties of the dutiful child* (xiàozǐ 孝子).

a. *Xiao Mao cites the following saying. Use the list of characters provided.* 把漢字填進去。／把汉字填进去。

不	在	孔	遠／远	子	母	遊／游	父

Fùmǔ zài, bù yuǎn yóu. —Kǒngzǐ

_____ _____ _____, _____ _____ _____。 — _____ _____

When your parents are alive, don't travel far. —Confucius

b. *Chen Feng refers to his own situation using a different saying. Use the list of characters provided.* 把漢字填進去。／把汉字填进去。

不	欲	而	親／亲	子	養／养	在

Zǐ yù yǎng ér qīn bú zài.

_____ _____ _____ _____ _____ _____ _____。

The child wishes to offer care, but the parents are no longer there.

FYI 供你参考

Filial piety in Chinese culture

The two expressions in 29.14 are typical of the kind of language that educated Chinese people often use to deepen their comments and connect to their past.

The first expression comes from the Analects of Confucius. The complete quote is as follows:

子曰：父母在，不遠遊，遊必有方。／子曰：父母在，不远游，游必有方。

Zǐ yuē: Fùmǔ zài, bù yuǎn yóu, yóu bì yǒu fāng.

"Master-say: father-mother-present, not-far-travel, travel-must-have-method"
(The Master said: When your parents are alive, don't travel far; if you travel, you must have a method.)

子 is a reference to 孔子 (*Kǒngzǐ*—Confucius). 曰 is the literary equivalent of 说／说. 在 means "to be present," or—by extension—"to be alive; to be present in this life." 方 usually has two interpretations. The first is that it refers to a definite residing place—if you must be far from your parents, then you have to be in a definite place where you can be reached easily. The other is that it means a legitimate reason—if you must be far away from your parents, then there has to be a legitimate reason.

Discussion questions: *Why do you think Confucius made this remark? Does it seem reasonable to you? Does it still apply to modern life?*

....

The second expression is actually one half of a couplet:

樹欲靜而風不止，子欲養而親不在。／树欲静而风不止，子欲养而亲不在。

Shù yù jìng ér fēng bù zhǐ, zǐ yù yǎng ér qīn bú zài.

"tree-wish-still-but-wind-not-cease, child-wish-care-but-parent-not-there"
(The tree wishes to be still, but the wind will not cease; the child wishes to care for his parents, but they are no longer alive.)

Couplets are common in literary Chinese. The natural phenomenon indicated in the first half of this expression (a tree blowing in a gusty wind) invokes a connection to the human condition indicated in the second half. A tree can't control a natural force any more than a person can control his or her destiny. Since life is fickle and unpredictable—just like blowing winds—all we can do is cherish the present and care for our parents while we can.

The first line of the couplet is matched in form to the second line—the two lines are parallel.

樹	靜	風	止
	欲	而	不
子	養	親	在
noun	verb	noun	verb

Challenge: *Can you find another couplet in your environment or online, decipher it, and share it with your class? You could make a poster for the classroom or post your couplet and explanation online.*

29.15 *Pair work: How would you describe your feelings—filial or otherwise—toward your own parent(s) or guardian(s)? Take some notes below, and then describe these feelings to a partner. Record how your partner feels. Repeat with someone else in your class, if time is available.*

Encounter 2   Reading and writing

29.16 *Read the following notes. The first was written by a student in Hong Kong to her friend Tang Li in Kunming, and the other was written in response.*

ⓐ 莉莉：

今天是清明節。我們一家人到我外公外婆的墳墓去掃墓，給他們燒了香和紙錢、獻了花、烤乳豬還有很多點心。完了以後我們把所有吃的東西都搬到我表哥家裡去吃午飯，聚了一整個下午。我表哥託我問候你。我們都很想念你，希望你不久能有機會再來香港玩。會的嗎？祝好！

白玉立

ⓑ 小白：

太久没和你联系了！清明那天我们也去扫墓。真的很难相信，我父亲过世已经有五年了。我很想念香港，特别怀念在你表哥家过的那个非常愉快的夜晚：吃、喝、打麻将、玩电子游戏、聊通宵。我希望将来有机会再去香港看你们，也希望你们可以来昆明啊！冬天的时候昆明尤其值得来一趟。昆明的气候四季如春。到时候我会带你们到石林去逛逛！你还记得我跟你提过我的外国笔友吗？他可能今年圣诞节的时候会来昆明玩。你要是那个时候也能过来的话，那该多好啊！

请代我问叔叔阿姨好。非常想念你们一家人！

唐莉

Pretend you're the foreign friend Tang Li refers to. Write her a brief note, wish her a happy Qingming Festival, and ask what her family did to celebrate. Mention anything your own family does to remember family members who have passed. Confirm that you'll be visiting at Christmas, and mention some things you look forward to doing while in Kunming (do some research if necessary).

Reading real-life texts

29.17 *Following are a number of signs on the way to the home in which Fang Lan and Emma live.*

a 用拼音填空。

Jǐng _____	*Warning*
_____ shēn wēixiǎn	*Danger, deep water*
_____ _____ kào _____	*Please do not get close*

b 用拼音填空。

Jīdòng _____ _____	*Motor vehicles*
_____ _____ _____ _____	*Please park to the left*

c 用拼音填空。

Xiāofáng _____ _____	*Fire lane*
_____ _____ _____ _____	*Parking prohibited*

d *Many services in China target people who have gone out drinking after work and need to get home.* 用英文填空。

e dài jià	*e–substitute driver*
22 diǎn qián	*before _____ P.M.*
10 gōnglǐ nèi ¥39	*within _____ kilometers ¥39*
Wēixìn	*Use WeChat*
jiào dài jià	*call for a substitute driver*
Jiùshì kuài!	*It's so _____!*
Qǐng wù jiǔhòu jiàchē	*_____ drive after _____*

e *Perhaps the service offered here is more straightforward. What is "dial-a-cab" in Chinese?*

漢字／汉字: ____ ____ ____ ____

拼音: _____ _____

f 請寫拼音。／请写拼音。

1. *China Post:* _____

2. *box for letters and newspapers:*

   _____

   (That's what's actually written on the box.)

g *Write* 拼音 *for these two signs.*

1. *recyclable trash:* _____

2. *non-recyclable trash:* _____

h *On the wall in the office in which Chen Feng and Xiao Mao talk about their parents and filial duty hangs this poster on the same topic. It is written in classical Chinese in the traditional format: top to bottom, right to left.*
請填拼音。／请填拼音。

中华美德	_____	*Chinese Virtues*
孝道	_____	*The Way of Filial Piety*
中华孝道与和谐社会	_____ yǔ héxié shèhuì	*Chinese Filialness and a Harmonious Society*
孝子之事亲也	_____	*This is how a dutiful son serves his parents.*

局则致其敬	Jú zé zhì qí jìng.	*In living together, he is maximally respectful.*
养则致其乐	_____ lè.	*In caring for them, he is as joyful as possible.*
病则致其忧	_____ yōu.	*When they fall ill, he is extremely concerned.*
丧则致其哀	Sāng _____ āi.	*When they die, he grieves hard.*
祭则致其严	Jì _____ yán.	*In observing funereal rites, he is absolutely formal.*
五者备矣	Wǔ zhě bèi yǐ,	*When all these five have been met,*
然后能事亲	_____.	*then he has served his parents as a dutiful son.*

29.18 *If you were making a similar poster about how you think children should ideally behave toward their parents, what would you write? Come up with three adjectives, and fill in the blanks below. Some suggestions have been provided; look up other possibilities or ask for help.* 請寫漢字。／请写汉字。

對待父母要 _____、_____、_____。

对待父母要 _____、_____、_____。

禮貌／礼貌 lǐmào *courteous*	體諒／体谅 tǐliàng *considerate*	寬容／宽容 kuānróng *tolerant*
尊重 zūnzhòng *respectful*	體貼／体贴 tǐtiē *thoughtful*	包容 bāoróng *inclusive*
服從／服从 fúcóng *obedient*	關心／关心 guānxīn *caring*	坦率 tǎnshuài *candid*
合作 hézuò *cooperative*	關愛／关爱 guān'ài *loving*	坦誠／坦诚 tǎnchéng *frank*
誠實／诚实 chéngshí *truthful*	理解 lǐjiě *understanding*	誠懇／诚恳 chéngkěn *sincere*

▌ Reading a story

29.19 故事： 生氣怎麼能孝順呢？ *Work with a partner or in a small group to read the story below.*

小虎十三歲了，上初二。他書讀得不怎麼樣，馬馬虎虎，可是他非常吸引人，朋友很多，大家都認為他特別的酷。他長得很帥，又高又瘦，身材很好，在學校裡老愛搞笑，上課的時候常讓老師生氣同學們樂，所以學生們都非常喜歡他。

可是他父母對他非常失望。小虎很聰明，人也很好，喜歡幫忙，討好別人。但他就不愛讀書，不聽話，有一點逆反心理。所以他父母老說他、罵他、盯著他，管他的一舉一動。小虎在家裡待不住，受不了，一有機會就往外跑，找他的朋友們去了。

他很生他父母的氣。他覺得父母和老師們一點都不理解他，只有他的朋友們理解他。他喜歡上學，是為了和朋友們在一起，搞笑，讓大家樂，不是為了學習。他覺得上課的內容特別無聊，沒意思，所以他不願意花時間讀書。他越不讀書，越讓父母生氣。父母越不高興，他就越不想呆在家裡了。

孝道第一件事是得多陪陪父母。小虎其實很愛他父母，只是受不了他們老管他。怎麼辦呢？

29.20 *Part 1: Write two pieces of advice, one to Xiao Hu and the other to his parents, and share them with your classmates. Take a survey of all the advice provided by members of your class, and see if any predominates. **Part 2:** Now write a short story that touches on relationships between young people and their parents or guardians. Have it edited by your teacher or someone else who is fluent in Chinese. Illustrate your story as best as you can before sharing it with your classmates.*

Encounter 3   Extension: Cultural mini-documentary

View the cultural mini-documentary for this unit and complete the exercises that follow.

▪ Part 1

怎樣看待和對待孩子／怎样看待和对待孩子

Zěnyàng kàndài hé duìdài háizi

How children are viewed and treated

29.21 *In the first part of this video (00:00–00:36), three speakers talk about how children are viewed and treated in China. For each speaker,* 用拼音填空. *Then write the number of the corresponding English summary.*

a. Zhōngguó de chuántǒng _____, háizi jiùshì . . . nǐ shēngmìng zhōng zuì _____ de . . . jiùshì zuì zuì zhòngyào de.

中國的傳統家庭，孩子就是……你生命中最重要的……就是最最重要的。／中国的传统家庭，孩子就是……你生命中最重要的……就是最最重要的。

Summary: ____

b. . . . tèbié shì zài Zhōngguó de _____ lǐtou, zhèi ge jìhuà shēngyù yǐhòu zàochéng de, zhèi ge, yí ge háizi _____ de zhè zhǒng bùjǐn shì _____ érqiě shì nì'ài.

……特別是在中國的社會裡頭，這個計劃生育以後造成的，這個，一個孩子父母的這種不僅是愛而且是溺愛。／……特別是在中国的社会里头，这个计划生育以后造成的，这个，一个孩子父母的这种不仅是爱而且是溺爱。

Summary: ____

c. Wǒ juéde, qíshí _____ bǎ tāmen dāng háizi lái kàndài háizi. Wǒ yào dāng tā shì _____. Wǒmen . . . wǒ gēn wǒ nǚ'ér de, wǒmen liǎng ge, gǎnjué shì, jiùshì _____ liǎng ge.

我覺得，其實不應該把他們當孩子來看待孩子。我要當他是朋友。我們……我跟我女兒的，我們兩個，感覺是，就是姐妹兩個。／我觉得，其实不应该把他们当孩子来看待孩子。我要当他是朋友。我们……我跟我女儿的，我们两个，感觉是，就是姐妹两个。

Summary: ____

1. In Chinese **society**, there's a kind of spoiling (not just **love**) that has arisen among **parents** with the advent of family planning.

2. I think one **should not** view children as children. I want the child to be a **friend**. We . . . my daughter and I, the two of us, the feeling is like two **sisters**.

3. In a traditional Chinese **family**, children are absolutely the most **important** thing in your life.

■ **Part 2**

對孩子的期待以及教育／对孩子的期待以及教育

Duì háizi de qīdài yǐjí jiàoyù

Expectations and education of children

29.22 *In the second part of the video (00:37–02:14), three speakers talk about their expectations for their children. For each speaker,* 用拼音填空. *Then write the number of the corresponding English summary.*

a.

Qíshí wǒ shì . . . wǒ de xiǎngfǎ jiùshì háizi yídìng yào . . . ràng tā _____, yángguāng, jiǎndān de chéngzhǎng, kuàilè de chéngzhǎng, bú shì xiàng dàduōshù rénjiā, jiùshì ràng tā bào hěn duō de zhè zhǒng péixùnbān, xiǎng ràng tā zěnme zěnmeyàng, wǒ jiùshì, xiǎngfǎ jiùshì, ràng tā yǒu ge _____ de tóngnián. Xiǎng shàng péixùnbān, kěyǐ shàng, jiùshì, tā zhǐyào xǐhuan cái shàng, rúguǒ bù _____ wǒ juéduì bú huì qù qiángjiā tā. Wǒ duì tā de yāoqiú jiùshì jiānglái _____ yǐhòu tā zhǐyào nénggòu shēntǐ jiànkāng, sīxiǎng jiànkāng, jiùshì hěn yángguāng, ránhòu nénggòu zìjǐ guò zìjǐ xiǎngyào de jiǎndān kuàilè de _____ jiù kěyǐ, wǒ bìng méiyǒu xiǎng tā huì qù shàng shénme míngpái dàxué, huòzhě shì _____ qù . . . qù zěnmeyàng, cónglái méiyǒu zhèyàng xiǎng, zhǐyào jiànkāng jiù hǎo, kuàilè jiù hǎo.

其實我是⋯⋯我的想法就是孩子一定要⋯⋯讓她健康、陽光、簡單地成長，快樂地成長，不是像大多數人家，就是讓她報很多的這種培訓班，想讓她怎麼怎麼樣，我就是，想法就是，讓她有個快樂的童年。想上培訓班，可以上，就是，她只要喜歡才上，如果不喜歡我絕對不會去強加她。我對她的要求就是將來長大以後她只要能夠身體健康，思想健康，就是很陽光，然後能夠自己過自己想要的簡單快樂的生活就可以，我並沒有想她會去上甚麼名牌大學，或者是出國去⋯⋯去怎麼樣，從來沒有這樣想，只要健康就好，快樂就好。／

其实我是⋯⋯我的想法就是孩子一定要⋯⋯让她健康、阳光、简单地成长，快乐地成长，不是像大多数人家，就是让她报很多的这种培训班，想让她怎么怎么样，我就是，想法就是，让她有个快乐的童年。想上培训班，可以上，就是，她只要喜欢才上，如果不喜欢我绝对不会去强加她。我对她的要求就是将来长大以后她只要能够身体健康，思想健康，就是很阳光，然后能够自己过自己想要的简单快乐的生活就可以，我并没有想她会去上什么名牌大学，或者是出国去⋯⋯去怎么样，从来没有这样想，只要健康就好，快乐就好。

Summary: ____

b.

Qíshí wǒ yě zhème xiǎng, jiùshì, wǒmen jiā _____ jiùshì . . . wǒ jiù yào . . . xiǎng ràng tā gēn wǒ zài [*place name*] guò de _____ yíyàng . . . jiù wúyōu-wúlǜ de zhèyàng ràng tā yǒu yí ge hěn hǎo de tóngnián. Zhèi diǎn _____ wǒmen liǎng ge cóng zhèi diǎn shang bǐjiào wěnhé yìxiē.

其實我也這麼想，就是，我們家小孩就是⋯⋯我就要⋯⋯想讓她跟我在 [*place name*] 過的童年一樣⋯⋯就無憂無慮的這樣讓她有一個很好的童年。這點可能我們兩個從這點上比較吻合一些。／

其实我也这么想，就是，我们家小孩就是……我就要……想让她跟我在 [place name] 过的童年一样……就无忧无虑的这样让她有一个很好的童年。这点可能我们两个从这点上比较吻合一些。

Summary: ____

c. Wǒmen jīběnshang lái jiǎng háishi cǎiqǔ fēicháng . . . yí ge shì _____ de yì zhǒng xiǎngfǎ, lìngwài bǐjiào fàngsōng, wǒ yě méiyǒu shuō nǐ zài shénme dìfang bìxū shuō Zhōngwén, nǐ zài shénme dìfang bìxū shuō Yīngwén děng děng, ràng tāmen zìjǐ cóngxiǎo _____ tā zìjǐ běnrén shì nénggòu yǒu zuò juédìng, érqiě nénggòu _____ de xiǎngshòu tā zhèi ge shēnghuó, xuéxí, xuéxí bù yīnggāi chéngwéi yì zhǒng fùdān, yīnggāi shì tā rènwéi búduàn jìnqǔ guòchéng dāngzhōng de yí ge hěn zhòngyào de yí _____.

我們基本上來講還是採取非常……一個是開放的一種想法，另外比較放鬆，我也沒有說你在甚麼地方必須說中文，你在甚麼地方必須說英文等等，讓他們自己從小認為他自己本人是能夠有做決定，而且能夠真正地享受他這個生活、學習，學習不應該成為一種負擔，應該是他認為不斷進取過程當中的一個很重要的一部份。／

我们基本上来讲还是采取非常……一个是开放的一种想法，另外比较放松，我也没有说你在什么地方必须说中文，你在什么地方必须说英文等等，让他们自己从小认为他自己本人是能够有做决定，而且能够真正地享受他这个生活、学习，学习不应该成为一种负担，应该是他认为不断进取过程当中的一个很重要的一部份。

Summary: ____

1. Basically we still take a very . . . on the one hand, **open** way of thinking, and also more relaxed. I never said you have to speak Chinese here and you have to speak English there. From childhood, we let them **feel** that they themselves could make decisions and could **truly** enjoy their lives and enjoy learning. Learning should not become a burden—they should see it as a very important **part** of the process of continuous improvement.

2. Actually, to my way of thinking a child must be . . . you have to allow her to grow up **healthy** and positive, to grow up simply, grow up happily. I'm not like most people—signing her up for so many of these training classes, to make her into something or other. I just . . . the idea is to let her have a **happy** childhood. If she wants to take a class, that's fine, but only if she wants to. If she didn't **like** it, I would definitely never impose it on her. As long as in the future, after she **grows up**, she is healthy, mentally sound, positive, and as long as she's able to live her own happy, simple **life**, that's enough. I've never thought she would go to some famous university, then **go abroad** to do whatever. I have never thought this way. As long as she is healthy and happy, that's enough.

3. Actually, I think that way too, that is, our **kid** is . . . I want to . . . let her have the same kind of **childhood** I had in [place name] . . . to let her have a good, carefree childhood. On this point, the two of us **maybe** have relatively similar views.

■ **Part 3**

帶孩子／带孩子

Dài háizi

Taking care of kids

29.23 *In the next part of the video (02:15–03:40), two parents mention challenges faced by Chinese parents regarding childcare, along with a number of possible solutions. Put checkmarks in the boxes to show which speaker(s) mention(s) which challenges and solutions. (Some may be mentioned by both speakers.)*

Challenges		
Young working parents have a hard time finding childcare solutions.	☐	☐
Childcare for two children is difficult for one person.	☐	☐
We have very little time to play with the kids because of our schedules.	☐	☐
Solutions		
Send the child to stay with the grandparents.	☐	☐
Hire a nanny to look after the children at home.	☐	☐
Hope that in the future we can spend more time with the kids.	☐	☐

■ **Part 4**

撫育孩子和贍養老人／抚育孩子和赡养老人

Fǔyù háizi hé shànyǎng lǎorén

Raising kids and taking care of elders

29.24 *In the last part of the video (03:41–05:07), a father addresses the related questions of childcare and elder care. The following statements are a trimmed-down version of what he says. First, number the statements to show the order in which they are mentioned. Then match each statement with its English summary by writing the appropriate letters in the blanks on page 194.*

_____ a. Guówài, rúguǒ shuō fùmǔ liǎng ge rén dōu gōngzuò, xūyào zhēnzhèng kào daycare huòzhě shì tuō'érsuǒ, yěshì hěn yǒu tiǎozhàn de.

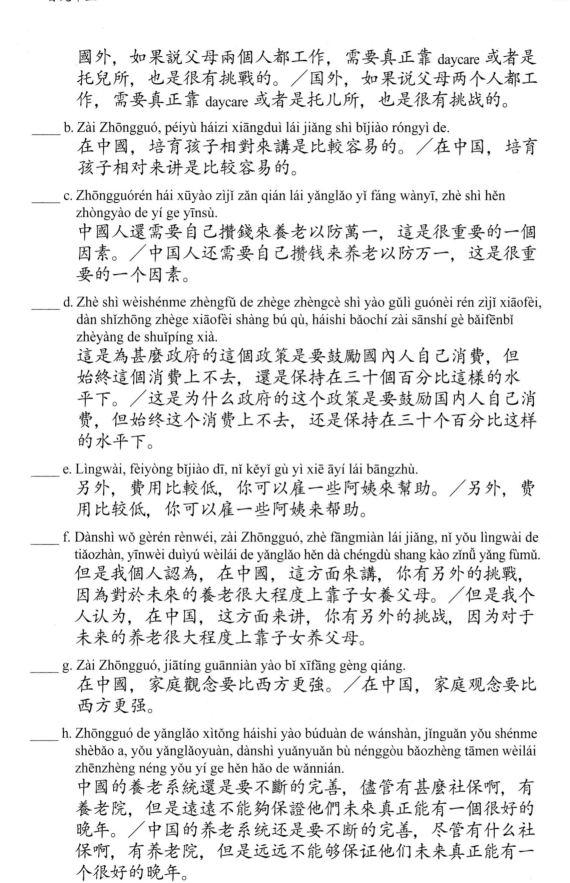

國外，如果说父母兩個人都工作，需要真正靠 daycare 或者是托兒所，也是很有挑戰的。／国外，如果说父母两个人都工作，需要真正靠 daycare 或者是托儿所，也是很有挑战的。

____ b. Zài Zhōngguó, péiyù háizi xiāngduì lái jiǎng shì bǐjiào róngyì de.
在中國，培育孩子相對來講是比較容易的。／在中国，培育孩子相对来讲是比较容易的。

____ c. Zhōngguórén hái xūyào zìjǐ zǎn qián lái yǎnglǎo yǐ fáng wànyī, zhè shì hěn zhòngyào de yí ge yīnsù.
中國人還需要自己攢錢來養老以防萬一，這是很重要的一個因素。／中国人还需要自己攒钱来养老以防万一，这是很重要的一个因素。

____ d. Zhè shì wèishénme zhèngfǔ de zhège zhèngcè shì yào gǔlì guónèi rén zìjǐ xiāofèi, dàn shǐzhōng zhège xiāofèi shàng bú qù, háishi bǎochí zài sānshí gè bǎifēnbǐ zhèyàng de shuǐpíng xià.
這是為甚麼政府的這個政策是要鼓勵國內人自己消費，但始終這個消費上不去，還是保持在三十個百分比這樣的水平下。／这是为什么政府的这个政策是要鼓励国内人自己消费，但始终这个消费上不去，还是保持在三十个百分比这样的水平下。

____ e. Lìngwài, fèiyòng bǐjiào dī, nǐ kěyǐ gù yì xiē āyí lái bāngzhù.
另外，費用比較低，你可以雇一些阿姨來幫助。／另外，费用比较低，你可以雇一些阿姨来帮助。

____ f. Dànshì wǒ gèrén rènwéi, zài Zhōngguó, zhè fāngmiàn lái jiǎng, nǐ yǒu lìngwài de tiǎozhàn, yīnwèi duìyú wèilái de yǎnglǎo hěn dà chéngdù shang kào zǐnǚ yǎng fùmǔ.
但是我個人認為，在中國，這方面來講，你有另外的挑戰，因為對於未來的養老很大程度上靠子女養父母。／但是我个人认为，在中国，这方面来讲，你有另外的挑战，因为对于未来的养老很大程度上靠子女养父母。

____ g. Zài Zhōngguó, jiātíng guānniàn yào bǐ xīfāng gèng qiáng.
在中國，家庭觀念要比西方更強。／在中国，家庭观念要比西方更强。

____ h. Zhōngguó de yǎnglǎo xìtǒng háishi yào búduàn de wánshàn, jǐnguǎn yǒu shénme shèbǎo a, yǒu yǎnglǎoyuàn, dànshì yuǎnyuǎn bù nénggòu bǎozhèng tāmen wèilái zhēnzhèng néng yǒu yí ge hěn hǎo de wǎnnián.
中國的養老系統還是要不斷的完善，儘管有甚麼社保啊，有養老院，但是遠遠不能夠保證他們未來真正能有一個很好的晚年。／中国的养老系统还是要不断的完善，尽管有什么社保啊，有养老院，但是远远不能够保证他们未来真正能有一个很好的晚年。

____ i. Dàjiē shang yéye nǎinai bàozhe sūnzi, sūnnǚ, shì fēicháng pǔbiàn de xiànxiàng.
大街上爺爺奶奶抱著孫子、孫女，是非常普遍的現象。／大街上爷爷奶奶抱着孙子、孙女，是非常普遍的现象。

_____ China has stronger family values than in the West.

_____ It is quite common to see grandparents on the street carrying a grandson or granddaughter.

_____ In addition, costs are relatively low; you can hire a nanny to help.

_____ In China, raising children is easier, relatively speaking.

_____ In other countries, if two people are working parents and need to really rely on a daycare or nursery, it is a real challenge.

_____ But I personally believe that in China, as far as this aspect is concerned, you have another challenge, because future elder care will to a large degree depend on parents being cared for by their children.

_____ China's pension system needs to continue to improve. Even though we have social insurance and nursing homes, we are far from being able to guarantee that people can really have a good old age in the future.

_____ This is why the government's policy is to encourage domestic consumption, but consumption never seems to be able to rise; it always stays around 30 percent.

_____ Chinese people still need to save money for their own elder care, just in case of the unexpected. This is a very important factor [that limits domestic consumption].

Recap

▶ Grammar

Classical Chinese in a few words

From ancient times until the early 20th century, classical Chinese—also known as literary Chinese—was the principal language of written communication in China and throughout all of East Asia and beyond. By the time of Confucius, around the 5th century BCE, the language had begun to stabilize and develop grammatical rules. Over the next two centuries, the first great flowering of Chinese writing occurred, including the great philosophical treatises and historical narratives.

Literary Chinese was and is a language with few rules and essentially no inflections. Comprehension depends less on grammar and more on a contextual understanding of the argument, along with knowledge of the past usage of particular characters. In pre-modern times, Chinese students of the literary language did not study a system of grammar (as, for example, when Western students learned Latin). Rather, students memorized classical texts and absorbed their meanings and rhythms. These ancient texts provided a template for later writers of the language.

Therefore, reading literary Chinese is largely a matter of knowing character meanings and which meanings occur in what situations. One can "master" the basic rules of grammar in a few weeks, but it takes years of study to become comfortable with the language.

Because literary Chinese was not phonetically based, it could be adopted by different cultures beyond China, eventually providing an international language that made communication possible among people over a vast area. Again, this recalls the role Latin played in the medieval West. Most educated men and women in Korea, Japan, and Vietnam could read (and often write) literary Chinese, which was pronounced according to the rules of the speaker's own language.

Much of this reminds us of the modern written language of China: relatively "simple" grammar, no inflections, can be read by speakers of different Chinese languages, and takes years of study to master.

So is literary Chinese important for students of the modern language? Yes—emphatically yes—because modern written Chinese (and, as we saw in this unit, to a large extent spoken Chinese) contains many phrases drawn from the classical language. To become a fluent reader of modern Chinese, the student needs a familiarity with literary Chinese. You will meet it in all sorts of articles, in works of art, on signs, in speech, and, as we hoped you've noticed, even in lesson titles! Remember this one from Unit 24?

愛美之心，人皆有之

Ài měi zhī xīn, rén jiē yǒu zhī.

"love beauty [的 de] heart people all possess it"
(It's only natural to want to look beautiful.)

Notice here that *zhī* 之 plays a double role: in the first clause, it is a particle of modification (like 的); in the second clause, it is the object of the verb *possess*.

Exercise: Look at the following sayings from other units in this book. Can you tell whether the 之 in each is

a. used like the particle 的 in modern Chinese
b. serving as the object of a verb

1. 君子愛財，取之有道 (U23)

Jūnzǐ ài cái, qǔ zhī yǒu dào

"good person love wealth, obtain 之 using moral path"
(A person of good character obtains wealth properly.)

Your answer: _____

2. 巧婦難為無米之炊 (U27)

Qiǎo fù nánwéi wúmǐzhīchuī

"clever wife difficult make no rice 之 cooking"
(Even the cleverest wife cannot cook without rice.)

Your answer: _____

3. 孝，德之本也 (U29)

Xiào, dé zhī běn yě

"filial piety, virtue 之 foundation"
(Filial piety is the foundation of all virtues.)

Your answer: _____

4. 既來之，則安之 (U30)

Jì lái zhī, zé ān zhī

"since come 之, then find peace 之"
(Since we've come, we might as well settle in.)

Your answer: _____

This has been just a taste of literary Chinese. We hope we have whetted your appetite for more! If you're interested, take a look at *A New Practical Primer of Literary Chinese* by Paul Rouzer (Cambridge, MA: Harvard University Asia Center, ©2007). Many of the remarks we make here are drawn from that fine book.

Answers:
君子愛財，取之有道 [之 is the object of the verb obtain]
巧婦難為無米之炊 [之 is like 的 "no rice [type] cooking"]
孝，德之本也 [之 is like 的 "virtue['s] foundation"]
既來之，則安之 [之 is used twice to mean "this place" and serves as the object of the verbs come and find peace]

▶ Vocabulary

Please refer to page R-2 for a list of grammatical abbreviations used throughout this book.

bào 抱 hold; carry in one's arms V

bàodá 報答／报答 repay; requite V

bǎohù 保護／保护 protect; safeguard V

chǎocài 炒菜 make a dish VO

chǎojià 吵架 argue; quarrel; have a spat VO

chōng 衝／冲 rush; charge; dash V

cónglái 從來／从来 + *negative* never A

děng...de shíhou 等⋯的時候／等⋯的时候 when PH

dīng 盯 gaze at; stare at V

dúshēng zǐnǔ 獨生子女／独生子女 only child N

fán 煩／烦 vexed; irritated; annoyed SV

fánrén 煩人／烦人 annoy VO; annoying; vexing; troubling SV

gānjìng 乾淨／干净 clean; neat; tidy SV

gǎnqíng 感情 feeling; emotion; sentiment N

guǎn 管 control; manage; run; have charge of V

hái hǎo 還好／还好 not bad; passable VP

hǎohāo 好好 carefully A

jiēguòlai 接過來／接过来 bring over to us; receive RV

juéwàng 絕望／绝望 lose/give up hope; despair V

kàn qǐlai 看起來／看起来 it seems; it appears; it looks as if VP

kěnqiú 懇求／恳求 earnestly plead for; implore; entreat V

làngfèi 浪費／浪费 waste; squander V

làngmàn 浪漫 romantic SV

Nǐ zài gànma? 你在幹嘛？／你在干吗？ What are you doing? PH

péibàn 陪伴 keep company with; spend time with; accompany V

shāo 燒／烧 burn V

sūnnǚ 孫女／孙女 granddaughter; son's daughter N

sūnzi 孫子／孙子 grandson; son's son N

wèilái 未來／未来 future; time to come N

wēixiào 微笑 smile V

xiàn 獻／献 offer V

xiāng 香 incense N

xiāngyān 香煙／香烟 cigarette N

xíngdòng búbiàn 行動不便／行动不便 unable to get about / move freely PH

xìngrén 杏仁 almond N

xìnrèn 信任 trust; have confidence in N/V

yǎnglǎo sòngzhōng 養老送終／养老送终 look after (one's parents) in their old age and give them a proper burial PH

yánlì 嚴厲／严厉 strict; stern; severe SV

yùnqi 運氣／运气 luck; fortune N

zhǎngdà 長大／长大 grow up; mature RV

zhàogu 照顧／照顾 take care of; look after; care for V

zhīchí 支持 support; back V

zhǐhuī 指揮／指挥 direct; command V

zhǐqián 紙錢／纸钱 paper money (for the deceased) N

zòu yí dùn 揍一頓／揍一顿 beat up; hit VP

zuò yí dùn (fàn) 做一頓(飯)／做一顿(饭) make a meal VP

zuòzhǔ 做主 make the decision; decide; take charge of VO

▶ Checklist of "can do" statements

After completing this unit, you should be able to perform each of the following tasks:

Listening and speaking

☐ Describe your relationship with your parents (or guardians).

☐ Converse with someone for three to five minutes about your relationship with your parents (or guardians).

Reading and writing

☐ Decipher some notes describing Qingming activities.

☐ Decipher some neighborhood signs.

☐ Read a short story about a teenager's relationship with his parents and write one about your own situation.

Understanding culture

☐ Make some accurate statements about aspects of Chinese filial piety.

☐ Make an accurate statement about Qingming activities.

☐ Make an accurate statement about sayings and couplets in literary Chinese.

☐ Make two or three accurate statements about how some Chinese parents say they relate to their children.

"Since we've come, we might as well settle in"

既來之，則安之

Jì lái zhī, zé ān zhī

Settling in a new place

In this unit, you will learn how to:

- describe your arrival in a new place.
- describe your feelings about being in an unfamiliar place.
- talk about the steps you might take to function in an unfamiliar place.

- decipher some notes related to settling in.
- comprehend a short story about settling in, and write one of your own.

Encounter 1   Talking about settling in a new place

30.1 *Fang Lan's parents—Lao Fang and Zhang Suyun—have invited Xiao Mao to their home to discuss Emma's recent bout of depression.* 請把中文跟英文對上。／ 请把中文跟英文对上。

____ a. chá qī hǎo le 茶沏好了

____ b. lǎo tí tā de jiārén 老提她的家人

____ c. xīnqíng bù hǎo 心情不好

____ d. xiǎngjiā le 想家了

____ e. bǐjiào kùnnán de jiēduàn 比較困難的階段／比较困难的阶段

____ f. jièshào gèng duō de péngyou rènshi 介紹更多的朋友認識／ 介绍更多的朋友认识

1. *(she has been) feeling down*
2. *always bringing up her family*
3. *introduce her to more friends*
4. *the tea has been brewed*
5. *a rather difficult period of time*
6. *(she is) homesick*

30.2 *View Episode 30, Vignette 1. Put the following events in the order in which they occur.*

_____ Xiao Mao tells Fang Lan's parents that their daughter is a lively thinker.

_____ Lao Fang demonstrates how to brew tea.

_____ Xiao Mao says that foreign students are often excited initially and then experience a period of depression.

_____ Lao Fang informs Xiao Mao that the tea is a special gift from the Fangs' hometown.

_____ Zhang Suyun says that Emma isn't talking much and asks if anything is wrong at school.

_____ Xiao Mao offers to introduce Emma to Mick.

_____ Lao Fang says that when he first got to Beijing, he used to write home constantly.

30.3 *At the beginning of the video, the Fangs and Xiao Mao make polite conversation for a few minutes.* 請再一次聽錄像片斷，然後圈選正確的答案。／ 请再一次听录像片断，然后圈选正确的答案。

Lǎo Fāng: Máo lǎoshī, nǐ hǎo.

Xiǎo Máo: Nǐ hǎo.

Lǎo Fāng: Huānyíng nǐ.

Xiǎo Máo: Gǎnxiè nǐmen _____ (yāoqiú *require* / yāoqǐng *invite*) wǒ lái.

Lǎo Fāng: Lái, qǐng zuò.

Zhāng Sūyún: Láiláilái, qǐng jìn, qǐng jìn.

Lǎo Fāng: Máo lǎoshī, lái, qǐng zuò, qǐng zuò.

Zhāng Sūyún: Bāor _____ (gē *put* / gěi *give*) zhè biān ba!

   Xiǎo Máo: Méishìr, méishìr, méiguānxi.

…

   Xiǎo Máo: Nǐmen jiā _____ (bù zhí *not worth* / bùzhì *decorate*) de hěn wēnxīn ma!

   Lǎo Fāng: Xièxie, xièxie!

Zhāng Sūyún: Jiùshì yǒudiǎnr _____ (làn *decrepit* / luàn *messy*)!

   Xiǎo Máo: Hái kěyǐ, hái kěyǐ! Tǐng hǎo de.

Zhāng Sūyún: Liǎ háizi zài xuéxiào gěi nín _____ (tiān máfan *were a bother* / bèi mà *were scolded*) le.

   Xiǎo Máo: Méiyǒu, méiyǒu. Fāng Lán hé Emma zài xuéxiào fēicháng hǎo. Yóuqí shì Fāng Lán, tā de sīwéi tèbié de _____ (huǒyào *gunpowder* / huóyuè *lively*) érqiě rén yě hěn rèqíng.

Zhāng Sūyún: Tāmen yàoshi yǒu zuòbuhǎo de dìfang, nín jǐnguǎn _____ (pīfā *wholesale* / pīpíng *criticize*) tā.

   Xiǎo Máo: Hǎo de, hǎo de. Wǒmen _____ (suíshí *constantly* / suíbiàn *casually*) gōutōng.

30.4 Group work: *Work in groups of three (double up if the numbers don't work out right) to read the script of the conversation among Lao Fang, Zhang Suyun, and Xiao Mao. Switch roles twice so you have a chance to role-play each character.*

老方: 毛老师，你好。

小毛: 你好。

老方: 欢迎你。

小毛: 感谢你们邀请我来。

老方: 来，请坐。

张苏云: 来来来，请进，请进。

老方: 毛老师，来，请坐，请坐。

张苏云: 包儿搁这边吧！

小毛: 没事儿，没事儿，没关系……

……

小毛: 你们家布置得很温馨嘛！

老方: 谢谢，谢谢！

张苏云: 就是有点儿乱！

小毛: 还可以，还可以！挺好的。

张苏云: 俩孩子在学校给您添麻烦了。

小毛: 没有，没有。方兰和 Emma 在学校非常好。尤其是方兰，她的思维特别的活跃而且人也很热情。

张苏云: 她们要是有做不好的地方，您尽管批评她。

小毛: 好的，好的。我们随时沟通。

30.5 Pair work: *Now you try it. Make polite conversation in Chinese with a partner for two to three minutes. Talk about anything you'd like.*

30.6 *As he explains how to make tea properly, Lao Fang explains his steps.* 請圈選正確的答案。／请圈选正确的答案。

Lǎo Fāng: Dì-yī _____ (bāo *packet* / pào *infusion*) xǐ chá, dì-èr _____ (bāo *packet* / pào *infusion*) cái shì zuì hǎo de shíhou. Lái, qǐng nín chángchang.

Xiǎo Máo: Xièxie! N, hěn _____ (xiāng *fragrant* / xiǎng *loud*) hěn _____ (xiāng *fragrant* / xiǎng *loud*). Wèidao hěn búcuò.

30.7 *After a while, Lao Fang and Zhang Suyun bring up the point of the visit.* 請再一次聽錄像片斷，然後圈選正確的答案。／请再一次听录像片断，然后圈选正确的答案。

Lǎo Fāng: Máo lǎoshī ya . . . _____ (yuè *month* / yuē *set up a meeting*) nǐ lái shì xiǎng hé nǐ tántan Àimǎ de shìr.

Xiǎo Máo: Àimǎ? Àimǎ zěnme le?

Lǎo Fāng: Zuìjìn wǒ fāxiàn Àimǎ lǎo gēn wǒmen _____ (tī *kick* / tí *bring up, mention*) tā de jiāxiāng, hái lǎo tí tā de jiārén.

Zhāng Sūyún: Shì zhè yàng de, wǒ juéde Àimǎ zuìjìn bù zěnme shuōhuà, hǎoxiàng _____ (xīnqíng *mood; disposition* / xiānqǐ *lift up*) bù hǎo. Wǒ xiǎng tā huìbuhuì zài xuéxiào, huòzhě zài wàibian huì yǒu shénme shìr? Suǒyǐ, jiù bǎ nín qǐng lái le.

Lǎo Fāng: Wǒmen shì dānxīn ya, Àimǎ kěnéng shì _____ (xiāngxià *countryside* / xiǎngjiā *be homesick*) le.

Xiǎo Máo: Ō, shì zhèyàng a. Qíshí, wǒ de xuésheng dāngzhōng yǒu bù shǎo wàiguó liúxuéshēng, tāmen gāng dào Zhōngguó de shíhou tèbié gāoxìng, tèbié _____ (xīngfèn *excited* / xìngfú *lucky*). Dàn wǎngwǎng zhè yàng de xuésheng, jǐn jiēzhe jiù huì jīnglì yí ge bǐjiào kùnnán de _____ (jiētóu *street corner* / jiēduàn *period; segment*). Zhè dōu shì fēicháng zhèngcháng de _____ (xiántán *chitchat* / xiànxiàng *phenomenon*).

30.8 Group work: *Again, work in groups of three (double up if the numbers don't work out right) to read the script of the conversation among Lao Fang, Zhang Suyun, and Xiao Mao. Switch roles twice so you have a chance to role-play each character.*

老方: 毛老师呀……约你来是想和你谈谈艾玛的事儿。

小毛: 艾玛？艾玛怎么了？

老方: 最近我发现艾玛老跟我们提她的家乡，还老提她的家人。

张苏云: 是这样的，我觉得艾玛最近不怎么说话，好像心情不好。我想她会不会在学校、或者在外边会有什么事儿？所以，就把您请来了。

老方: 我们是担心呀，艾玛可能是想家了。

小毛: 噢，是这样啊。其实，我的学生当中有不少外国留学生，他们刚到中国的时候特别高兴、特别兴奋。但往往这样的学生，紧接着就会经历一个比较困难的阶段。这都是非常正常的现象。

30.9 *Lao Fang compares Emma's homesickness to his own experience when he first moved to Beijing while his wife and young daughter remained at home.* 請再一次聽錄像片斷。／请再一次听录像片断。 *Put the following statements in order.*

Lǎo Fāng:

_____ Xīnlǐ tou yě hěn yāyì de.

_____ Wǒ zìjǐ yí ge rén xiàbān zhīhòu ne, huí dào kōng dàngdàng de sùshè.

_____ Wǒmen jiā Fāng Lán xiǎo, tā niáng liǎ zài lǎojiā.

_____ Yí ge rén zuòfàn, yí ge rén chīfàn, yě shì hěn jìmò.

_____ Nàge shíhou wǒ zài dānwèi, chúle nà jǐ ge tóngshì zhī wài shéi wǒ yě bú rènshi a.

Xiǎo Máo:

_____ yuǎnlí zìjǐ de qīnrén,

_____ yuǎnlí zìjǐ shúxī de jiāxiāng,

_____ nà zhǒng gǎnjué díquè bù hǎoshòu.

_____ Díquè a,

30.10 把英文跟漢字對上。／把英文跟汉字对上。

老方：

____ a. 我们家方兰小，她娘俩在老家。

____ b. 那个时候我在单位。

____ c. 我自己一个人下班之后呢，回到空荡荡的宿舍。

____ d. 心里头也很压抑的。

____ e. 除了那几个同事之外谁我也不认识啊。

____ f. 一个人做饭，一个人吃饭，也是很寂寞。

1. *I didn't know anyone other than a few colleagues.*

2. *After work, I returned alone to an empty dorm room.*

3. *Our Fang Lan was little; she and her mother were in our hometown.*

4. *At that time, I was with my unit.*

5. *I cooked alone, ate alone, and was very lonely.*

6. *I also felt very down at heart.*

小毛：

____ a. 远离自己熟悉的家乡

____ b. 的确啊

____ c. 那种感觉的确不好受

____ d. 远离自己的亲人

1. *and far away from your family*

2. *when you are far away from the home you are familiar with*

3. *oh, for sure*

4. *that kind of feeling is hard to bear*

30.11 *Pair work:* Work with a partner to make sure you know how to say each of the following statements in Chinese.

a. about Emma and other exchange students

was very happy and excited when she first arrived
is now experiencing a difficult time
keeps bringing up her hometown
keeps bringing up her family
doesn't talk much
seems to be feeling down
seems to be feeling homesick

b. about Lao Fang

was far away from his hometown
was far away from his family
returned to an empty dorm room after work
cooked alone
ate alone
was very down at heart

Now chat with your partner for a few minutes. Find out if either of you has ever had an experience such as Emma's or Lao Fang's—perhaps during the early days of this school year. See how many of these 13 phrases you can use in your conversation!

你們可以互相問：你經歷過這種情況嗎？／
你们可以互相问：你经历过这种情况吗？(情況/情况
　　　　　　　　qíngkuàng *situation*)

30.12 *To stay in touch with his family, Lao Fang had access to nothing except for mail service.* 請再一次聽錄像片斷。請用拼音填空，然後把拼音和漢字對上。／请再一次听录像片断。请用拼音填空，然后把拼音和汉字对上。

Nà ge shíhou yòu méiyǒu _____, dǎ ge _____ yòu bù fāngbiàn, suǒyǐ wǒ jiù lǎo _____. Nà ge shíhou, wǒ jīngcháng wǎng _____ pǎo, mǎi _____ dōu shì _____ de mǎi, lǎo gěi tāmen niáng liǎ _____. Wǒ de _____ a, dà bùfen dōu huā zài _____ shang la!

____ a. zhěng bǎn zhěng bǎn *sheet by sheet*   1. 郵票／邮票

____ b. gōngzī *wages*   2. 寫信／写信

____ c. xiěxìn *write letters*   3. 長途／长途

____ d. yóupiào *stamps*   4. 整版整版

____ e. jì bāoguǒ *send parcels*   5. 郵費／邮费

____ f. chángtú *long-distance phone call*   6. 郵局／邮局

____ g. yóufèi *postage*   7. 工資／工资

____ h. shǒujī *cell phone*   8. 手機／手机

____ i. yóujú *post office*   9. 寄包裹

30.13 *Pair work: Work with a partner to read Lao Fang's statement out loud.*

那個時候又没有手機，打個長途又不方便，所以我就老寫信。那個時候，我經常往郵局跑，買郵票都是整版整版地買，老給他們娘倆寄包裹。我的工資啊，大部分都花在郵費上啦！／那個時候又没有手机，打个长途又不方便，所以我就老写信。那个时候，我经常往邮局跑，买邮票都是整版整版地买，老给他们娘倆寄包裹。我的工资啊，大部分都花在邮费上啦！

Now try to retell his experience in your own words in Chinese.

30.14 *In Episode 30, Vignette 2, Emma, Xiao Mao, and Luo Xueting visit Mick at his teahouse. View Vignette 2, and identify who makes each of the following statements (presented in the order in which they are made).*

| a. Emma | b. Xiao Mao | c. Luo Xueting | d. Mick |

_____ 1. Very pleased to meet you.

_____ 2. I heard that you are even a specialist in Chinese tea.

_____ 3. Fine, treat us to a cup of tea!

_____ 4. The flavor of the tea today is very special!

_____ 5. You're homesick, right?

_____ 6. When I first got here, I was really excited, so I wasn't homesick at all.

_____ 7. When I got to China, I was really homesick.

_____ 8. Whenever anyone gets to a new place, there'll be a period of adjustment.

_____ 9. When I came to China I had no friends; I was all alone.

_____ 10. You make friends (in China), and your Chinese will become better and better.

_____ 11. In Chinese, we call that a "virtuous circle."

_____ 12. Friends and colleagues are extremely, extremely important. They'll give you lots of support and help.

_____ 13. I encourage you to make lots and lots of friends.

_____ 14. Let's use tea for wine and drink to Emma in hopes that she'll make more new friends!

30.15 請把下面的拼音跟上面的英文對上。／请把下面的拼音跟上面的英文对上。

_____ a. Xíng, qǐng wǒmen hē bēi chá ba!

_____ b. Nǐ xiǎngjiā, shìbushì?

_____ c. Wǒ gāng dào de shíhou hái tèbié xīngfèn, suǒyǐ hái yìdiǎnr yě bù xiǎngjiā.

_____ d. Wǒ lái Zhōngguó de shíhou méiyǒu péngyoumen, wǒ hěn gūdú de.

_____ e. Wǒ lái Zhōngguó de shíhou tèbié de xiǎngjiā.

_____ f. Péngyou hé tóngshì fēicháng fēicháng zhòngyào, tāmen huì gěi nǐ hěn duō zhīchí hé bāngzhù.

_____ g. Jīntiān zhè ge chá wèidao hěn tèbié.

_____ h. Nǐ duō jiāo péngyou, nǐ de Zhōngwén huì yuèlái-yuèhǎo de.

_____ i. Rènshi nǐ hěn gāoxìng.

_____ j. Wǒ gǔlì nǐ qù jiéjiāo hěn duō hěn duō de péngyou.

_____ k. Nà wǒmen jiù yǐ chá dài jiǔ, wèi Àimǎ zhùfú, zhùyuàn tā jiéjiāo gèng duō de xīn péngyou!

_____ l. Zhè zài Zhōngwén lǐmian jiù jiàozuò "liángxìng xúnhuán."

_____ m. Rènhé rén dào yí ge xīn de dìfang, huì yǒu yí ge shìyìng de guòchéng.

_____ n. Tīngshuō nǐ háishi yí ge Zhōngguó chádào de zhuānjiā.

30.16 _View Episode 30, Vignette 2 again, and follow along in the script below. Then work with three classmates to act out the scene. The roles are Mick, Emma, Xiao Mao, and Luo Xueting._

米克: 啊，你好，我的"学生"都到了，你好，你好。哈哈！（转向艾玛）你应该是艾玛。

艾玛: 对呀！认识你很高兴。

米克: 太好了，我应该跟你说中文，因为这个是罗大夫还有毛老师的要求。

小毛: 那谢谢你米克。艾玛知道我跟雪婷在一个澳大利亚人开的中心学做中国菜，感觉特别惊讶！所以她非常想认识你。

艾玛: 而且我听说你还是一个中国茶道的专家！

米克: 哪里，哪里。

小毛: 行，请我们喝杯茶吧！

米克: 当然。你们一起来吧。咱们来喝茶。

[Mick pours tea.]

小毛: 谢谢。今天这个茶味道很特别。米克，那就请你给艾玛分享一下你的经验吧！

米克: 可以。所以，艾玛，你在中国多长时间？

艾玛: 快两个月了。

米克: 你想家，是不是？

[Emma nods in embarrassment.]

艾玛: 对呀，我刚到的时候还特别兴奋，所以一点儿也不想家。但是现在我很想念我的父母，尤其是我妈妈。

罗雪婷: 你来中国很久了，是吧，米克？

米克: 差不多六年了。

小毛: 那你刚来的时候，有没有得思乡病呀？

米克: 当然有。我来中国的时候我特别想家。后来就是，来这边我一直在旅游。我骑自行车到好多地方在中国，然后每个地方有的时候去办事也对我很烦恼。

罗雪婷: 任何人到一个新的地方，会有一个适应的过程。

米克: 这个肯定的。就是，我来中国的时候没有朋友们，我很孤独的。你交朋友们在中国，你的中文会越来越好。

小毛: 这在中文里面就叫做"良性循环"。

艾玛: 我真希望能早点有这个，什么循环？

小毛: "良性循环"。

艾玛: 对，这个"良性循环"。

米克: 我现在也一点儿不想家。罗大夫，你怎么呢？

罗雪婷: 嗯，对我来说有一点儿不同，因为我的同事们都给了我很多支持和帮助。当然，医院的工作特别忙，也没多少时间想家。

小毛: 而且你现在不是有我了吗？

罗雪婷: 有你也还会想家的呀，思念父母啊！

小毛: 对，对，对。

罗雪婷: 我见过很多外国留学生都遇到同样的问题。我同意米克的说法，朋友和同事非常非常重要，他们会给你很多支持和帮助。所以艾玛，我鼓励你去结交很多很多的朋友。

艾玛: 好，我特别感谢你们对我这么这么好。你们非常关心我，我很感激。

米克: 艾玛！这个应该的，我和罗大夫是过来人。

小毛: 那我们就以茶代酒，为艾玛祝福，祝愿她结识更多的新朋友！

四人一起: 干杯！

30.17 Pair work: *Following the example of the conversation in 30.16, speak with a partner for a few minutes about your own experience when you first started at the school in which you are currently enrolled.*

Encounter 2 Reading and writing

▶ Reading real-life texts

30.18 *The following brief posts were made by five visitors to the United States upon arrival.* 請用英語填空。／请用英语填空。

a.

终于到美国了，这下可真是要开始讲英文了。

b.

这里的人们都很热情！先好好睡一觉，新的生活就要开始啦！^^

c.

噗，這地方實在太美麗了，天上人間

d.

好开心，我终于到了。这里的一切都让我兴奋。

e.

经过十三小时的飞行，飞机停在了芝加哥O'Hare国际机场，我们一家三口终于踏上了美国的土地。期待已久，心里的兴奋无法形容。

a. I've finally arrived in the United States; now I have to really start
_____.

b. The people here are so warmhearted! First, I'm going to
_____; my new life is about to begin!

c. Wow, this place is really _____—a heaven on Earth.

d. I'm so happy that I'm finally here. Everything about this place makes me
_____.

e. After 13 hours of flying, the plane landed at Chicago's O'Hare airport, and we
_____ finally stepped onto U.S. soil. We'd been looking
forward to this for so long that the _____ in our hearts was
indescribable.

30.19 *After some months, the same five people made the following posts about their lives in their new homes.* 请用英语填空。／请用英语填空。

a.

特别想念中国随处可吃的美食！！！妈吃的！我的胃已经开始想家了T^T

b.

哎，大家都在庆祝新年了。不知道爸爸妈妈还有咪咪在干什么？

c.

今天是中秋节，虽然吃到了可口的月饼，但是没能和家人在一起，好伤心。

d.

很想念家裏的食物及妈妈做的

e.

去学校，走路；上超市，走路……太不方便了。在美国没有车"车轮上的国家"，名不虚传。可是我还没摸过方向盘呢。

a. I really miss the wonderful food you can find everywhere in China!!! It's delicious! My stomach is beginning to feel _____.

b. Ah, everyone is celebrating _____. I wonder what Dad and Mom and Mimi are doing?

c. Today is the Mid-Autumn Festival. Although I had some tasty mooncakes, I can't be with my family. I feel very _____.

d. I really miss the food from my home and the _____ that Mom makes.

e. To go to school, I walk; to go to the supermarket, I walk; it is really _____ not to have a car in the United States. "A country on wheels"—this is not a misnomer. And yet I've not yet touched a steering wheel.

30.20 *Finally, after a year or more, the same five people made the following posts.* 請用英語填空。／请用英语填空。

a.

一切都靠自己真
不容易. 还是原来
运动队的生活好.
有吃有睡不用自己
操心.

b.

后来, 我们交了一些
朋友, 尤其是教会的
朋友, 他们带我们购物,
去教会, 去玩, 还教我
们开车. 太幸福了.

c.

人生就是这样,
求其放心吧!

d.

最近终于觉得我在
国外的生活已经逐渐
步入正轨了~希望爸
妈和朋友不要太想我.
哈哈~

e.

今天和爸妈视频
聊天, 告诉他们我
自己包了饺子. 看来
自己在异乡也能 过
得好好的.

a. It's really _____ to have to rely on oneself for everything. After all, my former life as an athlete was better: I could eat and _____ and not have to worry about anything.

b. Afterward, we _____, especially friends from church. They took us _____, took us to church and to have fun, and they even _____. We were so lucky.

c. This is how _____; might as well accept it!

d. Recently, I've finally begun to feel that my life overseas is on track. I hope Dad and Mom and my friends won't _____, ha ha. ;-)

e. Today, I had a _____ with my parents, and I told them I had made some jiaozi. Apparently, I can live _____ by myself in a foreign country.

▶ **Reading a story**

30.21 故事：　第一次離開家 *Read the following recollection.*

我上大學那年才16歲。我特別興奮，第一次要離開家，去一所離家500里的大學，準備住在一棟看起來很漂亮的宿舍裡。我不記得我在家的最後幾天做了些甚麼，準備帶甚麼東西去上學。快開學的時候，我爸爸、媽媽、姐姐和我把我的兩箱行李裝進我們的車，他們準備開車送我去學校。半路上我們停了一夜，去看我的二哥。他在另外一所大學上學。我們那天晚上過得很愉快。

到了我的學校以後，他們幾個人幫我把行李搬進我的房間，把衣服掛好，東西擺齊。我還有個室友，我們和她打了個招呼，就去吃晚飯了。那時候我還是很興奮，竟然等不及讓我家人快點走，好讓我開始認識一些新的朋友。

所以吃完飯以後，爸媽和姐姐就上路往回走了。他們決定在路上找個旅館過夜，第二天直接開回家。我們最後互相抱了抱，說了幾聲再見。我媽和姐都哭了，可是我沒哭，因為還是太興奮了。然後他們就上車走了。

他們離開以後，我的室友叫我和她的一些同學們一起去參加一個新生晚會。我們房間裡人很多，所以我挑了幾件衣服到浴室裡去換。可是一到浴室裡，關上門以後，一下子覺得非常非常難過，好像突然才意識到家裡的人都走了，只留下我自己一個人在這個陌生的地方。我真的不知道現在應該怎麼辦。我不認識我的室友，其實我在這個地方誰也不認識。一下子開始特別特別地想念家人，終於開始回過神兒來，原來我的爸爸媽媽和姐姐都已經離開，回家去了。我就很傷心地坐到馬桶上開始哭了。我室友叫我，我也不能回答，默默地流眼淚，不好意思哭出聲音來。過了一會兒，我說我不舒服，讓她們自己走吧。她們走了以後，我坐在廁所裡一連哭了好幾個鐘頭，一直哭到很晚，累了，上床繼續哭到睡著了，連枕頭都濕了。

那年秋天，我每天都在想家。一直到感恩節的時候，終於有機會回家一趟，看爸爸、媽媽和姐姐。在家裡過了溫暖的節日以後再回學校，思鄉病才好，才開始喜歡學校的生活，欣賞大學的環境。

經過那次的經驗，我才徹底地理解思鄉病讓人有多麼的痛苦啊！

What was your first experience away from home? Were you happy? Did you feel homesick? If so, how did you get over it? Write a narrative with as much detail as you can include. Have it checked, write a final draft, and then share it with your classmates.

Encounter 3   Extension: Cultural mini-documentary

 View the cultural mini-documentary for this unit and complete the exercises below.

30.22 *In this video, five different speakers offer their views on cultural and environmental differences that may prove challenging for newcomers in China. A selection of edited quotes from the speakers is presented here. Fill in the letter from the list of topics (on page 212) that best matches the topic of each quote.*

Měiguó de liúxuéshēng zài Zhōngguó kěnéng dì yī ge fǎnyìng shì . . . xìnxīliàng hěn dà, dàochù dōu shì bú rènshi de zì, dàochù dōu shì bù míngbai de shìqing [zài] fāshēng.

美國的留學生在中國可能第一個反應是 ……信息量很大，到處都是不認識的字，到處都是不明白的事情[在]發生。／

美国的留学生在中国可能第一个反应是……信息量很大，到处都是不认识的字，到处都是不明白的事情[在]发生。

Qíshí, nǐ shì ge kèren, nǐ lái bùtóng rénjiā de guójiā, suǒyǐ bié bǎ nǐ zìjǐ de wénhuà de guīzé fàng zai zhèlǐ de rén de shēnshang.

其實，你是個客人，你來不同人家的國家，所以別把你自己的文化的規則放在這裡的人的身上。／

其实，你是个客人，你来不同人家的国家，所以别把你自己的文化的规则放在这里的人的身上。

Xiànzài Měiguó wénhuà, Zhōngguó wénhuà yǒu hěn duō gòngtóngdiǎn . . . liúxíng gē dōu tīng yíyàng de gē, dōu shàng yíyàng de wǎng, dōu kàn yíyàng de diànshì . . . Tāmen hěn yǒu gòngtóngdiǎn, bú xiàng yǐqián.

現在美國文化、中國文化有很多共同點……流行歌都聽一樣的歌，都上一樣的網，都看一樣的電視……他們很有共同點，不像以前。／

现在美国文化、中国文化有很多共同点……流行歌都听一样的歌，都上一样的网，都看一样的电视……他们很有共同点，不像以前。

Zuò péngyou huòzhě jiāoliú qǐlai, zǒng yǒuxiē bùtóng de . . . Měiguórén juéde yǒuxiē fāngmiàn "Nǐ bú yòng guānxīn wǒ . . . Nǐ kěyǐ bú yòng bǎ wǒ dāngzuò xiǎoháir" . . . Dàn zhè shì Zhōngguórén jiāoliú de yí ge xíguàn ma, tā jiù "Wǒ guānxīn nǐ, wǒ yào bǎohù nǐ, wǒ yào bāngzhù nǐ."

做朋友或者交流起來，總有些不同的……美國人覺得有些方面"你不用關心我，……你可以不用把我當做小孩兒" ……但這是中國人交流的一個習慣嘛，他就"我關心你，我要保護你，我要幫助你。"／

做朋友或者交流起来，总有些不同的……美国人觉得有些方面"你不用关心我，……你可以不用把我当做小孩儿" ……但这是中国人交流的一个习惯嘛，他就"我关心你，我要保护你，我要帮助你。"

Nǐ jiāo péngyou de shíhou . . . rúguǒ tāmen yào qǐng nǐ qù cānjiā rènhé huódòng, nǐ zuìhǎo hái shì tóngyì qù . . . Nǐ děi kǎolǜ dào tāmen yǐjing qǐngle nǐ . . . Rúguǒ nǐ bú qù de huà, tāmen huì diūliǎn, diūmiànzi.

你交朋友的時候……如果他們要請你去參加任何活動，你最好還是同意去……你得考慮到他們已經請了你……如果你不去的話，他們會丟臉，丟面子。／

你交朋友的时候……如果他们要请你去参加任何活动，你最好还是同意去……你得考虑到他们已经请了你……如果你不去的话，他们会丢脸，丢面子。

Shàngkè de shíhou . . . bú yào wèn yìxiē fēicháng yǒu tiǎozhànxìng de wèntí, ràng lǎoshī gǎndào bù shūfu. Zhè ge zuòwéi xuésheng shì zuì jìhuì de . . . Měiguó bù yíyàng . . . Hěn yǒu tiǎozhànxìng de [wèntí] lǎoshī gèng huānyíng . . . Zhè zhǒng jiàoxué de fāngfǎ shì bù yíyàng [de].

上課的時候……不要問一些非常有挑戰性的問題，讓老師感到不舒服。這個作為學生是最忌諱的……美國不一樣……很有挑戰性的[問題]老師更歡迎……這種教學的方法是不一樣[的]。／

上课的时候……不要问一些非常有挑战性的问题，让老师感到不舒服。这个作为学生是最忌讳的……美国不一样……很有挑战性的[问题]老师更欢迎……这种教学的方法是不一样[的]。

. . . Kěyǐ shuō shì bù píngděng. Zhōngguórén huì juéde yīnwèi tāmen shì Huáyì, huòzhě wàimiàn shang shì Zhōngguórén de yàngzi, suǒyǐ tāmen xīnlǐ yīnggāi shì gēn Zhōngguórén de xiǎngfǎ yíyàng.

……可以說是不平等。中國人會覺得因為他們是華裔，或者外面上是中國人的樣子，所以他們心理應該是跟中國人的想法一樣。／

……可以说是不平等。中国人会觉得因为他们是华裔，或者外面上是中国人的样子，所以他们心理应该是跟中国人的想法一样。

Yīnggāi dào nǎr, yòng Zhōngwén lái jiǎng, "suíyù'ér'ān," yìsi jiùshì shuō, nǐ jìshì dào zhèr lái, nǐ yīnggāi zài zhè ge shèhuì lǐ néng xúnzhǎo nǐ rènwéi shì zuì hǎo de yì xiē dōngxi, néng shǐ nǐ zài Zhōngguó de jīnglì shì yí ge fēicháng zhèngmiàn de, ér bú shì yí ge miǎnqiáng de huòzhě fùmiàn de.

應該到哪兒，用中文來講，"隨遇而安"，意思就是說，你既是到這兒來，你應該在這個社會裡能尋找你認為是最好的一些東西，能使你在中國的經歷是一個非常正面的，而不是一個勉強的或者負面的。／

应该到哪儿，用中文来讲，"随遇而安"，意思就是说，你既是到这儿来，你应该在这个社会里能寻找你认为是最好的一些东西，能使你在中国的经历是一个非常正面的，而不是一个勉强的或者负面的。

Topics:

a. *Remembering your role as a guest in the host culture*

b. *Different expectations that Chinese have of foreigners from different ethnic backgrounds*

c. *Staying focused on the positive and shaping your own positive experience*

d. *How global culture is softening cultural boundaries*

e. *An overwhelming flood of information and impressions that is hard to sort out and understand*

f. *The importance of face and respect and not giving offense*

g. *Conflict between the cultural values of caring for the needs of others and maintaining personal boundaries and independence*

h. *Behaviors expected of students in class, such as not challenging the teacher*

Recap

▶ Grammar

之, 而, 以, 所, 為／为: Little words that pack a big punch

Writing differs from speech in all languages. In general, we don't speak the same way as something like an article in the *New York Times* is written. This is especially true for Chinese, where for centuries the written language was composed in *wényán* 文言—"classical literary language"—which was very different from how people actually spoke. This all changed during the first decades of the 20th century with the start of the movement to replace 文言 with *báihuà* 白話／白话—"vernacular language"—which is the language used in speech. After decades of controversy, the movement succeeded. Writing in so-called *báihuàwén* 白話文／白话文 replaced *wényánwén* 文言文 as the standard written language.

However, old traditions die hard. Certain features of 文言 are still extensively preserved in the modern written language, with words, phrases, and sentence patterns taken from 文言 style. This is especially true in the so-called *sì zì chéngyǔ* 四字成語／四字成语—"four character phrases"—several of which you have seen here. Because the "old" language can convey thought compactly, economically, and with considerable force, writers (and speakers) of modern Chinese turn to it for an inexhaustible supply of "just the word I'm looking for." To become fluent in Chinese, both written and spoken, students need to appreciate and study the interplay between the "old" and the "new." Expressions drawn from the classical language regularly make use of the "little words" referred to in the title of this grammar recap: 之, 而, 以, 所, 為／为. Let's look in detail at these words that pack such a big punch.

Exercise 1: In the following paragraphs, locate and understand the "classical" phrase and how it contributes to the meaning and force of the sentence. Try to link the classical constituent characters with words you already know. Read each twice at least, with context firmly in mind, and then complete the exercise.

Glossary

不公平　bù gōngpíng　*unfair; unjust*

到處都亂七八糟的／到处都乱七八糟的　dàochù dōu luànqībāzāo de　*everywhere is a mess*

減少不公平／减少不公平　jiǎnshǎo bù gōngpíng　*reduce injustice*

守時／守时　shǒushí　*be on time*

勇敢地　yǒnggǎn de　*bravely*

"After the party is over"

晚會過後，大家都走了，回自己家去了。可是我家呢？用過的紙杯、紙盤、空瓶子、餐巾紙，甚麼的，大家都一丟了之，到處都亂七八糟的。我父母一定會很生氣。／

晚会过后，大家都走了，回自己家去了。可是我家呢？ 用过的纸杯、纸盘、空瓶子、餐巾纸，什么的，大家都一丢了之，到处都乱七八糟的。我父母一定会很生气。

"A world traveler"

他特別喜歡到外國去旅行，每次回來以後他都把自己的所見所聞講給朋友聽，讓大家覺得好像他們自己也去了外國旅行一樣。／

他特别喜欢到外国去旅行，每次回来以后他都把自己的所见所闻讲给朋友听，让大家觉得好像他们自己也去了外国旅行一样。

"If you see something, say something"

有些人看到不公平的事情，覺得少說為妙，但是更好的做法是勇敢地說出來，告訴警察或者更多的人。只有這樣做才能有助於減少不公平的事發生。／

有些人看到不公平的事情，觉得少说为妙，但是更好的做法是勇敢地说出来，告诉警察或者更多的人。只有这样做才能有助于减少不公平的事发生。

"Timeliness is golden"

我的朋友常常遲到。別人說他的時候，他還不以為然，覺得遲到幾分鐘真的不算甚麼。可是就我而言，守時是非常重要的，因為讓別人等就是在浪費別人的時間，而浪費時間就是浪費生命。／

我的朋友常常迟到。别人说他的时候，他还不以为然，觉得迟到几分钟真的不算什么。可是就我而言，守时是非常重要的，因为让别人等就是在浪费别人的时间，而浪费时间就是浪费生命。

Exercise 2: 请把中文跟英文對上。／请把中文跟英文对上。

_____ a. yì diū liǎo zhī 一丢了之

_____ b. suǒ jiàn suǒ wén 所見所聞／所见所闻

_____ c. shǎo shuō wéi miào 少說為妙／少说为妙

_____ d. bùyǐwéirán 不以為然／不以为然

_____ e. jiù wǒ ér yán 就我而言

_____ f. ér 而

1. *as for me*
2. *tossed it and was done with it*
3. *everything he saw and heard*
4. *disagreed; didn't think that was so*
5. *the less said the better*
6. *and*

Exercise 3: Fill in the blanks with words from the word bank. Some words will be used more than once. 請用英文填空。／请用英文填空。

and	to be	this/it	all that is/was	take this

a. 一丢了之　one + toss + done with + _____

b. 所見所聞／所见所闻　_____ + seen + _____ heard

c. 少説為妙／少说为妙　less + speak + _____ fine

d. 不以為然／不以为然　not + _____ + _____ + so

e. 就我而言　focus on + me + _____ + speak

f. 而　_____

Vocabulary

Please refer to page R-2 for a list of grammatical abbreviations used throughout this book.

bāoguǒ　包裹　parcel; package; bundle　N

bāor　包兒／包儿　bag; sack; parcel　N

bù zěnme　不怎麼／不怎么　not very/ particularly　A

bùzhì　佈置／布置　decorate; arrange; fix up　V

chádào　茶道　tea ceremony; the Way of tea　N

chángtú　長途／长途　(short for) long-distance phone call　N

dàbùfen　大部份／大部分　major part　N

dānwèi　單位／单位　unit (in an organization)　N

díquè　的確／的确　for sure; certainly; surely　A

fánnǎo　煩惱／烦恼　troubled; vexed; worried　SV

fāxiàn　發現／发现　discover; find　V

fēnxiǎng　分享　share (joy, experience, etc.); partake of　V

gānbēi　乾杯／干杯　Cheers! Bottoms up!　IE

gǎnjī　感激　feel grateful/indebted　V

gē　擱／搁　put/place (aside)　V

gōngzī　工資／工资　wages; salary; pay　N

gōutōng　溝通／沟通　link up; communicate　V

gūdú　孤獨／孤独　lonely; lonesome　SV

gǔlì　鼓勵／鼓励　encourage; urge　V/N

guòchéng　過程／过程　course; process　N

guòláirén　過來人／过来人　someone who has had same experience　N

hǎoshòu　好受　feeling good　SV

huóyuè　活躍／活跃　active; dynamic; lively　SV

jiāo péngyou　交朋友　make friends with; be friends with　VO

jiēduàn　階段／阶段　stage; phase　N

jiéjiāo　結交／结交　make friends with; befriend　V

jìmò　寂寞　lonely; lonesome　SV

jǐn jiēzhe　緊接著／紧接着　immediately; right after　A

jǐnguǎn　儘管／尽管　feel free to; don't hesitate to　A

jīngyà　驚訝／惊讶　amazed; astounded　SV

jīngyàn　經驗／经验　experience; go through　V/N

kōng(kōng) dàngdàng　空（空）蕩蕩／空（空）荡荡　absolutely empty; deserted　VP

kùnnán　困難／困难　difficulty; problem　N

liǎ　倆／俩　two (informal; a fusion of liǎng and ge)　PR

liángxìng xúnhuán 良性循環／良性循环 a virtuous circle *(opposite of vicious circle)* N

luàn 亂／乱 messy; in disorder SV

lǚyóu 旅遊／旅游 travel for pleasure; tour; tourism V/N

niáng 娘 ma; mom; mother N

pào 泡 steep; soak; brew V

pīpíng 批評／批评 criticize; criticism V/N

qī chá 沏茶 brew/make/infuse tea VO

qīnrén 親人／亲人 close relatives; those dear to you N

shìyìng 適應／适应 get used to; get accustomed to V

shúxī 熟悉 know *(somebody or something)* very well V/SV

sīniàn 思念 miss; think of; long for V

sīwéi 思維／思维 thought; thinking N

sīxiāng bìng 思鄉病／思乡病 homesickness; nostalgia N

suíshí 隨時／随时 at any time; at all times; whenever A

tiān máfan 添麻煩／添麻烦 be a bother/trouble *(to somebody)* VP

tíqǐ 提起 bring up; mention; speak of RV

wǎngwǎng 往往 often; frequently; more often than not A

wèi 為／为 for; in the interests of PREP

wèidao 味道 taste; flavor N

wēnxīn 溫馨 warm and comfortable SV

xiāng 香 fragrant; appetizing; savory V

xiǎngjiā 想家 be homesick VO/SV

xiǎngniàn 想念 miss someone or something V

xiànxiàng 現象／现象 phenomenon; appearance N

xīngfèn 興奮／兴奋 excited SV

xìngfú 幸福 happiness N; fortunate SV

xīnqíng 心情 mood; state/frame of mind N

yāoqǐng 邀請／邀请 invitation N

yāoqiú 要求 demand; request; require; requirement V/N

yāyì 壓抑／压抑 depressing; feel down SV

yǐ chá dài jiǔ 以茶代酒 use tea as a replacement for alcohol PH

yóufèi 郵費／邮费 postage N

yóujú 郵局／邮局 post office N

yóupiào 郵票／邮票 postage stamp N

yóuqíshì 尤其是 especially VP

yuǎnlí 遠離／远离 be far away from V

yùdào 遇到 encounter; meet; come across; run into V

yuē 約／约 invite; make an appointment; arrange V

zhěng bǎn 整版 a full page; an entire sheet N

zhōngxīn 中心 center; heart; hub; focus N

zhuānjiā 專家／专家 expert; specialist N

zhùfú 祝福 wish happiness to/for V

zhùyuàn 祝願／祝愿 wish; in hopes that V

▶ Checklist of "can do" statements

After completing this unit, you should be able to perform each of the following tasks:

Listening and speaking

☐ Describe your arrival in a new place.

☐ Describe your feelings about being in an unfamiliar place.

☐ Talk about the steps you might take to function in an unfamiliar place.

Reading and writing

☐ Decipher some notes related to settling in.

☐ Read a short story about settling in, and write one of your own.

Understanding culture

☐ Make several accurate statements about what sorts of things might be challenging to newcomers in China, according to Chinese people and expatriates.

REFERENCE

Glossaries

The Chinese-English and English-Chinese glossaries list the words introduced in **Encounters** Book 3. Look upon this section as a sort of mini-dictionary. In addition, you may wish to refer to the glossary of measure words starting on page R-25. Traditional characters for each entry are given first, followed by simplified characters. The number refers to the unit in which the word first appears.

The following grammatical abbreviations are used throughout the glossaries:

A	adverb	PL	phonetic loan
ATTR	attributive	PR	pronoun
AV	auxiliary verb	PREF	prefix
BF	bound form	PREP	preposition
C	conjunction	PW	place word
CV	coverb	QW	question word
EV	equative verb	RF	reduplicated form
I	interjection	RV	resultative verb
IE	idiomatic expression	S	suffix
M	measure word	SP	specifier
N	noun	SV	stative verb
NP	noun phrase	TW	time word
NU	number	V	verb
P	particle	VO	verb object
PH	phrase	VP	verbal phrase

Chinese-English Glossary

A

. . . a 啊 P; **Chén Fēng a, tā búcuò.** 陳峰啊，他不錯。／陈峰啊，他不错。 Oh, Chen Feng, he's fine. 21

Āi 哎 Um/Hey! *(expresses surprise, dissatisfaction; attracts attention)* I, 21

āiyō 哎喲／哎哟 *(of surprise, pain)* I, 23

àn 按 press down; push V, 23

ànmó 按摩 massage V/N, 24

ànzhào 按照 according to; on the basis of C, 25

Àodàlìyà 澳大利亞／澳大利亚 Australia PW, 21

āsīpǐlín 阿司匹林 aspirin N, 22

B

bājiǎo 八角 (star) anise N, 27

bǎn 版 version, type, kind *(literally, "edition of book, newspaper")* N, 25

bàng 棒 good; fine; excellent SV; **Tài bàng le! Zhēn bàng a!** 太棒了！真棒啊！ That's great! 21

bànlǐ 辦理／办理 handle; set up V, 23

bào 抱 hold; carry in one's arms V, 29

bào yí ge bān 報一個班／报一个班 register for a class VP, 21

bǎobèi(r) 寶貝(兒)／宝贝(儿) darling N, 24

bàodá 報答／报答 repay; requite V, 29

bāoguǒ 包裹 parcel; package; bundle N, 30

bǎohù 保護／保护 protect; safeguard V, 29

bàomíng 報名／报名 sign up VO, 21

bāor 包兒／包儿 bag; sack; parcel N, 30

bèi 被 by *(someone or some agent)* [marker of passive voice; see Grammar Bits, p. 8] P, 21

bèi 倍 times; -fold M, 26

bèi 備／备 prepare; get (something) ready V, 26

běnrén 本人 oneself; in person N, 23

biānchǎo 煸炒 stir fry V, 27

biàndòng 變動／变动 change; transform V/N, 23

biǎo 表 chart; form; table; schedule N; **gōngkèbiǎo** 功課表／功课表 homework schedule, 23

biǎoyǎn 表演 perform; act; play V; performance; exhibition N, 28

biāozhì 標誌／标志 sign; mark; brand N, 26

bìnglì(běn) 病歷(本)／病历(本) medical record; case history N, 22

bìngrén 病人 patient N, 22

bǐrú shuō 比如說／比如说 for example/instance VP, 28

bìyào 必要 need N; necessary; indispensable SV, 22

bù zěnme 不怎麼／不怎么 not very/particularly A, 30

bú zhìyú 不至於／不至于 not necessarily IE, 26

bùdé bù 不得不 cannot but; have to VP, 28

bùzhì 佈置／布置 decorate; arrange; fix up V, 30

C

cái 才 just *(indicates emphatic tone)* A, 21

càipǔ 菜譜／菜谱 recipe; menu N, 27

cèyàn 測驗／测验 test; examination N; **xiǎo cèyàn** 小測驗／小测验 quiz, 22

chā 插 insert; stick into V, 23

chá 查 check; investigate; look up V; **chá zìdiǎn** 查字典 look it up in a dictionary, 23

chádào 茶道 tea ceremony; the Way of Tea N, 30

chǎng 場／场 *(for games, performances, etc.)* M, 23

chángdào 腸道／肠道 intestines N, 22

chángmìngbǎisuì 長命百歲／长命百岁 bless you *(said when someone sneezes)* IE, 22

chángtú 長途／长途 *(short for)* long-distance phone call N, 30

chǎo 炒 stir fry; sauté V, 27

chǎocài 炒菜 make a dish VO, 29

chǎojià 吵架 argue; quarrel; have a spat VO, 29

chāoshì 超市 supermarket N, 26

cháshì 茶室 tearoom N, 21

chéngshòu 承受 bear; endure V, 25

chénpí 陳皮／陈皮 dried tangerine/orange peel N, 27

chōng 衝／冲 rush; charge; dash V, 29

chuánméi 傳媒／传媒 communication media N, 21

chuānzhuó 穿著／穿着 apparel; dress; attire N, 26

chūchāi 出差 be away on a business trip VO, 21

chuīgān 吹乾／吹干 blow-dry V, 24

chūshì 出示 produce; show V, 23

chūxiàn 出現／出现 appear; arise; emerge V, 22

chúyì 廚藝／厨艺 art of cooking N, 21

chúyìbān|kè 廚藝班|課／厨艺班|课 cooking class N, 21

cōng 蔥／葱 green onion; scallion N, 27

cónglái 從來／从来 + *negative* never A, 29

cōngming 聰明／聪明 smart SV, 28

cù 醋 vinegar N, 27

cún 存 save; deposit V, 23

cúnkuǎn, cúnqián 存款, 存錢／存钱 deposit money VO, 23

D

dàbùfen 大部份／大部分 major part   N, 30

dàdūshì 大都市 metropolis   N, 21

dǎ pēntì 打噴嚏／打喷嚏 sneeze   VO, 22

dà shùn 大順／大顺 auspicious *(literally, "greatly favorable")*   IE, 25

dàbiàn 大便 defecate   V; feces   N, 22

dādàng 搭檔／搭档 partner up *(with)*; team up *(with)* VP; partner   N, 21

dǎdòng 打動／打动 move emotionally   RV, 28

dài 帶／带 carry something   V; **dài xīnghào(r) de zì** 帶星號(兒)的字／带星号(儿)的字 asterisked characters, 23

dài huài 帶壞／带坏 lead astray; corrupt   RV, 25

dàifu 大夫 doctor; physician   N, 22

dàjiē 大街 main street; avenue   N, 26

dàn 淡 light; pale *(in color)*   SV, 26

dāndān 單單／单单 only; alone   A, 24

dānwèi 單位／单位 unit *(in an organization)*   N, 30

dānxīn 擔心／担心 worry; feel anxious   SV/V/VO, 26

dānzi 單子／单子 list; bill; form   N, 23

dào 道 *(for course or dish of food)*   M, 27

dǎoyǎn 導演／导演 director   N; direct *(a film, play, etc.)*   V, 28

dàozhàng 到賬／到账 reach / been posted to *(my/the)* account   VO, 23

dàyuē 大約／大约 about; around; approximately   A, 27

... de huà ......的話／......的话 if ...   C, 24

dé lìng 得令 receive / take an order   VO, 23

děng ... de shíhou 等......的時候／等......的时候 when   PH, 29

déyì 得意 be proud of oneself; smug   VO, 26

dì 遞／递 hand to/over; pass to   V, 24

diàn qìng 店慶／店庆 anniversary of (our) store   N, 24

diànchí 電池／电池 (electric) battery   N, 25

diànfěn 澱粉／淀粉 starch   N, 27

diǎnjīlǜ 點擊率／点击率 click/strike rate *(on a keyboard or other device)*   N, 28

diànzǐ chǎnpǐn 電子產品／电子产品 electronic products   N, 26

dīng 盯 gaze at; stare at   V, 29

dīngr 丁兒／丁儿 cube   N, 27

díquè 的確／的确 for sure; certainly; surely   A, 30

dìxià 地下 underground; basement   N, 26

dìzhèn 地震 earthquake   N, 28

dòngbudòng 動不動／动不动 *(usually followed by* **jiù** 就*, indicating an act or situation occurring frequently and often unwished for)* frequently; easily; at every turn; apt to   A, 26

dù 度 *(for angles; degrees; temperature)*   M, 27

duàn 段 sections; strips   N, 27

duìhuàn 兌換／兑换 exchange   V, 23

dúshēng zǐnǚ 獨生子女／独生子女 only child   N, 29

dùzi 肚子 stomach; belly   N, 22

E

éi 誒／诶 *(expressing surprise, realization)*   I, 26

èn 摁 press with hand or fingertip   V, 22

ěxīn 噁心／恶心 feel nauseated; feel like vomiting; be sick   VO, 22

F

fā duǎnxìn 發短信／发短信 send a text message   VP, 21

fán 煩／烦 vexed; irritated; annoyed   SV, 29

fàngrù 放入 put into   VP, 27

fàngsōng 放鬆／放松 relax   V, 24

fàngxīn 放心 feel relieved; set one's mind to rest   RV, 22

fǎngzhì 仿製／仿制 copy; imitate   V, 25

fǎnmiàn 反面 negative side; reverse/wrong side   N, 28

fánnǎo 煩惱／烦恼 troubled; vexed; worried   SV, 30

fánrén 煩人／烦人 annoy   VO; annoying; vexing; troubling   SV, 29

fànwéi 範圍／范围 scope; extent; range; limits   N, 22

fǎnzhèng 反正 in any case; anyway; anyhow   A, 25

fāshāo 發燒／发烧 have a fever   VO, 22

fāxiàn 發現／发现 discover; find   V, 30

fàzhì 髮質／发质 hair quality/texture   N, 24

fèi 費／费 fee; charge   N; **yǎnchūfèi** 演出費／演出费 performance fee, 23

fèiyòng 費用／费用 fee; charge   N, 23

fēngshēngshuǐqǐ 風生水起／风生水起 burgeoning; successful *(said of an enterprise)*   IE, 21

fēnxiǎng 分享 share *(joy, experience, etc.)*; partake of   V, 30

fūliǎn 敷臉／敷脸 facial treatment; masque   N, 24

fúwù 服務／服务 service(s)   N; **fúwùyuán** 服務員／服务员 attendant; **fúwùtái** 服務台／服务台 service counter, 23

fùxí 複習／复习 review *(what has been learned)*   V, 22

fùxiè 腹瀉／腹泻 diarrhea   N, 22

fùyìn 複印／复印 photocopy; copy; duplicate   V, 23

fúzhuāng 服裝／服装 clothing   N, 26

G

gǎi zhǔyi 改主意 change one's mind   VO, 25

gǎiháng 改行 change to a new profession   VO, 21

gān 乾／干 dry   SV, 24

gǎn 感 feeling BF; **rèntónggǎn** 認同感／认同感 feeling/sense of identification, 28

gānbēi 乾杯／干杯 Cheers! Bottoms up! IE, 30

gānghǎo 剛好／刚好 just; exactly A, 25

gǎnjī 感激 feel grateful/indebted V, 30

gǎnjǐn 趕緊／赶紧 hurriedly; losing no time A, 21

gānjìng 乾淨／干净 clean; neat; tidy SV, 29

gǎnqíng 感情 feeling; emotion; sentiment N, 29

gǎnrǎn 感染 infect V; infection N, 22

gānzào 乾燥／干燥 dry; arid SV, 24

gāodàng 高檔／高档 top-quality; superior grade SV, 26

gē 擱／搁 put/place (aside) V, 30

gēbo 胳膊 arm N, 22

gēnjù 根據／根据 according to; on the basis of C; basis; grounds N, 24

gèxìng 個性／个性 individual character; personality N, 28

gōngbǎo jīdīng 宮保雞丁／宫保鸡丁 spicy diced chicken; gongbao chicken N, 27

gōngběn(r)fèi 工本(兒)費／工本(儿)費 production/ activation fee N, 23

gōngnéng 功能 function N, 23

gōngsī 公司 company; corporation N, 21

gōngyì 公益 public good; welfare; public service N, 28

gōngzī 工資／工资 wages; salary; pay N, 30

gōngzuò rìlì 工作日曆／工作日历 work schedule N, 21

gōutōng 溝通／沟通 link up; communicate V, 30

gòuwù 購物／购物 go shopping VO; shopping N, 27

guàhào 掛號／挂号 check in; register (to see a doctor) VO, 22

guàibude 怪不得 No wonder!; So that's why! RV, 21

guǎn 管 control; manage; run; have charge of V, 29

guàng 逛 stroll; ramble; roam V, 26

guǎnggào 廣告／广告 advertisement N, 21

guānxīn 關心／关心 be concerned about; worry about V, 22

guānzhào 關照／关照 look after V, 22

guānzhòng 觀眾／观众 spectator; audience N, 28

gūdú 孤獨／孤独 lonely; lonesome SV, 30

guǐ 鬼 ghost N, 23

guīnü 閨女／闺女 daughter (unmarried) N, 23

guìpí 桂皮 Chinese cinnamon N, 27

gūjì 估計／估计 estimate; appraise; looks as though V, 22

gǔlì 鼓勵／鼓励 encourage; urge V/N, 30

guóchǎn 國產／国产 product of a country; domestic product N, 25

guòchéng 過程／过程 course; process N, 30

guójì 國際／国际 international ATTR, 21

guòláirén 過來人／过来人 someone who has had the same experience N, 30

guòmǐn 過敏／过敏 have an allergy V; allergy N, 22

H

hái hǎo 還好／还好 not bad; passable VP, 29

hánjià 寒假 winter vacation N, 21

hǎohāo 好好 carefully A, 29

hǎohāo liáoliao 好好聊聊 have a good chat/talk VP, 21

hǎojiǔbújiàn 好久不見／好久不见 Long time no see! IE, 21

hǎoshòu 好受 feeling good SV, 30

háoyóu 蠔油／蚝油 oyster sauce N, 27

hǎoxiàng 好像 seems; seems as if A, 21

héduì 核對／核对 check figures/sums; proof RV, 23

hēitǐ zì 黑體字／黑体字 (printing) boldfaced letters N, 23

héshì 合適／合适 suitable; appropriate SV, 22

hézuò 合作 cooperate; work together; collaborate V, 21

huā 花 spend; expend V, 26

huāfěn 花粉 pollen N, 22

huājiāo 花椒 Sichuan peppers; peppercorns N, 27

huánggua 黃瓜 cucumber N, 27

huánjìng 環境／环境 environment; surroundings N, 21

huāshēngmǐ 花生米 shelled peanut N, 27

huāshēngyóu 花生油 peanut oil N, 27

huàyàn 化驗／化验 make a lab test V, 22

huí 回 (for times, occurrences) M, 23

húluóbo 胡蘿蔔／胡萝卜 carrots N, 27

huòbì 貨幣／货币 currency N, 23

huódòng 活動／活动 activity; program N, 24

huólì 活力 vigor; vitality; energy N, 28

huòwù 貨物／货物 goods; commodities; merchandise N, 26

huóyuè 活躍／活跃 active; dynamic; lively SV, 30

hútòng 胡同 lane; alley N, 21

hùtóu 戶頭／户头 account N, 23

hùzhào 護照／护照 passport N, 23

J

jí 急 anxious; worried SV, 28

jiā 加 plus V, 23

jiǎ 假 false; phony; fake; artificial SV, 25

jiā dào yèxià 夾到腋下／夹到腋下 place something in the armpit VP, 22

jiāchángcài 家常菜 homestyle cooking/food N, 21

jiàn 鍵／键 button; key (of a piano, computer, etc.) N, 23

jiǎn tóufa 剪頭髮／剪头发 get a haircut VO, 24

jiǎnchá 檢查／检查 inspect; examine V, 22

jiāng 薑／姜 ginger N, 27

jiǎngjiu 講究／讲究 be particular/fussy about SV, 26

jiǎngkè 講課／讲课 teach; lecture VO, 21

jiāngshī 殭屍／僵尸 zombie N, 23

jiǎngxuéjīn 獎學金／奖学金 scholarship; stipend N, 23

jiàngyóu 醬油／酱油　soy sauce　N, 27

jiànmiàn 見面／见面　meet each other　VO, 21

jiāo péngyou 交朋友　make friends with; be friends with　VO, 30

jiāoyì 交易　transaction; deal　N, 23

jiārù 加入　add; mix; put in　VP, 27

jiàwèi 價位／价位　price range　N, 25

jiāxiāng 家鄉／家乡　hometown; native place　N, 28

jìdé 記得／记得　remember　V, 22

jié 節／节　(for classes measured in periods)　M, 22

jiēduàn 階段／阶段　stage; phase　N, 30

jiēguòlai 接過來／接过来　welcome over to us; receive　RV, 29

jiéjiāo 結交／结交　make friends with; befriend　V, 30

jièshào 介紹／介绍　introduction/guide (to service, contents, etc.)　N, 24

jiéshù 結束／结束　end; conclude; close　V, 24

jiēzhe 接著／接着　continue to; keep on　VP, 28

jílì 吉利　lucky; fortuitous; auspicious　SV; good luck　N, 25

jìmò 寂寞　lonely; lonesome　SV, 30

jǐn jiēzhe 緊接著／紧接着　immediately; right after　A, 30

jīn'é 金額／金额　amount/sum of money　N, 23

jīngcháng 經常／经常　frequently; constantly; regularly; often　A, 21

jīngdiǎn 經典／经典　classic; "best of the lot"　ATTR, 25

jīngjìrén 經紀人／经纪人　broker; agent; middleman　N, 23

jīnglì 經歷／经历　experience　N; go through; experience; undergo　V, 28

jǐnguǎn 儘管／尽管　feel free to; don't hesitate to　A, 30

jīngyà 驚訝／惊讶　amazed; astounded　SV, 30

jīngyàn 經驗／经验　experience; go through　V/N, 30

jìnxíng 進行／进行　carry out; conduct　V, 22

jīnzhēngū 金針菇／金针菇　enoki mushrooms　N, 27

jīpí 雞皮／鸡皮　chicken skin　N, 27

jīròu 雞肉／鸡肉　chicken meat　N, 27

jītuǐ ròu 雞腿肉／鸡腿肉　chicken leg (meat)　N, 27

jiǔdiàn 酒店　hotel　N, 26

jīxiōng ròu 雞胸肉／鸡胸肉　chicken breast (meat)　N, 27

jīzi 機子／机子　small machine　N, 25

jù 句　(sentence)　M; **yí jù huà** 一句話／一句话　a sentence; **zhèi jù huà** 這句話／这句话　this sentence; **jùzi** 句子　sentence, 23

juésè 角色　role; part　N, 28

juéwàng 絕望／绝望　lose/give up hope; despair　V, 29

jù(ju) 聚(聚)　get together (for a chat, meeting, etc.)　V, 21

jùnnán měinǚ 俊男美女　handsome man and beautiful woman　N, 26

K

kǎ 卡　card　N, 23

kāi 開／开　open (a course, a business)　V, 21

kāi kǎ 開卡／开卡　open a card (account) (for ATM, etc.)　VO, 23

kāiyào 開藥／开药　prescribe; write out a prescription　VO, 22

kàn qǐlai 看起來／看起来　it seems; it appears; it looks as if　VP, 29

kànbìng 看病　see a doctor; see a patient　VO, 22

kàngshēngsù 抗生素　antibiotic　N, 22

kàngshǐ 抗使　stands up to use; wears well; long-lasting　VO, 25

kǎochá 考察　check over; examine　V, 22

kǎolǜ 考慮／考虑　to consider; think about; think over　V, 24

kě 可　actually; remarkably　A, 26

kě'ài 可愛／可爱　loveable; lovely; cute　SV, 26

kěbù zěnmeyàng 可不怎麼樣／可不怎么样　nothing to speak of; not very good　IE, 25

kěndìng 肯定　definitely; surely; for sure　A, 25

kěnqiú 懇求／恳求　earnestly plead for; implore; entreat　V, 29

kěpà 可怕　scary　SV, 23

kěshì 可是　be indeed　C, 26

késòu 咳嗽　cough　V, 22

kǒngbù 恐怖　fearful; horrible　SV, 23

kōng(kōng) dàngdàng 空（空）蕩蕩／空（空）荡荡　absolutely empty; deserted　VP, 30

kòuchú 扣除　deduct　RV, 23

kǒudàir 口袋兒／口袋儿　pocket　N, 26

kù 酷　"cool"　PL /SV, 28

kuǎn 款　type; style　N, 25

kuǎnxíng 款型　style; pattern; design　N, 25

kùnnán 困難／困难　difficulty; problem　N, 30

kùzi 褲子／裤子　pants; trousers　N, 26

L

lā dùzi 拉肚子　suffer from diarrhea; have loose bowels　VO, 22

láizì 來自／来自　come/originate/stem from　VP, 27

làjiāo 辣椒　hot pepper; chili　N, 27

làngfèi 浪費／浪费　waste; squander　V, 29

làngmàn 浪漫　romantic　SV, 29

lǎochōu 老抽　thick soy sauce　N, 27

lǎogōng 老公　husband　N, 26

liǎ 倆／俩　two (informal; a fusion of liǎng and ge)　PR, 30

liáng 量　measure　V, 22

liángxìng xúnhuán 良性循環／良性循环　virtuous circle (opposite of vicious circle)　N, 30

liǎnpǔ 臉譜／脸谱　types of theatrical makeup; mask　N, 23

liàojiǔ 料酒　cooking wine　N, 27

lìdù 力度　strength; pressure; intensity　N, 24

límǐ 厘米　centimeter　M, 27

língshí 零食　snacks　N, 26

lǐpǐn 禮品／礼品　gifts　N, 26

liú 留　(let) grow　V, 24

liú bítì   流鼻涕   have a runny nose   VO, 22

liúliàng   流量   storage capacity   N, 25

liúxià   留下   leave (something for someone)   RV, 21

liúxuéshēng   留學生／留学生   foreign student; student studying abroad   N, 22

luàn   亂／乱   messy; in disorder   SV, 30

lǚyóu   旅遊／旅游   travel for pleasure; tour; tourism   V/N, 30

M

. . . ma!   嘛   (indicates that something speaks for itself)   P; **Nǐ de shēngyi búcuò ma!**   你的生意不錯嘛！／你的生意不错嘛！   Wow, your business sure is good!   21

máfan nǐ   麻煩你／麻烦你   May I trouble you to . . . ?   Will you please . . . ?   IE, 21

mǎi yī zèng yī   買一贈一／买一赠一   buy one, get one free   N, 24

máyóu   麻油   sesame oil   N, 27

měibái   美白   skin toning   N, 24

Měiguó Huárén   美國華人／美国华人   American-born Chinese person   N, 21

měinǚ   美女   beautiful woman; beauty   N, 28

měiróng   美容   improve one's looks   VO; cosmetology   N, 24

měiyuàn   美院   (= **měishù xuéyuàn** 美術學院／美术学院); school of arts   N, 26

miànduì   面對／面对   face; confront   V, 28

miànbù hùlǐ   面部護理／面部护理   facial conditioning; skin protection   N, 24

miǎnfèi   免費／免费   be free of charge   VO, 24

miànshì   面試／面试   interview; audition   VO/N, 26

mìmǎ(r)   密碼(兒)／密码(儿)   secret code; password   N, 23

mǐngǎn   敏感   sensitive; susceptible; allergic   SV, 23

mìnglìng   命令   order; command   V/N, 24

míngpiàn   名片   business card   N, 21

míxìn   迷信   superstition   N; have blind faith in   V, 25

mùjiàng   木匠   carpenter   N, 26

mùlù   目錄／目录   list; table of contents; menu of services   N, 24

mǔyīng   母嬰／母婴   mother and baby   N, 26

N

ná yào   拿藥／拿药   fill a prescription   VO, 22

nánguā dēng   南瓜燈／南瓜灯   jack-o'-lantern   N, 23

nánzhuāng   男裝／男装   men's clothing   N, 26

nánzǐhàn   男子漢／男子汉   a real man (in the macho sense)   N, 24

nào dùzi   鬧肚子／闹肚子   have diarrhea   VO, 22

náshǒu   拿手   be good at doing something   SV, 21

nèikē   内科   internal medicine   N; **wàikē**   外科   surgical department, 22

nèiróng   内容   content; essence   N, 22

nénggàn   能幹／能干   capable; competent   SV, 23

ng   嗯   (indicates hesitation)   I, 21

Nǐ zài gànma?   你在幹嘛？／你在干吗？   What are you doing?   PH, 29

niánfèi   年費／年费   annual fee/charge   N, 23

niáng   娘   ma; mom; mother   N, 30

nòng   弄   make; do; handle   V, 22

nuó   喏   look; see; there (dialect) (used to call attention to something)   I, 26

nǚzhuāng   女裝／女装   women's clothing   N, 26

O

Ò, duì le   哦，對了／哦，对了   Oh, that reminds me (expresses realization)   I, 21

P

pāi   拍   take (a picture); shoot (a film)   V, 28

páichú   排除   eliminate   RV, 22

pāizhào   拍照   take (a picture); shoot (a film)   VO, 25

pào   泡   steep; soak; brew   V, 30

péi   陪   accompany; keep somebody company   V, 24

péibàn   陪伴   keep company with; spend time with; accompany   V, 29

pèitào   配套   form a set   VO, 25

pí   皮   skin   N, 27

piàn   騙／骗   deceive; fool   V, 24

piàoliang   漂亮   pretty   SV, 28

piàoyǒu   票友   amateur performer   N, 23

pífū   皮膚／皮肤   skin   N, 24

píngmù   屏幕   screen   N, 25

píngpíng   平平   average; mediocre; so-so   RF, 28

pǐnpái   品牌   trademark; brand   N, 25

pǐnzhì   品質／品质   quality   N, 26

pīpíng   批評／批评   criticize; criticism   V/N, 30

píqi hǎo   脾氣好／脾气好   good-tempered   SV, 28

píqi huài   脾氣壞／脾气坏   bad-tempered   SV, 28

Q

qī chá   沏茶   brew/make/infuse tea   VO, 30

qiángzhì   強制   force; compel; coerce   V, 25

qiānxū   謙虛／谦虚   modest; unassuming   SV, 26

qiānzì, qiānmíng   簽字／签字, 簽名／签名   sign one's name; signature   VO/N, 23

qiáo   瞧   look at   V, 26

qiēchéng   切成   cut into pieces; slice; dice   RV, 27

qīn'ài de   親愛的／亲爱的   dear; beloved   IE, 24

qīng   輕／轻   gentle; light; soft   SV, 24

qīngchūndòu   青春痘   acne; pimple   N, 28

qíngkuàng   情況／情况   situation; condition; state of affairs   N, 22

qīngwēi 輕微／轻微 trivial; slight; mild SV, 22
qīnrén 親人／亲人 close relatives; those dear to you N, 30
qíquán 齊全／齐全 complete; all in readiness SV, 26
qíshí 其實／其实 in fact; as a matter of fact; actually A, 21
qítā 其他 others; the rest PR, 27
qíyú 其餘／其余 others; the rest PR, 27
qǔ 取 get; take; obtain V, 23
qūbié 區別／区别 difference; distinction N; distinguish; differentiate V, 26
qùdiào 去掉 get rid of RV, 27
quē 缺 be short of; lack V, 24
quèdìng 確定／确定 be sure; confirm V, 23
quèrèn 確認／确认 confirm; identify with certainty V, 21
qūjìngtōngyōu 曲徑通幽／曲径通幽 a winding path leading to a secluded spot IE, 21
qǔkuǎn, qǔqián 取款, 取錢／取钱 withdraw money VO, 23
qúnzi 裙子 skirt N, 26

R

rǎnfà 染髮／染发 dye/tint/color the hair VO, 24
ràng 讓／让 let; allow CV, 23
rěn 忍 bear; endure V, 24
rén hǎo 人好 kind; nice (person) SV, 28
rēng 扔 throw away; discard; throw; toss V, 23
rènhé 任何 any; whatever ATTR, 27
rénjiā 人家 (somebody) else; people (in general) PR, 26
rèntóng 認同／认同 identify V; identification N, 28
rénwù 人物 character; personage; character in literature N, 28
rényuán 人員／人员 staff N, 25
rèqíng 熱情／热情 enthusiastic; passionate SV, 28
rìyòngpǐn 日用品 daily-use items N, 26
róngqì 容器 container N, 27
ròu 肉 meat N, 27
ruǎn 軟／软 soft (to the touch); yielding SV, 24
rùnfū 潤膚／润肤 skin toning N, 24

S

sè-xiāng-wèi jùquán 色香味俱全 look, smell, and taste great IE, 27
shǎguā 傻瓜 fool N, 24
shàng 上＋[number] up to (preceding numbers) BF;
　shàngwàn 上萬／上万 more than ten thousand, 26
shāngchǎng 商場／商场 market; bazaar; mall N, 26
shāngdiàn 商店 shop; store N, 26
shāngshà 商廈／商厦 high-rise commercial building N, 26
shàngwǎng 上網／上网 go online; be on the Internet VO, 25

shànliáng 善良 kindhearted; decent SV, 28
shānzhài 山寨 phony; fake; knockoff (literally, "mountain fastness") N, 25
shāo 燒／烧 heat; cook V, 27; burn V, 29
shāo děng yíxià 稍等一下 just a moment; a moment, please VP, 21
shāowēi 稍微 slightly; a bit A, 25
shēn 身 (for an outfit, suit of clothing) M, 26
shēncéng qīngjié 深層清潔／深层清洁 deep (skin) cleansing N, 24
shēnfènzhèng 身份證／身份证 personal ID N, 23
shēngāo 身高 height (of a person) N, 28
shēngchōu 生抽 thin soy sauce N, 27
shēnghuó jīnglì 生活經歷／生活经历 life experience N, 28
shēngjiāng 生薑／生姜 fresh ginger N, 27
shēngyi 生意 business; trade N, 21
shēnqǐng biǎo 申請表／申请表 application form N, 23
shèzhì 設置／设置 (computers) configure; set up V, 23
shīfu 師傅／师傅 (general term of address or title for service workers) N, 24
shìhé X yòng 適合X用／适合X用 appropriate/good for X IE, 25
shíjiānbiǎo 時間表／时间表 schedule; timetable N, 21
shípǐn 食品 foods N, 26
shìpín 視頻／视频 video N, 25
shísān xiāng 十三香 13-spice (powder) N, 27
shíxí 實習／实习 work as an intern V, 21
shìxì 試戲／试戏 audition VO, 28
shìyìng 適應／适应 get used to; get accustomed to V, 30
shǐyòng 使用 use; utilize; employ V, 24
shìzhōng 適中／适中 moderate; appropriate; just right VP, 26
shōu 收 receive; accept V, 21
shòu dàjiā de xǐhuan/huānyíng 受大家的喜歡｜歡迎／受大家的喜欢｜欢迎 well liked/welcomed by all PH, 27
shǒujīhào 手機號／手机号 cell phone number N, 25
shòuliáng 受涼／受凉 catch a chill/cold VO, 22
shuàigē 帥哥／帅哥 handsome young man N, 24
shuāngrénjiān 雙人間／双人间 double room N, 24
shūcài 蔬菜 vegetable N, 27
shùnbiàn 順便／顺便 in passing; conveniently A, 23
shuō fǎn le 說反了／说反了 get it backward RV, 26
shuōfú (shuìfú) 說服／说服 persuade; convince someone V, 28
shūrù 輸入／输入 (computers) input V, 23
shúxī 熟悉 know (somebody or something) very well V/SV, 30
shùzì 數字／数字 numeral; number; figure; digit N, 23
Sìchuān 四川 (province in southwestern China known for its very spicy cuisine) PW, 21
sīniàn 思念 miss; think of; long for V, 30
sīwéi 思維／思维 thought; thinking N, 30

sīxiāng bìng 思鄉病／思乡病   homesickness; nostalgia   N, 30

suàn 蒜   garlic   N, 27

suíshēn 隨身／随身   take or have with oneself   VO, 23

suíshí 隨時／随时   at any time; at all times; whenever   A, 30

sūnnǚ 孫女／孙女   granddaughter; son's daughter   N, 29

sūnzi 孫子／孙子   grandson; son's son   N, 29

suǒyǒu 所有   all; every   ATTR, 23

T

táng 糖   sugar   N, 27

tàng 燙／烫   scald   V; burning hot   SV, 22

tàng 燙／烫   perm (hair)   V, 24

tǎngxià 躺下   lie down   RV, 26

tǎnzi 毯子   blanket   N, 26

tàocān 套餐   set package (of food, services, etc.)   N, 24

tèdà 特大   especially/exceptionally large   VP, 28

téng 疼   ache; painful   SV, 22

tèsè 特色   characteristic; special feature; hallmark   N, 21

tí 提   mention; refer to; bring up   V, 23

tián 填   fill in/out (a form, etc.)   V, 23

tiān máfan 添麻煩／添麻烦   be a bother/trouble (to somebody)   VP, 30

tiāo 挑   choose; select   V, 26

tiāohuāyǎn 挑花眼   eyes blur with so many choices   VO, 25

tiáojiàn 條件／条件   condition; factor; term   N, 28

tiǎorǎn 挑染   give hair tinted highlights   VO, 24

tiáowèipǐn 調味品／调味品   flavoring; seasoning; condiment   N, 27

tiāoxuǎn 挑選／挑选   choose; select; pick   V, 28

tígōng 提供   supply; furnish; offer   V, 23

tīng 聽／听   heed; obey   V, 24

tíqǐ 提起   bring up; mention; speak of   RV, 30

tǐwēnbiǎo 體溫表／体温表   thermometer   N, 22

tíxǐng 提醒   remind; alert to   V, 25

tǐzhòng 體重／体重   (body) weight   N, 28

tòng 痛   painful   SV, 24

tóngshí 同時／同时   at the same time   A, 24

tōngzhī 通知   notify   V, 23

tóngzhuāng 童裝／童装   children's clothing   N, 26

tóurù 投入   absorbed; concentrated; devoted   SV, 28

tóuténg 頭疼／头疼   have a headache   VO, 22

tóuyūn 頭暈／头晕   dizzy   VP, 22

tù 吐   vomit; throw up   V, 22

tuī 推   push; promote   V, 25

tuì (chūlái) 退 (出來／出来)   quit; withdraw from; eject   V, 23

tuījiàn 推薦／推荐   recommend   V, 25

tuīsòng 推送   promote   V, 23

W

wàixíng 外形   appearance; external form   N, 28

Wángfǔjǐng 王府井   (major shopping area in Beijing)   PW, 26

wǎngwǎng 往往   often; frequently; more often than not   A, 30

wǎnhuì 晚會／晚会   evening event; soiree   N, 21

wánjù 玩具   toy; plaything   N, 26

wánle 完了   and then   VP, 25

wánměi 完美   perfect; flawless   SV, 22

Wànshèngjié 萬聖節／万圣节   Halloween   N, 23

wànyī 萬一／万一   just in case; supposing; if by any chance   C, 26

wèi 為／为   for; in the interests of   C, 30

wèidao 味道   taste; flavor   N, 30

wèihūnqī 未婚妻   fiancée   N, 21

wèikǒu 胃口   appetite   N, 22

wèilái 未來／未来   future; time to come   N, 29

wèile 為了／为了   for the sake of; for   C, 24

wēixiào 微笑   smile   V, 29

wēnxīn 溫馨   warm and comfortable   SV, 30

Wò'ěrmǎ 沃爾瑪／沃尔玛   Walmart   N, 26

wǒ méishì 我沒事   I'm fine; nothing wrong; no problem   IE, 22

wǔguānduānzhèng 五官端正   have a regular, symmetrical face (with five facial features in the right places)   VP, 28

wùpǐn 物品   articles; goods   N; **suíshēn wùpǐn** 隨身物品／随身物品   personal items, 23

wūpó 巫婆   witch   N, 23

X

xì 戲／戏   drama; play; show   N; **kàn xì** 看戲／看戏   watch a show, 23

xǐ jiǎn chuī 洗剪吹   wash, cut, and blow-dry   IE, 24

xǐ nù āi lè 喜怒哀樂／喜怒哀乐   happiness, anger, sorrow, joy   IE, 28

xiàn 獻／献   offer   V, 29

xiāng 香   incense   N, 29

xiāng 香   fragrant; appetizing; savory   SV, 30

xiàng 項／项   (for itemized things) item   M, 24

xiàng 像   be like; resemble   V, 26

xiāngchà 相差   difference   N; differ (by)   V, 26

xiānggū 香菇   shiitake mushroom   N, 27

xiǎngjiā 想家   be homesick   VO/SV, 30

xiàngmào 相貌   looks; appearance   N, 28

xiàngmù 項目／项目   project   N, 23

xiǎngniàn 想念   miss (someone or something)   V, 30

xiǎngshòu 享受   enjoy   V; enjoyment; treat   N, 24

xiāngyān 香煙／香烟   cigarette   N, 29

xiànxiàng 現象／现象   phenomenon; appearance   N, 30

xiào yīyuàn 校醫院／校医院 school hospital; student health center N, 21

xiǎoqū 小區／小区 city/town district; residential area PW, 26

xiāoshòu 銷售／销售 sell; market V, 25

xiàrén 嚇人／吓人 frightening SV, 23

xiē 歇 have a rest V, 26

xiédiàn 鞋店 shoe store N, 26

xiéyīn 諧音／谐音 homophone; homonym N, 25

xīfāng 西方 west; the West; the Occident; Western world N, 27

xīfú 西服 Western-style suit/clothes N, 26

xǐhǎo 洗好 washed (fully) RV, 27

xíngdòng búbiàn 行動不便／行动不便 unable to get about / move freely PH, 29

xīngfèn 興奮／兴奋 excited SV, 30

xìngfú 幸福 happiness N; fortunate SV, 30

xìnghǎo 幸好 fortunately; luckily IE, 26

xìngjiàbǐ 性價比／性价比 quality-price ratio N, 25

xìngrén 杏仁 almond N, 29

xìngyùn 幸運／幸运 good fortune; good luck N; fortunate; lucky SV, 21

xīnjiàn 新建 newly built ATTR, 26

xīnqíng 心情 mood; state/frame of mind N, 30

xìnrèn 信任 trust; have confidence in N/V, 29

xìnxī 信息 information; news; message N, 23

xìnxīn 信心 confidence; faith; belief N, 26

xiōngdì péngyou 兄弟朋友 very close friends N, 28

xìtǒng 系統／系统 system; process N, 23

xǐtóu 洗頭／洗头 wash (one's) hair VO, 24

xīxuèguǐ 吸血鬼 vampire N, 23

xīyī 西醫／西医 Western medicine; doctor trained in Western medicine N, 22

xīyǐn 吸引 attract; draw one's attention to V, 21

xuéqī 學期／学期 semester N, 21

xuéshengzhèng 學生證／学生证 student ID N, 22

xuèyā 血壓／血压 blood pressure N, 22

Y

yáchǐ 牙齒／牙齿 tooth; teeth N, 28

yālì 壓力／压力 pressure; burden; strain N, 21

yán 鹽／盐 salt N, 27

yǎn 演 perform; play V, 23

yánggāng zhī qì 陽剛之氣／阳刚之气 manliness; virility N, 24

yǎnglǎo sòngzhōng 養老送終／养老送终 look after (one's parents) in their old age and give them a proper burial PH, 29

Yángshuò 陽朔／阳朔 (a popular tourist town in southwest China's Guangxi Province, famous for its spectacular mountain scenery of karst topography) PW, 26

yánlì 嚴厲／严厉 strict; stern; severe SV, 29

yǎnxì 演戲／演戏 put on or act in a play VO, 23

yǎnyuán 演員／演员 performer; actor N, 28

yānzhì 醃製／腌制 soak; marinate; cure V, 27

yánzhòng 嚴重／严重 serious; grave; critical SV, 22

yāo 么／幺 one (used when saying the number 1 in phone numbers, etc.) NU, 25

yào bùrán 要不然 otherwise; or else; or C, 23

yàobu(shi) 要不(是) otherwise; or else C, 21

yàodiǎn 要點／要点 main points; essentials; gist N, 22

yàome ... yàome ... 要麼……要麼……／要么……要么…… ~ V1 (~ V2) either . . . or . . . C, 24

yāoqǐng 邀請／邀请 request; ask of (someone); invite V, 21; invitation N, 30

yāoqiú 要求 demand; request; require; requirement V/N, 30

yàoshuǐ 藥水／药水 medicinal liquid; lotion N, 24

yāyì 壓抑／压抑 depressing; feel down SV, 30

yèwù 業務／业务 business N, 23

yèxià 腋下 armpit N, 22

yèyú 業餘／业余 amateur; spare time ATTR, 23

yǐ 椅 chair BF; **yǐzi** 椅子 chair, 26

yǐ chá dài jiǔ 以茶代酒 use tea as a replacement for alcohol PH, 30

yī fēn jiàqián yī fēn huò 一分價錢一分貨／一分价钱一分货 "You get what you pay for" IE, 26

yījǔliǎngdé 一舉兩得／一举两得 accomplish two results with one effort; kill two birds with one stone IE, 23

yímín 移民 migrate; immigrate VO, 21

yīmóyīyàng 一模一樣／一模一样 be exactly alike IE, 23

yìng 硬 hard; stiff (to the touch) SV, 24

(yīng) gāi (應)該／(应)该 ought to; should A, 21

yīng'ér 嬰兒／婴儿 baby; infant N, 26

yīngjùn 英俊 handsome SV, 28

yǐngxiǎng 影響／影响 influence V/N, 28

yínháng 銀行／银行 bank N, 23

yǐnliào 飲料／饮料 drinks; beverages N, 26

yīshí'èrniǎo 一石二鳥／一石二鸟 kill two birds with one stone IE, 23

yìshù 藝術／艺术 art; skill N, 23

yìshùjiā 藝術家／艺术家 artist N, 26

yìshùpǐn 藝術品／艺术品 work of art N, 26

yīyuàn 醫院／医院 hospital N, 22

yízhèn yízhèn de 一陣一陣地／一阵一阵地 wave after wave (of pain) A, 22

yìzhí 一直 (indicates a constant state) A; **Tā yìzhí chūchāi.** 她一直出差。 She's always away on business. 21; (indicates a constant direction) A; **Yìzhí zǒu.** 一直走。 Go straight ahead. 21

yònggōng 用功 hardworking; studious SV, 28

yòngpǐn 用品 articles for use; appliances N, 26

yǒu qí mǔ bì yǒu qí nǚ 有其母必有其女 like mother, like daughter IE; **yǒu qí fù bì yǒu qí zǐ** 有其父必有其子 like father, like son, 23

yǒu shénme hǎo ne 有甚麼好呢／有什么好呢 What's so good about that? PH, 26

yòu xiàjiǎo 右下角 lower-right corner N, 23

yǒudeshì 有的是 have plenty of; no lack of IE, 26

yóufèi 郵費／邮费 postage N, 30

yóuguō 油鍋／油锅 frying pan N, 27

yōuhuì 優惠／优惠 preferential treatment; discount N, 24

yóujú 郵局／邮局 post office N, 30

yōumògǎn 幽默感 sense of humor N, 28

yóupiào 郵票／邮票 postage stamp N, 30

yóuqíshì 尤其是 especially VP/A, 27, 30

yǒushàn 友善 friendly; amicable SV, 28

yóuxì 遊戲／游戏 game (for recreation) N; play V, 25

yóuxiāng dìzhǐ 郵箱地址／邮箱地址 e-mail address N, 21

yuánlái 原來／原来 so . . .; so, after all N, 24

yuǎnlí 遠離／远离 be far away from V, 30

yuánliào 原料 material; raw material N, 27

yùdào 遇到 encounter; meet; come across; run into V, 30

yuē 約／约 invite; make an appointment; arrange V, 30

yūn 暈／晕 dizzy SV, 26

yùnqi 運氣／运气 luck; fortune N, 29

Z

zài X zhī nèi 在 X 之内 within X IE, 25

zài xiào 在校 at school; currently enrolled VO, 28

zán liǎ 咱倆／咱俩 we two; you and I PR, 26

zánmen 咱們／咱们 we; you and I PR, 26

zhǎng 長／长 grow; grow up; increase V, 26

zhǎngdà 長大／长大 grow up; mature RV, 29

zhànghù 帳戶／帐户 (business/bank) account N, 23

zhǎngxiàng 長相／长相 features (of a face) N, 28

zhào 兆 (computer) mega; million NU, 25

zhāo(r) 招(兒)／招(儿) trick; device; move N, 21

zhàogu 照顧／照顾 take care of; look after; care for V, 29

zhēnchéng 真誠／真诚 sincere; genuine; true SV; sincerity N, 28

zhěng bǎn 整版 a full page; an entire sheet N, 30

zhèngcháng 正常 normal SV, 22

zhènghǎo 正好 happen to; as it happens VP, 21

zhènghǎo de 正好的 exactly A, 23

zhèngjiàn 證件／证件 credentials; ID N, 22

zhèngmiàn 正面 positive ATTR, 28

zhěngqí 整齊／整齐 neat; tidy; in good order SV, 28

zhèngqián 掙錢／挣钱 earn/make money VO, 26

zhèngshì 正式 formal (of actions, speeches, etc.) SV, 26

zhèngzhuàng 症狀／症状 symptoms N, 22

zhèngzōng 正宗 authentic; genuine; authoritative SV, 27

zhēnjiǔ 針灸／针灸 acupuncture and moxibustion (traditional Chinese medicine made from mugwort) N, 22

zhì 至 to; until; till CV, 27

zhīchí 支持 support; back V, 29

zhídé 值得 merit; deserve; worth it SV/AV, 26

zhǐhuī 指揮／指挥 direct; command V, 29

zhǐjia hùlǐ 指甲護理／指甲护理 manicure/pedicure N, 24

zhìliàng 質量／质量 quality N, 25

zhìnéngjī 智能機／智能机 smartphone (literally, "intelligent machine") N, 25

zhìyuànzhě 志願者／志愿者 volunteer N, 28

Zhōngcān 中餐 Chinese cuisine/meal/food N, 27

Zhōngcǎoyào 中草藥／中草药 Chinese herbal medicine N, 22

zhōngxīn 中心 center; heart; hub; focus N, 30

Zhōngyī 中醫／中医 traditional Chinese medicine; a doctor trained in traditional Chinese medicine N, 22

zhōudào 周到 thorough; attentive; considerate; thoughtful SV, 28

zhōunián 週年／周年 anniversary N, 24

zhuàn 轉／转 turn; shift; rotate; revolve; stroll around V, 26

zhuānjiā 專家／专家 expert; specialist N, 30

zhuānmàidiàn 專賣店／专卖店 specialty store N, 26

zhuānmén 專門／专门 special SV, 21

zhuānyè 專業／专业 major (in a university) N, 28

zhǔchí 主持 take charge of; host; direct; manage V, 21

zhǔchírén 主持人 host; hostess; anchorperson N, 21

zhùfú 祝福 wish happiness to/for V, 30

zhǔyào 主要 main; principal; major; chief ATTR; primarily A, 22

zhùyì 注意 pay attention; take note of V, 22

zhùyuàn 祝願／祝愿 wish; in hopes that V, 30

zìdòng 自動／自动 automatically A, 23

(zìdòng) qǔkuǎnjī (自動)取款機／(自动)取款机 ATM N, 23

zìfèi 自費／自费 pay one's own expenses V, 22

zìjǐ shēnshang 自己身上 one's own self PH, 26

zījīn 資金／资金 fund; capital N, 23

zìliàn 自戀／自恋 be full of oneself; narcissism; narcissistic N/SV, 28

zǐxì 仔細／仔细 careful; attentive; meticulous SV; carefully; with care A, 22

zǒuhuǒrùmó 走火入魔 be obsessed with something IE, 23

zòu yí dùn 揍一頓／揍一顿 beat up; hit VP, 29

zuò yí dùn (fàn) 做一頓(飯)／做一顿(饭) make a meal VP, 29

zuòfǎ 做法 way of doing something N, 27

zuòliǎn 做臉／做脸 have a facial VO, 24
zuòpǐn 作品 works *(of literature, art)* N, 26
zuòwèi 座位 seat; place N, 23

zuòyǐ 座椅 chair; seat N, 26
zuòzhǔ 做主 make the decision; decide; take charge of VO, 29

English-Chinese Glossary

A

about dàyuē 大約／大约 A

absorbed tóurù 投入 SV

accept shōu 收 V

accompany péi; péibàn 陪; 陪伴 V

according to gēnjù; ànzhào 根據／根据; 按照 C

account hùtóu 戶頭／户头 N

account *(business/bank)* zhànghù 帳戶／帐户 N

account: been posted to (my/the) account dàozhàng 到賬／到账 VO

accustom: get accustomed to shìyìng 適應／适应 V

ache téng 疼 SV

acne qīngchūndòu 青春痘 N

act in a play yǎnxì 演戲／演戏 VO

activation fee gōngběn(r)fèi 工本(兒)費／工本(儿)费 N

active huóyuè 活躍／活跃 SV

activity huódòng 活動／活动 N

actor yǎnyuán 演員／演员 N

actually kě; qíshí 可; 其實／其实 A

acupuncture zhēnjiǔ 針灸／针灸 N

add jiārù 加入 VP

advertisement guǎnggào 廣告／广告 N

agent jīngjìrén 經紀人／经纪人 N

alike: be exactly alike yīmóyīyàng 一模一樣／一模一样 IE

all suǒyǒu 所有 ATTR

allergic mǐngǎn 敏感 SV

allergy guòmǐn 過敏／过敏 N

allergy: have an allergy guòmǐn 過敏／过敏 V

alley hútòng 胡同 N

allow ràng 讓／让 CV

almond xìngrén 杏仁 N

alone *(only)* dāndān 單單／单单 A

always *(indicates a constant state)* yìzhí 一直 A

amateur yèyú 業餘／业余 ATTR

amateur performer piàoyǒu 票友 N

amazed jīngyà 驚訝／惊讶 SV

American-born Chinese person Měiguó Huárén 美國華人／美国华人 N

amicable yǒushàn 友善 SV

anchorperson zhǔchírén 主持人 N

anise bājiǎo 八角 N

anniversary zhōunián 週年／周年 N

anniversary of (our) store diàn qìng 店慶／店庆 N

annoyed fán; fánnǎo 煩／烦; 煩惱／烦恼 SV

annoying fánrén 煩人／烦人 SV

annual fee/charge niánfèi 年費／年费 N

antibiotic kàngshēngsù 抗生素 N

anxious jí 急 SV

anxious: feel anxious dānxīn 擔心／担心 SV/V/VO

any rènhé 任何 ATTR

any: in any case; anyway; anyhow fǎnzhèng 反正 A

apparel chuānzhuó 穿著／穿着 N

appear chūxiàn 出現／出现 V

appear: it appears kàn qǐlai 看起來／看起来 VP

appearance wàixíng; xiàngmào 外形; 相貌 N

appetite wèikǒu 胃口 N

appetizing xiāng 香 SV

application form shēnqǐng biǎo 申請表／申请表 N

appointment: make an appointment yuē 約／约 V

appraise gūjì 估計／估计 V

appropriate héshì 合適／合适 SV

appropriate shìzhōng 適中／适中 VP

approximately dàyuē 大約／大约 A

apt to *(usually followed by* jiù 就, *indicating an act or situation occurring frequently and often unwished for)* dòngbudòng 動不動／动不动 A

argue chǎojià 吵架 VO

arid gānzào 乾燥／干燥 SV

arm gēbo 胳膊 N

armpit yèxià 腋下 N

art yìshù 藝術／艺术 N

articles for use yòngpǐn 用品 N

artist yìshùjiā 藝術家／艺术家 N

aspirin āsīpǐlín 阿司匹林 N

asterisked characters dài xīnghào(r) de zì 帶星號(兒)的字／带星号(儿)的字 N

astounded jīngyà 驚訝／惊讶 SV

ATM (zìdòng) qǔkuǎnjī (自動) 取款機／(自动) 取款机 N

attendant fúwùyuán 服務員／服务员 N

attention: draw one's attention to xīyǐn 吸引 V

attention: pay attention zhùyì 注意 V/N

attentive zhōudào; zǐxì 周到; 仔細／仔细 SV

attire chuānzhuó 穿著／穿着 N

attract xīyǐn 吸引 V

audience guānzhòng 觀眾／观众 N

audition *(interview)* miànshì 面試／面试 VO/N

audition *(for a performance)* shìxì 試戲／试戏 VO

auspicious dà shùn 大順／大顺 IE

auspicious jílì 吉利 SV

Australia Aòdàlìyà 澳大利亚／澳大利亚 PW

authentic zhèngzōng 正宗 SV

automatically zìdòng 自動／自动 A

average píngpíng 平平 RF

away on a business trip chūchāi 出差 VO

B

baby   yīng'ér   嬰兒／婴儿   N
bad: not bad   hái hǎo   還好／还好   VP
bad-tempered   píqi huài   脾氣壞／脾气坏   SV
bag   bāor   包兒／包儿   N
bank   yínháng   銀行／银行   N
basis   gēnjù   根據／根据   N
basis: on the basis of   gēnjù; ànzhào   根據／根据; 按照   C
battery   diànchí   電池／电池   N
bazaar   shāngchǎng   商場／商场   N
bear   chéngshòu; rěn   承受; 忍   V
beat up   zòu yí dùn   揍一頓／揍一顿   VP
beautiful woman   měinǚ   美女   N
belief   xìnxīn   信心   N
belly   dùzi   肚子   N
beloved   qīn'ài de   親愛的／亲爱的   IE
beverages   yǐnliào   飲料／饮料   N
bit: a bit   shāowēi   稍微   A
blanket   tǎnzi   毯子   N
bless you *(said when someone sneezes)*   chángmìngbǎisuì   長命百歲／长命百岁   IE
blood pressure   xuèyā   血壓／血压   N
blow-dry   chuīgān   吹乾／吹干   V
boldfaced letters *(printing)*   hēitǐ zì   黑體字/黑体字   N
Bottoms up!   gānbēi   乾杯／干杯   IE
brand   biāozhì; pǐnpái   標誌／标志; 品牌   N
broker   jīngjìrén   經紀人／经纪人   N
burgeoning *(said of an enterprise)*   fēngshēngshuǐqǐ   風生水起／风生水起   IE
business   shēngyi; yèwù   生意; 業務／业务   N
business card   míngpiàn   名片   N
buy one, get one free   mǎi yī zèng yī   買一贈一／买一赠一   N
by *(someone or some agent) [marker of passive voice; see Grammar Bits, p. 8]*   bèi   被   P

C

cannot but; have to   bùdé bù   不得不   VP
capable   nénggàn   能幹／能干   SV
capital   zījīn   資金／资金   N
card   kǎ   卡   N
care: take care of; care for   zhàogu   照顧／照顾   V
carefully   zǐxì   仔細／仔细   A
carpenter   mùjiàng   木匠   N
carrot   húluóbo   胡蘿蔔／胡萝卜   N
carry *(something)*   dài   帶／带   V
carry out   jìnxíng   進行／进行   V
catch a chill/cold   shòuliáng   受涼／受凉   VO
cell phone number   shǒujīhào   手機號／手机号   N
center   zhōngxīn   中心   N
centimeter   límǐ   厘米   M
certainly   díquè   的確／的确   A

chair   yǐzi; zuòyǐ   椅子; 座椅   N
chance: if by any chance   wànyī   萬一／万一   C
change   biàndòng   變動／变动   V/N
change one's mind   gǎi zhǔyi   改主意   VO
change to a new profession   gǎiháng   改行   VO
character   rénwù   人物   N
characteristic   tèsè   特色   N
charge   fèi; fèiyòng   費／费; 費用／费用   N
charge *(dash, hurry)*   chōng   衝／冲   V
charge: take charge of   guǎn   管   V; zuòzhǔ   做主   VO
chart   biǎo   表   N
chat: have a good chat   hǎohāo liáoliao   好好聊聊   VP
check   chá   查   V
check figures/sums   héduì   核對／核对   RV
check over   kǎochá   考察   V
Cheers!   gānbēi   乾杯／干杯   IE
chicken breast *(meat)*   jīxiōng ròu   雞胸肉／鸡胸肉   N
chicken leg *(meat)*   jītuǐ ròu   雞腿肉／鸡腿肉   N
chicken meat   jīròu   雞肉／鸡肉   N
chicken skin   jīpí   雞皮／鸡皮   N
children's clothing   tóngzhuāng   童裝／童装   N
chili   làjiāo   辣椒   N
Chinese cuisine/meal/food   Zhōngcān   中餐   N
Chinese herbal medicine   Zhōngcǎoyào   中草藥／中草药   N
Chinese medicine   Zhōngyī   中醫／中医   N
choose   tiāo; tiāoxuǎn   挑; 挑選／挑选   V
cinnamon (Chinese)   guìpí   桂皮   N
classic   jīngdiǎn   經典／经典   ATTR
clean   gānjìng   乾淨／干净   SV
click/strike rate *(on a keyboard or other device)*   diǎnjīlǜ   點擊率／点击率   N
close relatives   qīnrén   親人／亲人   N
clothing   fúzhuāng   服裝／服装   N
coerce   qiángzhì   強制／强制   V
cold: catch a cold   shòuliáng   受涼／受凉   VO
collaborate   hézuò   合作   V
color (one's) hair   rǎnfà   染髮／染发   VO
come across   yùdào   遇到   V
command   mìnglìng   命令   N
command   zhǐhuī   指揮／指挥   V
commodities   huòwù   貨物／货物   N
communicate   gōutōng   溝通／沟通   V
communication media   chuánméi   傳媒／传媒   N
company   gōngsī   公司   N
company: keep somebody company   péi; péibàn   陪; 陪伴   V
compel   qiángzhì   強制／强制   V
competent   nénggàn   能幹／能干   SV
complete   qíquán   齊全／齐全   SV
concern: be concerned about   guānxīn   關心／关心   V
conclude   jiéshù   結束／结束   V
condiment   tiáowèipǐn   調味品／调味品   N

condition qíngkuàng 情況／情况 N

conduct jìnxíng 進行／进行 V

confidence xìnxīn 信心 N

confidence: have confidence in xìnrèn 信任 N/V

configure (computers) shèzhì 設置／设置 V

confirm quèdìng; quèrèn 確定／确定; 確認／确认 V

confront miànduì 面對／面对 V

consider kǎolǜ 考慮／考虑 V

considerate zhōudào 周到 SV

constantly jīngcháng 經常／经常 A

container róngqì 容器 N

content nèiróng 內容 N

contents: table of contents mùlù 目錄／目录 N

continue to jiēzhe 接著／接着 VP

control guǎn 管 V

conveniently shùnbiàn 順便／顺便 A

cook shāo 燒／烧 V

cooking: art of cooking chúyì 廚藝／厨艺 N

cooking class chúyìbān, kè 廚藝班, 課／厨艺班,课 N

cooking wine liàojiǔ 料酒 N

"cool" kù 酷 PL/SV

cooperate hézuò 合作 V

copy fǎngzhì 仿製／仿制 V

corporation gōngsī 公司 N

corrupt dài huài 帶壞／带坏 RV

cosmetology měiróng 美容 N

cough késòu 咳嗽 V

course (process) guòchéng 過程／过程 N

credentials zhèngjiàn 證件／证件 N

critical yánzhòng 嚴重／严重 SV

criticism pīpíng 批評／批评 N

criticize pīpíng 批評／批评 V

cube dīngr 丁兒／丁儿 N

cucumber huánggua 黃瓜 N

currency huòbì 貨幣／货币 N

cut (into pieces) qiēchéng 切成 RV

cute kě'ài 可愛／可爱 SV

D

daily-use items rìyòngpǐn 日用品 N

darling bǎobèi(r) 寶貝(兒)／宝贝(儿) N

dash chōng 衝／冲 V

daughter (unmarried) guīnü 閨女／闺女 N

deal jiāoyì 交易 N

dear qīn'ài de 親愛的／亲爱的 IE

deceive piàn 騙／骗 V

decent shànliáng 善良 SV

decide: make the decision; decide zuòzhǔ 做主 VO

decorate bùzhì 佈置／布置 V

deduct kòuchú 扣除 RV

deep (skin) cleansing shēncéng qīngjié 深層清潔／深层清洁 N

defecate dàbiàn 大便 V

definitely kěndìng 肯定 A

demand yāoqiú 要求 V

deposit money cúnkuǎn; cúnqián 存款; 存錢／存钱 VO

depressing yāyì 壓抑／压抑 SV

deserted kōng(kōng) dàngdàng 空(空)蕩蕩／空(空)荡荡 VP

deserve zhídé 值得 SV/AV

design kuǎnxíng 款型 N

despair juéwàng 絕望／绝望 V

devoted tóurù 投入 SV

diarrhea fùxiè 腹瀉／腹泻 N

diarrhea: have diarrhea lā dùzi; nào dùzi 拉肚子; 鬧肚子／闹肚子 VO

dice qiēchéng 切成 RV

differ (by) xiāngchà 相差 V

difference qūbié; xiāngchà 區別／区别; 相差 N

differentiate qūbié 區別／区别 V

difficulty kùnnán 困難／困难 N

digit shùzì 數字／数字 N

direct zhǐhuī 指揮／指挥 V

direct (a film, play, etc.) dǎoyǎn 導演／导演 V

director dǎoyǎn 導演／导演 N

discard rēng 扔 V

discount yōuhuì 優惠／优惠 N

discover fāxiàn 發現／发现 V

distinction qūbié 區別／区别 N

distinguish qūbié 區別／区别 V

dizzy tóuyūn 頭暈／头晕 VP; yūn 暈／晕 SV

do nòng 弄 V

doctor dàifu 大夫 N

doctor: see a doctor kànbìng 看病 VO

domestic product guóchǎn 國產／国产 N

double room shuāngrénjiān 雙人間／双人间 N

drama xì 戲／戏 N

dried tangerine/orange peel chénpí 陳皮／陈皮 N

drinks yǐnliào 飲料／饮料 N

dry gān; gānzào 乾／干; 乾燥／干燥 SV

duplicate fùyìn 複印／复印 V

dye (one's) hair rǎnfà 染髮／染发 VO

dynamic huóyuè 活躍／活跃 SV

E

earn money zhèngqián 掙錢／挣钱 VO

earthquake dìzhèn 地震 N

edition bǎn 版 N

either . . . or . . . yàome . . . yàome . . . 要麼……要麼……／要么……要么…… C

eject tuì (chūlái) 退(出來／出来) V

electronic products diànzǐ chǎnpǐn 電子產品／电子产品 N

eliminate páichú 排除 RV

else: or else yào bùrán; yàobu(shi) 要不然; 要不(是) C

e-mail address yóuxiāng dìzhǐ 郵箱地址／邮箱地址 N

emerge   chūxiàn   出現／出现   V
emotion   gǎnqíng   感情   N
employ   shǐyòng   使用   V
empty: absolutely empty   kōng(kōng) dàngdàng   空(空)荡荡／空(空)荡荡   VP
encounter   yùdào   遇到   V
encourage   gǔlì   鼓勵／鼓励   V/N
end   jiéshù   結束／结束   V
endure   chéngshòu; rěn   承受; 忍   V
energy   huólì   活力   N
enjoy   xiǎngshòu   享受   V
enjoyment   xiǎngshòu   享受   N
enoki mushroom   jīnzhēngū   金针菇／金针菇   N
enroll: currently enrolled   zài xiào   在校   VO
enthusiastic   rèqíng   熱情／热情   SV
entreat   kěnqiú   懇求／恳求   V
environment   huánjìng   環境／环境   N
especially   yóuqíshì   尤其是   VP/A
estimate   gūjì   估計／估计   V
evening event   wǎnhuì   晚會／晚会   N
exactly   gānghǎo; zhènghǎo de   剛好／刚好; 正好的   A
examination   cèyàn   測驗／测验   N
examine   jiǎnchá; kǎochá   檢查／检查; 考察   V
example: for example   bǐrú shuō   比如说／比如说   VP
excellent   bàng   棒   SV
exchange   duìhuàn   兑換／兑换   V
excited   xīngfèn   興奮／兴奋   SV
experience   jīnglì   經歷／经历   N/V
expert   zhuānjiā   專家／专家   N
extent   fànwéi   範圍／范围   N
eyes blur with so many choices   tiāohuāyǎn   挑花眼   VO

F

face: have a regular, symmetrical face (with five facial features in the right places)   wǔguānduānzhèng   五官端正   VP
facial: have a facial   zuòliǎn   做臉／做脸   VO
facial conditioning   miànbù hùlǐ   面部護理／面部护理   N
facial treatment/masque   fūliǎn   敷臉／敷脸   N
fact: in fact; as a matter of fact   qíshí   其實／其实   A
factor   tiáojiàn   條件／条件   N
faith   xìnxīn   信心   N
faith: have blind faith in   míxìn   迷信   V
fake   jiǎ   假   SV
fake   shānzhài   山寨   N
far away from   yuǎnlí   遠離／远离   V
fearful   kǒngbù   恐怖   SV
features (of a face)   zhǎngxiàng   長相／长相   N
feces   dàbiàn   大便   N
fee   fèi; fèiyòng   費／费; 費用／费用   N
feel down   yāyì   壓抑／压抑   SV
feel free to   jǐnguǎn   儘管／尽管   A

feel grateful   gǎnjī   感激   V
feel indebted   gǎnjī   感激   V
feel like vomiting   ěxīn   噁心／恶心   VO
feel nauseated   ěxīn   噁心／恶心   VO
feel relieved   fàngxīn   放心   RV
feeling   gǎnqíng   感情   N
feeling good   hǎoshòu   好受   SV
feeling/sense of identification   rèntónggǎn   認同感／认同感   N
fever: have a fever   fāshāo   發燒／发烧   VO
fiancée   wèihūnqī   未婚妻   N
fill in/out (a form, etc.)   tián   填   V
find   fāxiàn   發現／发现   V
flavor   wèidao   味道   N
flavoring   tiáowèipǐn   調味品／调味品   N
flawless   wánměi   完美   SV
foods   shípǐn   食品   N
fool   piàn   騙／骗   V
fool   shǎguā   傻瓜   N
force   qiángzhì   强制   V
foreign student   liúxuéshēng   留學生／留学生   N
form   biǎo   表   N
form a set   pèitào   配套   VO
formal (of actions, speeches, etc.)   zhèngshì   正式   SV
fortuitous   jílì   吉利   SV
fortunate   xìngfú; xìngyùn   幸福; 幸運／幸运   SV
fortunately   xìnghǎo   幸好   IE
fortune   yùnqi   運氣／运气   N
fragrant   xiāng   香   V
free of charge   miǎnfèi   免費／免费   VO
frequently   jīngcháng   經常／经常   A
friend: close friends   xiōngdì péngyou   兄弟朋友   N
friend: make friends with; befriend   jiāo péngyou   交朋友   VO; jiéjiāo   結交／结交   V
friendly   yǒushàn   友善   SV
frightening   xiàrén   嚇人／吓人   SV
from: come from; originate from; stem from   láizì   來自／来自   VP
frying pan   yóuguō   油鍋／油锅   N
full of oneself   zìliàn   自戀／自恋   SV
function   gōngnéng   功能   N
fund   zījīn   資金／资金   N
fussy: be fussy about   jiǎngjiu   講究／讲究   SV
future   wèilái   未來／未来   N

G

game (for recreation)   yóuxì   遊戲／游戏   N
garlic   suàn   蒜   N
gaze at   dīng   盯   V
gentle   qīng   輕／轻   SV
genuine   zhēnchéng   真誠／真诚   SV
genuine (in a traditional sense)   zhèngzōng   正宗   SV
get   qǔ   取   V
get accustomed to   shìyìng   適應／适应   V

get it backward shuō fǎn le 说反了／说反了 RV

get rid of qùdiào 去掉 RV

get together (for a chat, meeting, etc.) jù(ju) 聚(聚) V

get used to shìyìng 適應／适应 V

ghost guǐ 鬼 N

gift lǐpǐn 禮品／礼品 N

ginger jiāng 薑／姜 N

ginger: fresh ginger shēngjiāng 生薑／生姜 N

gist yàodiǎn 要點／要点 N

give hair tinted highlights tiǎorǎn 挑染 VO

go online shàngwǎng 上網／上网 VO

go shopping gòuwù 購物／购物 VO

go through jīnglì 經歷／经历 V

gongbao chicken gōngbǎo jīdīng 宮保雞丁／宫保鸡丁 N

good bàng 棒 SV

good: not very good kěbù zěnmeyàng 可不怎麼樣／可不怎么样 IE

good at doing something náshǒu 拿手 SV

good for X shìhé X yòng 適合X用／适合X用 IE

good fortune; good luck jílì; xìngyùn 吉利; 幸運／幸运 N

goods huòwù; wùpǐn 貨物／货物; 物品 N

good-tempered píqi hǎo 脾氣好／脾气好 SV

granddaughter sūnnǚ 孫女／孙女 N

grandson sūnzi 孫子／孙子 N

grateful: feel grateful gǎnjī 感激 V

grave yánzhòng 嚴重／严重 SV

green onion cōng 蔥／葱 N

grow zhǎng 長／长 V

grow: let grow liú 留 V

grow up zhǎngdà 長大／长大 RV

H

hair: dye one's hair; tint one's hair; color one's hair rǎnfà 染髮／染发 VO

hair quality/texture fàzhì 髮質／发质 N

haircut: get a haircut jiǎn tóufa 剪頭髮／剪头发 VO

Halloween Wànshèngjié 萬聖節／万圣节 N

hand to/over dì 遞／递 V

handle bànlǐ 辦理／办理 V

handsome yīngjùn 英俊 SV

handsome man and beautiful woman jùnnán měinǚ 俊男美女 N

handsome young man shuàigē 帥哥／帅哥 N

happen to; as it happens zhènghǎo 正好 VP

happiness xìngfú 幸福 SV

happiness, anger, sorrow, joy xǐ nù āi lè 喜怒哀樂／喜怒哀乐 IE

hard (to the touch) yìng 硬 SV

hardworking yònggōng 用功 SV

headache: have a headache tóuténg 頭疼／头疼 VO

heed tīng 聽／听 V

height (of a person) shēngāo 身高 N

herb: Chinese herbal medicine Zhōngcǎoyào 中草藥／中草药 N

hesitate: don't hesitate to jǐnguǎn 儘管／尽管 A

highlight: give hair tinted highlights tiǎorǎn 挑染 VO

high-rise commercial building shāngshà 商廈／商厦 N

hit zòu yí dùn 揍一頓／揍一顿 VP

hold bào 抱 V

homesick xiǎngjiā 想家 VO/SV

homesickness sīxiāng bìng 思鄉病／思乡病 N

homestyle cooking/food jiāchángcài 家常菜 N

hometown jiāxiāng 家鄉／家乡 N

homework schedule gōngkèbiǎo 功課表／功课表

homophone, homonym xiéyīn 諧音／谐音 N

hope: in hopes that zhùyuàn 祝願／祝愿 V

hope: lose/give up hope juéwàng 絕望／绝望 V

horrible kǒngbù 恐怖 SV

hospital yīyuàn 醫院／医院 N

host (a ceremony, activity) zhǔchí 主持 V

hot: burning hot tàng 燙／烫 SV

hot pepper làjiāo 辣椒 N

hotel jiǔdiàn 酒店 N

hub zhōngxīn 中心 N

hurriedly gǎnjǐn 趕緊／赶紧 A

hurry chōng 衝／冲 V

husband lǎogōng 老公 N

I

ID (card) zhèngjiàn 證件／证件 N

identical: be identical yīmóyīyàng 一模一樣／一模一样 IE

identification rèntóng 認同／认同 N

identify rèntóng 認同／认同 V

if X X dehuà X的話／X的话 C

I'm fine wǒ méishì 我没事 IE

imitate fǎngzhì 仿製／仿制 V

immediately jǐn jiēzhe 緊接著／紧接着 A

immigrate yímín 移民 VO

implore kěnqiú 懇求／恳求 V

improve one's looks měiróng 美容 VO

increase zhǎng 長／长 V

indebted: feel indebted gǎnjī 感激 V

indispensable bìyào 必要 SV

individual character gèxìng 個性／个性 N

infant yīng'ér 嬰兒／婴儿 N

infect gǎnrǎn 感染 V

infection gǎnrǎn 感染 N

influence yǐngxiǎng 影響／影响 V/N

information xìnxī 信息 N

input (computers) shūrù 輸入／输入 V

insert chā 插 V

inspect jiǎnchá 檢查／检查 V

instance: for instance bǐrú shuō 比如说／比如说 VP

intensity lìdù 力度 N

interest: in the interests of wèi; wèile 為／为; 為了／为了 C

intern: work as an intern shíxí 實習／实习 V

internal medicine nèikē 内科 N

international guójì 國際／国际 ATTR

interview miànshì 面試／面试 VO/N

intestines chángdào 腸道／肠道 N

introduction (to service, contents, etc.) jièshào 介紹／介绍 N

investigate chá 查 V

invitation yāoqǐng 邀請／邀请 N

invite yāoqǐng; yuē 邀請／邀请; 約／约 V

J

jack-o'-lantern nánguā dēng 南瓜燈／南瓜灯 N

just cái; gānghǎo 才; 剛好／刚好 A

just in case wànyī 萬一／万一 C

K

keep on (continue) jiēzhe 接著／接着 VP

key (of a piano, computer, etc.) jiàn 鍵／键 N

kill two birds with one stone yījǔliǎngdé; yīshí'èrniǎo 一舉兩得／一举两得; 一石二鳥／一石二鸟 IE

kind (person) rén hǎo 人好 SV

kindhearted shànliáng 善良 SV

knockoff shānzhài 山寨 N

know (somebody or something) **very well** shúxī 熟悉 V/SV

L

lack quē 缺 V

lane hútòng 胡同 N

large: especially large tèdà 特大 VP

lead astray dài huài 帶壞／带坏 RV

leave (something for someone) liúxià 留下 RV

lecture jiǎngkè 講課／讲课 VO

let ràng 讓／让 CV

lie down tǎngxià 躺下 RV

life experience shēnghuó jīnglì 生活經歷／生活经历 N

light (in color) dàn 淡 SV

like: be like xiàng 像 V

like father, like son yǒu qí fù bì yǒu qí zǐ 有其父必有其子 IE

like mother, like daughter yǒu qí mǔ bì yǒu qí nǚ 有其母必有其女 IE

list dānzi 單子／单子 N

lively huóyuè 活躍／活跃 SV

load into fàngrù 放入 VP

lonely; lonesome gūdú; jìmò 孤獨／孤独; 寂寞 SV

Long time no see! hǎojiǔbújiàn 好久不見／好久不见 IE

long-distance phone call chángtú (diànhuà) 長途（電話）／长途（电话） N

long-lasting kàngshǐ 抗使 VO

look (used to call attention to something) nuó 喏 I

look after (one's parents) in their old age and give them a proper burial yǎnglǎo sòngzhōng 養老送終／养老送终 PH

look after guānzhào; zhàogu 關照／关照; 照顧／照顾 V

look at qiáo 瞧 V

look: it looks as if kàn qǐlai 看起來／看起来 VP

look, smell, and taste great sè-xiāng-wèi jùquán 色香味俱全 IE

look up chá 查 V

look up in a dictionary chá zìdiǎn 查字典

looks xiàngmào 相貌 N

lotion yàoshuǐ 藥水／药水 N

loveable kě'ài 可愛／可爱 SV

lovely kě'ài 可愛／可爱 SV

lower-right corner yòu xiàjiǎo 右下角 N

luck yùnqi 運氣／运气 N

luckily xìnghǎo 幸好 IE

lucky xìngyùn 幸運／幸运 SV

M

main zhǔyào 主要 ATTR

main points yàodiǎn 要點／要点 N

main street dàjiē 大街 N

major zhǔyào 主要 ATTR

major (in a university) zhuānyè 專業／专业 N

major part dàbùfen 大部份／大部分 N

make nòng 弄 V

make a dish chǎocài 炒菜 VO

make a lab test huàyàn 化驗／化验 V

make a meal zuò yí dùn (fàn) 做一頓(飯)／做一顿(饭) VP

make money zhèngqián 掙錢／挣钱 VO

makeup: theatrical makeup liǎnpǔ 臉譜／脸谱 N

mall shāngchǎng 商場／商场 N

manage guǎn 管 V

manicure zhǐjia hùlǐ 指甲護理／指甲护理 N

manliness yánggāng zhī qì 陽剛之氣／阳刚之气 N

marinate yānzhì 醃製／腌制 V

mark biāozhì 標誌／标志 N

market shāngchǎng 商場／商场 N

mask liǎnpǔ 臉譜／脸谱 N

massage ànmó 按摩 V/N

master of ceremonies zhǔchírén 主持人 N

material yuánliào 原料 N

May I trouble you to . . . ? máfan nǐ 麻煩你／麻烦你 IE

meal: Chinese meal Zhōngcān 中餐 N

measure liáng 量 V

meat ròu 肉 N

medical record bìnglì(běn) 病歷(本)／病历(本) N
medicine: Chinese medicine Zhōngyī 中醫／中医 N
mediocre píngpíng 平平 RF
meet each other jiànmiàn 見面／见面 VO
mega *(computer)* zhào 兆 M
men's clothing nánzhuāng 男裝／男装 N
mention tí 提 V; tíqǐ 提起 RV
menu of services mùlù 目錄／目录 N
merchandise huòwù 貨物／货物 N
messy luàn 亂／乱 SV
meticulous zǐxì 仔細／仔细 SV
metropolis dàdūshì 大都市 N
middleman jīngjìrén 經紀人／经纪人 N
migrate yímín 移民 VO
million zhào 兆 NU
mind: state/frame of mind xīnqíng 心情 N
miss *(someone or something)* sīniàn; xiǎngniàn 思念; 想念 V
moderate shìzhōng 適中／适中 VP
modest qiānxū 謙虛／谦虚 SV
mom; ma; mother niáng 娘 N
moment: just a moment; a moment, please shāo děng yíxià 稍等一下 VP
money: amount of money; sum of money jīn'é 金額／金额 N
mood xīnqíng 心情 N
more often than not wǎngwǎng 往往 A
mother; mom; ma niáng 娘 N
mother and baby mǔyīng 母嬰／母婴 N
move emotionally dǎdòng 打動／打动 RV

N

narcissism zìliàn 自戀／自恋 N
narcissistic zìliàn 自戀／自恋 SV
nauseated: feel nauseated ěxīn 噁心／恶心 VO
neat zhěngqí 整齊／整齐 SV
necessarily: not necessarily bú zhìyú 不至於／不至于 IE
necessary bìyào 必要 SV
need bìyào 必要 N
negative side fǎnmiàn 反面 N
never cónglái bù; cónglái méi 從來不／从来不; 從來沒／从来没 A
nice *(person)* rén hǎo 人好 SV
no wonder guàibude 怪不得 RV
normal zhèngcháng 正常 SV
nose: have a runny nose liú bítì 流鼻涕 VO
nostalgia sīxiāng bìng 思鄉病／思乡病 N
not bad hái hǎo 還好／还好 VP
not necessarily bú zhìyú 不至於／不至于 IE
not very/particularly bù zěnme 不怎麼／不怎么 A
note: take note of zhùyì 注意 V
nothing to speak of kěbù zěnmeyàng 可不怎麼樣／可不怎么样 IE

notify tōngzhī 通知 V
number shùzì 數字／数字 N
numeral shùzì 數字／数字 N

O

obsessed with zǒuhuǒrùmó 走火入魔 IE
obtain qǔ 取 V
offer tígōng 提供 V
often jīngcháng 經常／经常 A
Oh, that reminds me *(expresses realization)* Ò, duì le 哦, 對了／哦, 对了 I
one *(used when saying the number 1 in phone numbers, etc.)* yāo 么／幺 NU
one's own self zìjǐ shēnshang 自己身上 PH
oneself běnrén 本人 N
online: go online shàngwǎng 上網／上网 VO
only child dúshēng zǐnǚ 獨生子女／独生子女 N
open a card *(account) (for ATM, etc.)* kāi kǎ 開卡／开卡 VO
order mìnglìng 命令 V/N
order: receive an order; take an order dé lìng 得令 VO
others qítā; qíyú 其他; 其餘／其余 PR
otherwise yào bùrán; yàobu(shi) 要不然; 要不(是) C
ouch āiyō 哎喲／哎哟 I
ought to (yīng) gāi (應)該／(应)该 A
oyster sauce háoyóu 蠔油／蚝油 N

P

package bāoguǒ 包裹 N
page: a full page zhěng bǎn 整版 N
painful téng; tòng 疼; 痛 SV
pale *(in color)* dàn 淡 SV
pants kùzi 褲子／裤子 N
parcel bāoguǒ 包裹 N
particular: be particular about jiǎngjiu 講究／讲究 SV
particularly: not particularly bù zěnme 不怎麼／不怎么 A
partner dādàng 搭檔／搭档 N
partner up *(with)* dādàng 搭檔／搭档 VP
pass to dì 遞／递 V
passable hái hǎo 還好／还好 VP
passionate rèqíng 熱情／热情 SV
passport hùzhào 護照／护照 N
password mìmǎ(r) 密碼(兒)／密码(儿) N
path: a winding path leading to a secluded spot qūjìngtōngyōu 曲徑通幽／曲径通幽 IE
patient bìngrén 病人 N
patient: see a patient kànbìng 看病 VO
pattern kuǎnxíng 款型 N
pay one's own expenses zìfèi 自費／自费 V
peanut *(shelled)* huāshēngmǐ 花生米 N
peanut oil huāshēngyóu 花生油 N

pedicure zhǐjia hùlǐ 指甲護理／指甲护理 N

people *(in general)* rénjiā 人家 PR

peppercorns huājiāo 花椒 N

perfect wánměi 完美 SV

perform biǎoyǎn; yǎn 表演; 演 V

performance biǎoyǎn 表演 N

performance fee yǎnchūfèi 演出費／演出费 N

performer yǎnyuán 演員／演员 N

perm *(hair)* tàng 漫／烫 V

person: in person běnrén 本人 N

personage rénwù 人物 N

personal ID shēnfènzhèng 身份證／身份证 N

personal items suíshēn wùpǐn 隨身物品／随身物品 N

personality gèxìng 個性／个性 N

persuade; convince someone shuōfú (shuìfú) 説服／说服 V

phase jiēduàn 階段／阶段 N

phenomenon xiànxiàng 現象／现象 N

phony jiǎ 假 SV

phony shānzhài 山寨 N

photocopy fùyìn 複印／复印 V

physician dàifu 大夫 N

pimple qīngchūndòu 青春痘 N

place *(aside)* gē 擱／搁 V

place something in the armpit jiā dào yèxià 夾到腋下／夹到腋下 VP

play xì 戲／戏 N

plenty: have plenty of yǒudeshì 有的是 IE

plus jiā 加 V

pocket kǒudàir 口袋兒／口袋儿 N

pollen huāfěn 花粉 N

positive zhèngmiàn 正面 ATTR

post office yóujú 郵局／邮局 N

postage yóufèi 郵費／邮费 N

postage stamp yóupiào 郵票／邮票 N

preferential treatment yōuhuì 優惠／优惠 N

prepare bèi 備／备 V

prescribe; write a prescription kāiyào 開藥／开药 VO

prescription: fill a prescription ná yào 拿藥／拿药 VO

press *(with hand or fingertip)* èn 摁 V

press down àn 按 V

pressure yālì 壓力／压力 N

pretty piàoliang 漂亮 SV

price range jiàwèi 價位／价位 N

primarily zhǔyào 主要 A

problem kùnnán 困難／困难 N

process guòchéng 過程／过程 N

program huódòng 活動／活动 N

project xiàngmù 項目／项目 N

promote tuī; tuīsòng 推; 推送 V

protect bǎohù 保護／保护 V

proud: be proud of oneself déyì 得意 VO

public good/service gōngyì 公益 N

push àn; tuī 按; 推 V

put *(aside)* gē 擱／搁 V

put in jiārù 加入 VP

Q

quality pǐnzhì; zhìliàng 品質／品质; 質量／质量 N

quality-price ratio xìngjiàbǐ 性價比／性价比 N

quarrel chǎojià 吵架 VO

quit tuì (chūlai) 退(出來／出来) V

quiz xiǎo cèyàn 小測驗／小测验 N

R

range fànwéi 範圍／范围 N

raw material yuánliào 原料 N

ready: all in readiness qíquán 齊全／齐全 SV

real: a real man *(in the macho sense)* nánzǐhàn 男子漢／男子汉 N

receive shōu 收 V

recipe càipǔ 菜譜／菜谱 N

recommend tuījiàn 推薦／推荐 V

refer to tí 提 V; tíqǐ 提起 RV

register *(for a class)* bào yí ge bān 報一個班／报一个班 VP

register *(to see a doctor)* guàhào 掛號／挂号 VO

regularly jīngcháng 經常／经常 A

relax fàngsōng 放鬆／放松 V

relieved: feel relieved fàngxīn 放心 RV

remember jìdé 記得／记得 V

remind tíxǐng 提醒 V

repay bàodá 報答／报答 V

request yāoqiú 要求 V

require yāoqiú 要求 V

requirement yāoqiú 要求 N

resemble xiàng 像 V

residential area xiǎoqū 小區／小区 PW

rest: have a rest xiē 歇 V

rest: the rest qítā; qíyú 其他; 其餘／其余 PR

reverse side fǎnmiàn 反面 N

review *(what has been learned)* fùxí 複習／复习 V

revolve zhuàn 轉／转 V

rid: get rid of qùdiào 去掉 RV

right after *(immediately)* jǐn jiēzhe 緊接著／紧接着 A

roam guàng 逛 V

role juésè 角色 N

romantic làngmàn 浪漫 SV

rotate zhuàn 轉／转 V

run into yùdào 遇到 V

rush chōng 衝／冲 V

S

sack bāor 包兒／包儿 N

safeguard bǎohù 保護／保护 V

sake: for the sake of wèi; wèile 為／为; 為了／为了 C

salary gōngzī 工資／工资 N

salt yán 鹽／盐 N

sauté chǎo 炒 V

save *(money)* cún 存 V

savory xiāng 香 V

scald tàng 燙／烫 V

scalding tàng 燙／烫 SV

scallion cōng 蔥／葱 N

scary kěpà 可怕 SV

schedule shíjiānbiǎo 時間表／时间表 N

scholarship jiǎngxuéjīn 獎學金／奖学金 N

school: at school zài xiào 在校 VO

school hospital xiào yīyuàn 校醫院／校医院 N

school of arts měiyuàn 美院 (= měishù xuéyuàn 美術學院／美术学院) N

scope fànwéi 範圍／范围 N

screen píngmù 屏幕 N

seasoning tiáowèipǐn 調味品／调味品 N

seat zuòwèi 座位 N

secret code mìmǎ(r) 密碼(兒)／密码(儿) N

sections duàn 段 N

seem: it seems kàn qǐlai 看起來／看起来 VP

seems; seems as if hǎoxiàng 好像 A

select tiāo; tiāoxuǎn 挑; 挑選／挑选 V

sell xiāoshòu 銷售／销售 V

semester xuéqī 學期／学期 N

send a text message fā duǎnxìn 發短信／发短信 VP

sense of humor yōumògǎn 幽默感 N

sensitive mǐngǎn 敏感 SV

sentence jùzi 句子 N

sentiment gǎnqíng 感情 N

serious yánzhòng 嚴重／严重 SV

service(s) fúwù 服務／服务 N

service counter fúwùtái 服務台／服务台 N

sesame oil máyóu 麻油 N

set package *(of food, services, etc.)* tàocān 套餐 N

set up *(install)* shèzhì 設置／设置 V

share *(joy, experience, etc.)* fēnxiǎng 分享 V

sheet: an entire sheet zhěng bǎn 整版 N

shiitake mushroom xiānggū 香菇 N

shoe store xiédiàn 鞋店 N

shoot *(a film)* pāi 拍 V; pāizhào 拍照 VO

shop shāngdiàn 商店 N

shopping gòuwù 購物／购物 N; **go shopping** gòuwù 購物／购物 VO

short of *(lack)* quē 缺 V

should (yīng) gāi (應)該／(应)该 A

show chūshì 出示 V

show xì 戲／戏 N

show: watch a show kàn xì 看戲／看戏

Sichuan *(province in southwestern China known for its very spicy cuisine)* Sìchuān 四川 PW

Sichuan pepper huājiāo 花椒 N

sign biāozhì 標誌／标志 N

sign one's name qiānzì; qiānmíng 簽字／签字; 簽名／签名 VO

sign up bàomíng 報名／报名 VO

signature qiānzì; qiānmíng 簽字／签字; 簽名／签名 N

sincere zhēnchéng 真誠／真诚 SV

sincerity zhēnchéng 真誠／真诚 N

situation qíngkuàng 情況／情况 N

skin pí; pífū 皮; 皮膚／皮肤 N

skin toning rùnfū 潤膚／润肤 N

skin whitening měibái 美白 N

skirt qúnzi 裙子 N

slice qiēchéng 切成 RV

slight qīngwēi 輕微／轻微 SV

slightly shāowēi 稍微 A

small machine jīzi 機子／机子 N

smart cōngming 聰明／聪明 SV

smartphone zhìnéngjī 智能機／智能机 N

smile wēixiào 微笑 V

smug déyì 得意 VO

snack língshí 零食 N

sneeze dǎ pēntì 打噴嚏／打喷嚏 VO

so, after all yuánlái 原來／原来 N

soak pào 泡 V

soft qīng 輕／轻 SV

soft *(to the touch)* ruǎn 軟／软 SV

soiree wǎnhuì 晚會／晚会 N

someone who has had same experience guòláirén 過來人／过来人 N

so-so píngpíng 平平 RF

soy sauce jiàngyóu 醬油／酱油 N

soy sauce *(thick)* lǎochōu 老抽 N

soy sauce *(thin)* shēngchōu 生抽 N

special zhuānmén 專門／专门 SV

special feature tèsè 特色 N

specialist zhuānjiā 專家／专家 N

specialty store zhuānmàidiàn 專賣店／专卖店 N

spectator guānzhòng 觀眾／观众 N

spend huā 花 V

squander làngfèi 浪費／浪费 V

staff rényuán 人員／人员 N

stage *(phase)* jiēduàn 階段／阶段 N

stand up to use kàngshǐ 抗使 VO

star anise bājiǎo 八角 N

starch diànfěn 澱粉／淀粉 N

stare at dīng 盯 V

steep pào 泡 V

stern yánlì 嚴厲／严厉 SV

stick into chā 插 V

stiff *(to the touch)* yìng 硬 SV

stir fry biānchǎo; chǎo 煸炒; 炒 V

stomach dùzi 肚子 N

storage capacity liúliàng 流量 N

store shāngdiàn 商店 N

straight (indicates a constant direction)   yìzhí   一直   A
strain   yālì   壓力／压力   N
strength   lìdù   力度   N
strict   yánlì   嚴厲／严厉   SV
stroll   guàng   逛   V
student health center   xiào yīyuàn   校醫院／校医院   N
student ID   xuéshengzhèng   學生證／学生证   N
studious   yònggōng   用功   SV
successful (said of an enterprise)   fēngshēngshuǐqǐ   風生水起／风生水起   IE
sugar   táng   糖   N
suitable   héshì   合適／合适   SV
superior grade   gāodàng   高檔／高档   SV
supermarket   chāoshì   超市   N
superstition   míxìn   迷信   N
supply   tígōng   提供   V
support   zhīchí   支持   V
supposing   wànyī   萬一／万一   C
sure: surely; for sure   díquè; kěndìng   的確／的确; 肯定   A
surgical department   wàikē   外科
surroundings   huánjìng   環境／环境   N
susceptible   mǐngǎn   敏感   SV
symptoms   zhèngzhuàng   症狀／症状   N
system   xìtǒng   系統／系统   N

T

table of contents   mùlù   目錄／目录   N
take   qǔ   取   V
take (a picture)   pāi   拍   V; pāizhào   拍照   VO
take or have with oneself   suíshēn   隨身／随身   VO
talk: have a good talk   hǎohāo liáoliao   好好聊聊   VP
taste   wèidao   味道   N
tea: brew tea; make tea   qī chá   沏茶   VO
tea ceremony   chádào   茶道   N
teach   jiǎngkè   講課／讲课   VO
team up (with)   dādàng   搭檔／搭档   VP
tearoom   cháshì   茶室   N
term   tiáojiàn   條件／条件   N
test   cèyàn   測驗／测验   N
theatrical makeup   liǎnpǔ   臉譜／脸谱   N
then: and then   wánle   完了   VP
thermometer   tǐwēnbiǎo   體溫表／体温表   N
think about/over   kǎolǜ   考慮／考虑   V
think of   sīniàn   思念   V
thinking   sīwéi   思維／思维   N
thirteen-spice (powder)   shísān xiāng   十三香   N
thought   sīwéi   思維／思维   N
thoughtful   zhōudào   周到   SV
throw away   rēng   扔   V
throw up   tù   吐   V
tidy   gānjìng; zhěngqí   乾淨／干净; 整齊／整齐   SV
till (until)   zhì   至   CV

time: at any time; at all times   suíshí   隨時／随时   A
time: at the same time   tóngshí   同時／同时   A
timetable   shíjiānbiǎo   時間表／时间表   N
tint (one's) hair   rǎnfà   染髮／染发   VO
tooth/teeth   yáchǐ   牙齒／牙齿   N
top-quality   gāodàng   高檔／高档   SV
toss   rēng   扔   V
tour; tourism   lǚyóu   旅遊／旅游   V/N
toy   wánjù   玩具   N
trade   shēngyi   生意   N
trademark   pǐnpái   品牌   N
transaction   jiāoyì   交易   N
treat   xiǎngshòu   享受   N
trick   zhāo(r)   招(兒)／招(儿)   N
trivial   qīngwēi   輕微／轻微   SV
trouble: be a bother/trouble (to somebody)   tiān máfan   添麻煩／添麻烦   VP
troubled   fán; fánnǎo   煩／烦; 煩惱／烦恼   SV
troubling   fánrén   煩人／烦人   SV
trousers   kùzi   褲子／裤子   N
trust   xìnrèn   信任   N/V
turn   zhuàn   轉／转   V
two (informal)   liǎ   倆／俩   PR
type   kuǎn   款   N

U

Um   Āi   哎   I
unable to get about / move freely   xíngdòng búbiàn   行動不便／行动不便   PH
unassuming   qiānxū   謙虛／谦虚   SV
undergo   jīnglì   經歷／经历   V
underground   dìxià   地下   N
unit (in an organization)   dānwèi   單位／单位   N
until   zhì   至   CV
up to (preceding numbers)   shàng   上 + [number]   BF
upscale   gāodàng   高檔／高档   ATTR
urge   gǔlì   鼓勵／鼓励   V/N
use   shǐyòng   使用   V
use tea as a replacement for alcohol   yǐ chá dài jiǔ   以茶代酒   PH
used: get used to   shìyìng   適應／适应   V
utilize   shǐyòng   使用   V

V

vampire   xīxuèguǐ   吸血鬼   N
vegetable   shūcài   蔬菜   N
version   bǎn   版   N
very: not very   bù zěnme   不怎麼／不怎么   A
vexed   fán; fánnǎo   煩／烦; 煩惱／烦恼   SV
vexing   fánrén   煩人／烦人   SV
video   shìpín   視頻／视频   N
vigor   huólì   活力   N
vinegar   cù   醋   N

virility yánggāng zhī qì 陽剛之氣／阳刚之气 N

virtuous circle (*opposite of* vicious circle) liángxìng xúnhuán 良性循環／良性循环 N

vitality huólì 活力 N

volunteer zhìyuànzhě 志願者／志愿者 N

vomit tù 吐 V

vomit: feel like vomiting ěxīn 噁心／恶心 VO

W

wages gōngzī 工資／工资 N

Walmart Wò'ěrmǎ 沃爾瑪／沃尔玛 N

Wangfujing (*major shopping area in Beijing*) Wángfǔjǐng 王府井 PW

warm and comfortable wēnxīn 溫馨 SV

wash, cut, and blow-dry xǐ jiǎn chuī 洗剪吹 IE

wash hair xǐtóu 洗頭／洗头 VO

washed (*fully*) xǐhǎo 洗好 RV

waste làngfèi 浪費／浪费 V

watch a show kàn xì 看戲／看戏 VO

wave after wave (*of pain*) yízhèn yízhèn de 一陣一陣地／一阵一阵地 A

way of doing something zuòfǎ 做法 N

we two zán liǎ; zánmen 咱倆／咱俩; 咱們／咱们 PR

weight (*body*) tǐzhòng 體重／体重 N

well liked/welcomed by all shòu dàjiā de xǐhuan/huānyíng 受大家的喜歡｜歡迎／受大家的喜欢｜欢迎 PH

Western medicine xīyī 西醫／西医 N

Western-style suit/clothes xīfú 西服 N

Western world; the West xīfāng 西方 N

What are you doing? Nǐ zài gànma? 你在幹嘛？／你在干吗？ PH

what's so good about that yǒu shénme hǎo ne 有甚麼好呢／有什么好呢 PH

when děng . . . de shíhou 等……的時候／等……的时候 PH

whenever suíshí 隨時／随时 A

Will you please . . . ? máfan nǐ 麻煩你／麻烦你 IE

winding: a winding path leading to a secluded spot qūjìngtōngyōu 曲徑通幽／曲径通幽 IE

winter vacation hánjià 寒假 N

wish zhùyuàn 祝願／祝愿 V

wish happiness to/for zhùfú 祝福 V

witch wūpó 巫婆 N

withdraw from tuì (chūlai) 退 (出來／出来) V

withdraw money qǔkuǎn; qǔqián 取款; 取錢／取钱 VO

within X zài X zhī nèi 在 X 之内 IE

women's clothing nǚzhuāng 女裝／女装 N

work of art yìshùpǐn 藝術品／艺术品 N

work schedule gōngzuò rìlì 工作日曆／工作日历 N

works (*of literature, art*) zuòpǐn 作品 N

worried jí 急 SV

worry dānxīn 擔心／担心 SV/V/VO

worry about guānxīn 關心／关心 V

worth it zhídé 值得 SV/AV

Y

Yangshuo (*a popular tourist town in southwest China's Guangxi Province, famous for its spectacular mountain scenery of karst topography*) Yángshuò 陽朔／阳朔 PW

yielding (*to the touch*) ruǎn 軟／软 SV

you and I zán liǎ; zánmen 咱倆／咱俩; 咱們／咱们 PR

You get what you pay for yī fēn jiàqián yī fēn huò 一分價錢一分貨／一分价钱一分货 IE

Z

zombie jiāngshī 殭屍／僵尸 N

Glossary of Measure Words

Following is a list of some common measure words, along with the nouns each of them is usually associated with. The nouns listed here are by no means exhaustive. They represent the ones you have encountered so far as well as some other common nouns. Note that a few measure words are themselves nouns and are not followed by other nouns; for example: *kè* 課／课, *suì* 歲／岁, *tiān* 天. We encourage you to add more measure words and nouns to this list as your Chinese advances.

bǎ 把 *(for things you can grasp in your hand)*
    dāo 刀 *(knife)*
    mǐ 米 *([a handful of] rice)*
    qián 錢／钱 *([a fistful of] money)*
    sǎn 傘／伞 *(umbrella)*
    shuāzi 刷子 *(brush)*
    shūzi 梳子 *(comb)*
    yàoshi 鑰匙／钥匙 *(key)*
    yǐzi 椅子 *(chair)*

bān 班 *(for crowds, scheduled transport vehicles)*
    chē 車／车 *(bus [run])*
    fēijī 飛機／飞机 *(airplane [flight])*
    xuésheng 學生／学生 *([class of] students)*

bàn 半 *(half [of something])*

bàng 磅 *(pound)*
    shuǐguǒ 水果 *(fruit)*

bāo 包 *(pack; package)*
    táng(guǒ) 糖(果) *(candy)*
    (xiāng)yān (香)煙／(香)烟 *(cigarettes)*
    yáxiàn 牙線／牙线 *(floss)*
    yīfu 衣服 *(clothing)*

bēi 杯 *(cup; glass)*
    chá 茶 *(tea)*
    kāfēi 咖啡 *(coffee)*
    shuǐ 水 *(water)*

bèi 倍 *(times [as much])*

běn 本 *(for books, periodicals, files, etc.)*
    shū 書／书 *(book)*
    xiǎoshuō 小説／小说 *(novel)*
    zázhì 雜誌／杂志 *(magazine)*
    zìdiǎn 字典 *(dictionary)*

bǐ 筆／笔 *(lump sum)*
    qián 錢／钱 *(money)*

biàn 遍 *(occasions; times; occurrences)*

bù 部 *(for film, large books, machines, etc.)*
    diànyǐng 電影／电影 *(movie)*

cè 冊 *(volume [of books])*
    shū 書／书 *(book)*

céng 層／层 *(story [in buildings])*
    lóu 樓／楼 *(building)*

chǎng 場／场 *(for games, performances, etc.)*
    diànyǐng 電影／电影 *(movie [showing])*
    qiúsài 球賽／球赛 *(ball game)*

chǐ 尺 *(foot [length])*

chuàn 串 *(bunch)*
    pútao 葡萄 *(grapes)*
    yàoshi 鑰匙／钥匙 *(keys)*

cì 次 *(occasions; times; occurrences)*
    kǎoshì 考試／考试 *(exam)*
    lǚxíng 旅行 *(journey)*

cùn 寸 *(inch [length])*

dá 打 *(dozen)*
    jīdàn 雞蛋／鸡蛋 *(eggs)*

dào 道 *(course [of food]; dish)*
    cài 菜 *(food; dish)*

diǎn 點／点 *(clock time: hour on the clock)*
    zhōng 鐘／钟 *(clock)*

dǐng 頂／顶 *(for hats, sedan chairs)*
    màozi 帽子 *(hat)*

dòng 棟／栋 *(for houses)*
    fángzi 房子 *(house)*
    lóu 樓／楼 *(building)*

dù 度 *(angles; degrees; temperature)*

duàn 段 *(section; part)*
    huà 話／话 *(remarks)*

duì 對／对 *([matching] pair)*
    huāpíng 花瓶 *(vases)*

dùn 頓／顿 *(for meals, occurrences)*
    fàn 飯／饭 *(meal)*

duǒ 朵 *(for flowers, clouds, etc.)*
    huār 花兒／花儿 *(flower)*

fēn 分 *(clock time: minute)*
    zhōng 鐘／钟 *(clock)*

fēn 分 *(unit of money: "cent")*
    qián 錢／钱 *(money)*

fèn 份 *(for copies of newspapers)*
    bào(zhǐ) 報(紙)／报(纸) *(newspaper)*
    gōngzuò 工作 *(job)*

fēng 封 *(for letters)*
　xìn 信 *(letter)*
fú 幅 *(for cloth, paintings)*
　huàr 畫兒／画儿 *(painting)*
fù 副 *(for sets of things, facial expressions)*
　shǒutào 手套 *([pair of] gloves)*
　yǎnjìng 眼鏡／眼镜 *([pair of] eyeglasses)*
　yào 藥／药 *([dose of] medicine)*

ge 個／个 *(non-specific measure word)*
　bǐjìběn 筆記本／笔记本 *(notebook)*
　dìfang 地方 *(place)*
　jìniànpǐn 紀念品／纪念品 *(souvenir)*
　lǐbài 禮拜／礼拜 *(week)*
　qiú 球 *(ball)*
　qǐyè 企業／企业 *(business establishment)*
　rén 人 *(person)*
　shǒujī 手機／手机 *(cell phone)*
　wèntí 問題／问题 *(question; problem)*
　xiǎoshí 小時／小时 *(hour)*
　xīngqī 星期 *(week)*
　zhōngtóu 鐘頭／钟头 *(hour)*
gēn 根 *(for long, slender objects)*
　shéngzi 繩子／绳子 *(rope)*
　(xiāng)yān (香)煙／(香)烟 *(cigarette)*
　yáxiàn 牙線／牙线 *(floss)*

háng 行 *(line; row)*
　Hànzì 漢字／汉字 *(Chinese characters)*
hào 號／号 *(days of the month)*
hào 號／号 *(numbered things or people)*
　duìyuán 隊員／队员 *(team member)*
　lóu 樓／楼 *(building)*
hé 盒 *(box; case; pack)*
　huǒchái 火柴 *(matches)*
　qiǎokèlì 巧克力 *(chocolate)*
　yáxiàn 牙線／牙线 *(floss)*
hú 壺／壶 *(pot)*
　chá 茶 *(tea)*
hù 戶／户 *(for families, households)*
　rénjiā 人家 *(household)*
huí 回 *(occasions; times; occurrences)*

jiā 家 *(for families, businesses)*
　fànguǎnr 飯館兒／饭馆儿 *(restaurant)*
　shāngdiàn 商店 *(shop; store)*
jià 架 *(for planes, radios)*
　fēijī 飛機／飞机 *(airplane)*
jiān 間／间 *(for rooms)*
　bàngōngshì 辦公室／办公室 *(office)*
　fángjiān 房間／房间 *(room)*
　wūzi 屋子 *(room)*
jiàn 件 *(for articles, items)*
　chènshān 襯衫／衬衫 *(shirt)*

　jiákè 夾克／夹克 *(jacket)*
　máoyī 毛衣 *(sweater)*
　shìqing 事情 *(affairs, matters)*
　T-xùshān T-恤衫 *(T-shirt)*
　wàitào 外套 *(overcoat)*
　xíngli 行李 *(baggage, luggage)*
　yīfu 衣服 *(clothing)*
jié 節／节 *(for class sections)*
　kè 課／课 *(class session)*
jīn 斤 *(catty [Chinese unit of weight]; half kilogram)*
　shuǐguǒ 水果 *(fruit)*
jù 句 *(sentence)*
　huà 話／话 *(remarks)*
juǎn(r) 卷(兒)／卷(儿) *(for rolls, spools, reels)*
　wèishēngzhǐ 衛生紙／卫生纸 *(toilet paper)*

kē 棵 *(for trees, cabbages)*
　shù 樹／树 *(tree)*
kè 課／课 *(lesson [in a book])*
　dì sān kè 第三課／第三课 *(Lesson Three)*
kè 刻 *(clock time: quarter-hour)*
　zhōng 鐘／钟 *(clock)*
kǒu 口 *(for mouthfuls, people, wells)*
　rén 人 *([number of] people [in a family])*
kuài 塊／块 *(for pieces, slices)*
　(shǒu)biǎo (手)錶／(手)表 *(wristwatch)*
　bīngkuàir 冰塊兒／冰块儿 *(ice cube)*
　bù 布 *(cloth)*
　dàngāo 蛋糕 *(cake)*
　féizào 肥皂 *(soap)*
　ròu 肉 *(meat)*
　shǒujuàn 手絹／手绢 *(handkerchief)*
　táng 糖 *(candy)*
kuài 塊／块 *(unit of money: "dollar")*
　qián 錢／钱 *(money)*

lèi 類／类 *(type; category)*
　dōngxi 東西／东西 *(stuff; thing)*
lǐ 里 *(Chinese mile)*
　lù 路 *(road)*
lì 粒 *(for grainlike things)*
　yào 藥／药 *(medicine [pills])*
liàng 輛／辆 *(for vehicles)*
　gōng(gòng) (qì)chē 公(共汽)車／公(共汽)车 *(bus)*
　kǎchē 卡車／卡车 *(truck)*
　mótuōchē 摩托車／摩托车 *(motorcycle)*
　qìchē 汽車／汽车 *(car, automobile)*
　zìxíngchē 自行車／自行车 *(bicycle)*
liè 列 *(for [train] cars)*
　huǒchē 火車／火车 *(train)*
lóu 樓／楼 *(story [in buildings])*
lù 路 *(bus route)*
　chē 車／车 *(bus)*

luò 摞 *(for stacks of things)*
    zhǐ 紙／纸 *(paper)*

máo 毛 *(unit of money: "dime")*
    qián 錢／钱 *(money)*
mén 門／门 *(for courses of study)*
    kè 課／课 *(course)*
mǐ 米 *(meter)*
miàn 面 *(for mirrors, flags)*
    jìngzi 鏡子／镜子 *(mirror)*
miǎo 秒 *(clock time: second)*
    zhōng 鐘／钟 *(clock)*

nián 年 *(year)*
niánjí 年級／年级 *(year in school)*

pái 排 *(for rows of things)*
    zuòwèi 座位 *(seats)*
pán 盤／盘 *(for coils, dishes, etc.)*
    qí 棋 *([game of] chess)*
    shuǐguǒ 水果 *([plate of] fruit)*
pǐ 匹 *(for horses, mules, bolts of cloth)*
    mǎ 馬／马 *(horse)*
piān 篇 *(for articles, chapters, etc.)*
    wénzhāng 文章 *(article; essay)*
piàn 片 *(for slices of things)*
    miànbāo 麵包／面包 *(bread)*
píng 瓶 *(bottle)*
    hùfàsù 護髮素／护发素 *(hair conditioner)*
    píjiǔ 啤酒 *(beer)*
    xǐfàshuǐ 洗髮水／洗发水 *(shampoo)*

shēn 身 *(for outfits, suits of clothing)*
    yīfu 衣服 *(clothing)*
shǒu 首 *(for poems, songs)*
    gē 歌 *(song)*
    shī 詩／诗 *(poem)*
shù 束 *(for bunches of things)*
    huār 花兒／花儿 *(flowers)*
shuāng 雙／双 *(a pair of)*
    kuàizi 筷子 *(chopsticks)*
    shǒu 手 *(hands)*
    wàzi 襪子／袜子 *(socks)*
    xiézi 鞋子 *(shoes)*
    yǎnjīng 眼睛 *(eyes)*
suì 歲／岁 *(years of age)*
suǒ 所 *(for houses)*
    gōngyù 公寓 *(apartment)*
    xuéxiào 學校／学校 *(school)*
    yīyuàn 醫院／医院 *(hospital)*

tái 台 *(for performances, engines, etc.)*
    diànnǎo 電腦／电脑 *(computer)*
    diànshì 電視／电视 *(television)*

zhàoxiàngjī 照相機／照相机 *(camera)*
táng 堂 *(class period)*
    kè 課／课 *(class session)*
tàng 趟 *(for times [of trips])*
    huǒchē 火車／火车 *(train trip)*
    lù 路 *(trip)*
tào 套 *(set)*
    gōngyù 公寓 *(apartment)*
    shū 書／书 *(books)*
    yīfu 衣服 *(clothes)*
tiān 天 *(day)*
tiáo 條／条 *(for long, narrow things)*
    duǎnkù 短褲／短裤 *(shorts)*
    hé 河 *(river)*
    jiē 街 *(street)*
    kùzi 褲子／裤子 *(pants; trousers)*
    lóng 龍／龙 *(dragon)*
    lù 路 *(road)*
    máojīn 毛巾 *(towel)*
    miànbāo 麵包／面包 *(bread)*
    qúnzi 裙子 *(skirt)*
    shé 蛇 *(snake)*
    tǎnzi 毯子 *(blanket)*
    yú 魚／鱼 *(fish)*
tóu 頭／头 *(for livestock)*
    niú 牛 *(cow; ox)*
    zhū 豬／猪 *(pig)*

wǎn 碗 *(bowl)*
    fàn 飯／饭 *(rice)*
wèi 位 *(for people [polite form])*
    kèren 客人 *(guest)*
    lǎoshī 老師／老师 *(teacher)*

xiàng 項／项 *(for itemized things)*
xiē 些 *(small, indefinite amounts; some)*
    dōngxi 東西／东西 *(stuff, things)*
    rén 人 *(people)*
    shìqing 事情 *(affairs, matters)*

yàng 樣／样 *(type; kind)*
    dōngxi 東西／东西 *(stuff; thing)*
yè 夜 *(night)*
yìdiǎn(r) 一點(兒)／一点(儿) *(a little bit; small amount)*
    qián 錢／钱 *(money)*
yuán 元 *(dollar)*

zhàn 站 *(stop [train, bus, etc.])*
zhāng 張／张 *(for flat things)*
    chuáng 床 *(bed)*
    dìtú 地圖／地图 *(map)*
    huàr 畫兒／画儿 *(painting)*
    míngxìnpiàn 明信片 *(postcard)*
    piào 票 *(ticket)*

shūzhuō 書桌／书桌 (desk)
xìnyòngkǎ 信用卡 (credit card)
zhǐ 紙／纸 (paper)
zhuōzi 桌子 (table)
zhāng 章 (chapter [in a book])
　dì sān zhāng 第三章 (Chapter Three)
zhī 支 (for slender objects)
　máobǐ 毛筆／毛笔 (writing brush)
　yágāo 牙膏 (toothpaste)
　yáshuā 牙刷 (toothbrush)
zhī 隻／只 (for animals, one of a pair of things)
　gǒu 狗 (dog)
　jī 雞／鸡 (chicken)
　lǎohǔ 老虎 (tiger)
　lǎoshǔ 老鼠 (mouse; rat)

māo 貓／猫 (cat)
niǎo 鳥／鸟 (bird)
shǒu 手 (hand)
tùzi 兔子 (rabbit)
xié 鞋 (shoe)
yā 鴨／鸭 (duck)
yǎnjīng 眼睛 (eye)
zhū 豬／猪 (pig)
zhǒng 種／种 (kind; type)
　dòngwù 動物／动物 (animal)
zuò 座 (for mountains, bridges, etc.)
　dàshà 大廈／大厦 (high-rise building)
　qiáo 橋／桥 (bridge)
　shān 山 (mountain)

Index

Credits

Illustrations:

Illustrations by Nora Guo unless otherwise noted.
Maps on pp. 17 and R-32 by Nora Guo.
Map on inside back cover by Patti Isaccs/Parrot Graphics.

Photos:

Photos are taken from the video material for *Encounters,* unless otherwise noted.

frontispiece © testing/Shutterstock.com.
p. 7 © Jon Bilous/Shutterstock.com.
p. 10 (*left*) © JingAiping/Shutterstock.com; (*middle*) © trekandshoot/Shutterstock.com; (*right*) © S.Borisov/Shutterstock.com.
p. 47 (*left*) © Natali Glado/Shutterstock.com; (*right*) © Hung Chung Chih/Shutterstock.com.
p. 50 © IS_ImageSource/iStockphoto.
p. 71 © Andresr/Shutterstock.com (blow-dry); © racorn/Shutterstock.com (perm); © Voyagerix/Shutterstock.com (hair dye); © Yuri/iStockphoto/iStockphoto (hair highlights); © Poznyakov/Shutterstock.com (splashing water).
p. 72 © Lucky Business/Shutterstock.com (skin tones); © prudkov/Shutterstock.com (facial mask); © maskpro/iStockphoto (facial massage); © prudkov/Shutterstock.com (massage); © Tamara83/Shutterstock.com (manicure).
p. 73 © Juanmonino/iStockphoto (#1); © Cameron Whitman/iStockphoto (#2); © Cameron Whitman/iStockphoto (#3); © proxyminder/iStockphoto (#4).
P. 78 (*middle*) © antmishch/iStockphoto.
p. 89 © shuchunke/iStockphoto.
p. 119 © Alexander Hoffmann/Shutterstock.com (jade); © LVV/Shutterstock.com (colored stones); © Madlen/Shutterstock.com (crystal); © Ewa Studio/Shutterstock.com (pearls); © ZIGROUP-CREATIONS/Shutterstock.com (bracelet); © mirabellart/iStockphoto (necklace); © Toria/Shutterstock.com (ring); © plavevski/Shutterstock.com (earrings).
p. 131 © bonchan/Shutterstock.com (sweet-and-sour pork); © Razmarinka/Shutterstock.com (string beans); © cobraphotography/Shutterstock.com (vegetables); © Xidong Luo/Shutterstock.com (dumplings); © KateSmirnova/iStockphoto (noodles); © bonchan/Shutterstock.com (tofu).

Realia:

Realia photos on the following pages by Cynthia Y. Ning: pp. 12–13, 33–35, 53–57, 74, 76, 96–97, 115–117, 137–139, 161–163, 185–186, 206–208.
Spa menus on p. 75 by Nora Guo.
China Mobile logo on p. 96 courtesy of China Mobile.

Outline of China's Geography

Borders:
- To the east: Sea of Japan, Yellow Sea, East China Sea, Taiwan Strait, and South China Sea.
- To the north, west, and south: North Korea, Russia, Mongolia, Kazakhstan, Khirghizstan (Kyrgyzstan), Tadjikstan (Tajikistan), Afghanistan, Pakistan, India, Nepal, Bhutan, Myanmar, Laos, and Vietnam.

Area: About 9.6 million square kilometers (3.7 million square miles). China is the third-largest country in the world, behind Russia and Canada. Its land mass is similar in size to the United States.

Topography: 1) the Northeast Plain, 2) the North Plain, and 3) the Southern Hills in eastern China; 4) Xinjiang-Mongolia in the west; and 5) the Tibetan Highlands of the southwest. Overall, the land is high in the west and descends to the coast in the east.

Major rivers:
- **Yangtze** (長江／长江), the third-longest in the world (after the Amazon and the Nile), which begins in Tibet, flows through central China, and enters the East China Sea near Shanghai.
- **Yellow River** (黄河), which begins in Qinghai and flows through north China, entering the Bohai Gulf of the Yellow Sea, through the Shandong Peninsula.
- **Heilongjiang** (黑龍江／黑龙江 Black Dragon River), which flows for the first three quarters of its length through northeast China and the last quarter through Russia, where it is known as the Amur.
- **Zhujiang** (珠江 Pearl River) of south China, which forms a fertile delta near Guangzhou, Macau, and Hong Kong.

Administrative divisions:
- **23 provinces** (shěng 省): Anhui, Fujian, Gansu, Guangdong, Guizhou, Hainan, Hebei, Heilongjiang, Henan, Hubei, Hunan, Jiangsu, Jiangxi, Jilin, Liaoning, Qinghai, Shaanxi, Shandong, Shanxi, Sichuan, Taiwan [currently governed by the Republic of China], Yunnan, Zhejiang.

- **5 autonomous regions** (zìzhìqū 自治區／自治区): Guangxi Zhuang, Inner Mongolia, Ningxia Hui, Tibet, Xinjiang Uighur.
- **4 autonomous municipalities** (zhíxiáshì 直轄市／直辖市): Beijing, Chongqing, Shanghai, Tianjin.
- **2 special administrative regions** (SARS, tèbié xíngzhèngqū 特別行政區／特别行政区): Hong Kong, Macau.

Agricultural divisions:
- One demarcation is made by the Qinling mountain range and the Huai River. To the north is the North China Plain—drier wheat and millet country; to the south are the wetter rice cultivation regions of the Yangtze River watershed.
- The other major division is east-west, based on the availability of arable lands. Western China is deserts and uplands; this is 57% of the land that is populated by only 6% of China's people (in 2002). Eastern China is arable lowlands; it constitutes 43% of the land but supports 94% of the population (in 2002).